FRANCIS BACON

THE ARENSBERG LECTURES

Edited by W. H. Werkmeister

FIRST SERIES: *Facets of the Renaissance*
SECOND SERIES: *Francis Bacon: His Career and His Thought*

FRANCIS BACON

HIS CAREER AND HIS THOUGHT

FULTON H. ANDERSON

Professor of Philosophy, University of Toronto

GREENWOOD PRESS, PUBLISHERS
WESTPORT, CONNECTICUT

Library of Congress Cataloging in Publication Data

Anderson, Fulton Henry, 1895-
  Francis Bacon, his career and his thought.

    Reprint of the ed. published by the University of
Southern California Press, Los Angeles, which was issued
as 1957 of the Arensberg lectures.
    Includes index.
    1. Bacon, Francis, Viscount St. Albans, 1561-1626--
Addresses, essays, lectures. 2. Philosophers--England--
Biography--Addresses, essays, lectures. I. Title.
II. Series: The Arensberg lectures ; 1957.
[B1197.A5 1978]   192 [B]   77-18070
ISBN 0-313-20108-0

ACKNOWLEDGMENTS

DURING THE SPRING SEMESTER of 1957, Fulton H. Anderson was the Arensberg Visiting Professor in the School of Philosophy, University of Southern California. In April of that year he gave three public lectures on "The Philosophy of Francis Bacon." The present book is an expansion of these lectures. Both Dr. Anderson's Visiting Professorship and his public lectures were sponsored by The Francis Bacon Foundation, Inc., Claremont. This foundation has also made possible the publication of the lectures as here presented.

For its interest in, and generous support of, these scholarly activities, I wish to thank The Francis Bacon Foundation on behalf of myself, the School of Philosophy, and the University of Southern California.

W. H. WERKMEISTER, *Director*
School of Philosophy
University of Southern California

PREFACE

THIS STUDY IS AN ENLARGEMENT of a series of lectures delivered at the University of Southern California in the spring of 1957 as part of the Arensberg Lectures sponsored by that institution.

Now printed in book form, on the occasion of the four-hundredth anniversary of Francis Bacon's birth, the study is, in design, an account of that thinker's place within the perspectives of his time. It is hoped that its appearance may mark an advance, however modest, in Baconian exegesis through its attempt to relate certain of Bacon's opinions to traditional and contemporary philosophies; by its emphasis on his originality as a systematic thinker and not merely an exponent of scientific method; by its statement of reasons for his political support of the Royal Prerogative; and by its stress on the place in his thinking of the generic conception of the three kingdoms—of nature, of politics, and of Divine Grace.

This conception, in the writer's opinion, is basic to the pluralistic philosophy which contains within its structure the widely diverse principles of Verulam's thought. Not all, by any means, of his more striking and characteristic undertakings are recorded in the present book—lest, as the saying goes, the reader should fail to see the wood for the trees—but mainly those which have occasioned continuous controversy since that statesman and philosopher first became the subject of biography and commentary.

The writer gratefully acknowledges help received, during the period of years since he first became interested in Bacon's philosophy, from many historians, biographers, commentators, and editors of documents. Among these he would mention James Spedding, E. A. Abbott, R. W. Church, J. G. Crowther, S. R. Gardiner, John Nichol, and Francis Paget. Use has been made freely of such evidence as they, and others, have collected and interpreted. Sometimes, in the present study, particulars stressed in their assembled evidence have been regarded as the more cogent when disagreement with their verdicts has been the more pronounced.

The author thanks three of his colleagues in the University of Toronto for their generous aid in preparing this writing for publication. Professor C. W. Webb drastically reduced the bulk of the manuscript. Professor J. M. O. Wheatley critically examined the typescript and galley prints. Professor William Dray has read the page proof.

F. H. A.

CONTENTS

FRANCIS BACON

I

BACON'S REPUTATION

IN THIS STUDY WE ARE DEALING WITH A PHILOSOPHER and public servant whose life and place in history have occasioned much dispute among biographers, critics, historians, and expositors for more than three hundred years. It is our hope that some of this repetitious conflict may be resolved by the simple device of recording without presupposition immediate evidence from Bacon's circumstances, writings, and political undertakings. We are of the opinion that the reading of this author's character and the discounting of his endeavor have been reckless, uninformed, even at times malevolent.

Francis Bacon played many roles in the Late English Renaissance: he was courtier, literary artist, Parliamentarian, jurist, advisor of monarchs, and statesman. But pre-eminently he was a philosopher. As a philosopher he professed, in addition to a metaphysics, definite theological, political, and ethical principles. To these several principles he adhered consistently throughout his career. The "character studies" which purport to represent his life abound in philosophical, ethical, theological, and political praecognita which he himself would not have found tenable or even theoretically congruent. It is mainly through these presuppositions that Bacon has been represented as a man without principle and a philosopher without a "system of truth," even indeed as a combination of a Judas Iscariot and a Pontius Pilate.

To speak bluntly, Bacon's reputation has been reduced or destroyed through the philosophical naivety of biographers and historians. Those who have passed the severest judgment on his career and his thought have been amateurs in ethics and persons but little acquainted with the sequences and consequences of historical and systematic philosophy. Most of his literary biographers have shown, in what they call "moral" exposition, not the slightest regard to either a system or a hierarchy of virtues. They seem never to assign appropriate places in an ethics to reasoned wisdom, reasoned charity, and reasoned prudence in well-weighed circumstances. Some of their assumptions are ridiculous, and their several conclusions when placed together prove shockingly contradictory. One finds in their writings, for example, the presumption that all the theological and cardinal virtues are to be rendered subsidiary to something called "honor"—especially when dealing with the case of Essex. Readers are told in succession that Bacon failed in virtue because he had no "reasoned ethics"; because he was a "rationalist" in ethics; because his ethics rested on the dogmas of religious faith; because his ethics was "Machiavellian" and without principle.

Those "liberal" clerics among Bacon's critics who regard Christian apologetics as an unbroken journey from natural science to divinity, or in a more sophisticated way from metaphysical being to God, condemn their author as a retrograde thinker for his segregation of the realm of Divine Grace from the areas of natural science and a naturalistic metaphysics. Others, who agree in his rejection of liberal theology and welcome his supplanting of Platonic, Aristotelian, Stoic, Epicurean, and other pagan principles in ethics by the placets of Scripture, turn a deaf ear to his materialistic naturalism. Prepared to accept the teaching that the source of ethics is Divine Revelation, they, like the seventeenth-century "saints," proceed to damn their Elizabethan author for his failure to walk in the byways of what was deemed by Elizabethan churchmen a lawless, obscurely motivated, ever-changing, ever-meandering thing, without philosophically or theologically ordered foundation, the vaguely principled "Nonconformist conscience."

Clerics who habitually associate high thinking with scanty existence and plain fare can rarely abide the supposition that a courtier who lived lavishly, as Bacon undoubtedly did, could ever have been the author of a serious philosophy and ever have put into practice an elevated ethics. Such of their number as can encompass this comprehensive thought will yet have it that Bacon the advisor of monarchs on church affairs, the scholar at Court, the philosopher in politics, the savant on the bench, was but a truant from the academy. In his truancy they discern vices and sins commensurate with great powers wrongly used: inordinate flattery of sovereigns and aggravated vanity; support of the Royal Prerogative in denying the rights of subjects and their Parliament; sycophantic compliance with rulers in the doctrine of the divine right of kings; duplicity, after a shrewd assessment of political circumstances; the sundering of the placets of revealed religion from axioms derived through rational inquiry; illiberal opposition to Sir Edward Coke, the deliverer of the courts of common law from the interference of kings and privy councils; disdain for the "consciences" of Nonconformists; bribery of a judge by litigants; dishonor in the prosecution of the Earl of Essex; and, to end the list of complainings, a literary man's uttering, on his political downfall, a literary and therefore insincere psalm of confession to his Maker.

Those political historians who think that the "common man"

is endowed by nature with "rights" and sovereign "initiative," deplore as retrograde, even iniquitous, Bacon's profession on biblical grounds of the doctrine of divine right. The same historians are commonly prone to treat Bacon's opinions in constitutional law as a besmirched foil for the mediocrities of the politically and juristically ambitious lawyer Edward Coke.

The vicissitudes of Bacon's philosophical reputation are even more striking than those which have beset his "morality." Because of the Platonic and Aristotelian training and attitudes of persons in Court, church, and state, to whom his writings on science were at first addressed, Bacon's philosophy was treated in the beginning with neglect, hostility, or derision. Yet, a generation after his death, his works were accorded a veneration rarely, if ever, given the writings of a naturalistic philosopher. Members of the Royal Society and other investigators with kindred interests hailed Bacon as the sovereign of the kingdom of nature, "the great restorer of physics," "the great architect of experimental history," and the prophet of a "real" philosophy and a "solid" learning. In response to certain entreaties contained in his writings, an unprecedented host of inquirers undertook the collecting and interpreting of scientific data of wide range under the shield of his defending and directing philosophical induction. Impressed by his original classification of the sciences and his institution of a new mode of inquiry, Bacon's followers regarded him as the "modern Aristotle." For his refusal to accept the magisterial impositions of the a priori and the transcendental upon experimental science, they called him "nature's secretary." It was their belief that through the pursuit of a new induction natural philosophy was finally to come into its own. Yet, because their very enthusiasm for their prophet's method led them to the point of disregarding many of his major principles, these early disciples were to detract in perpetuity from his reputation as a systematic philosopher.

Educators of the seventeenth century saw in the scientific regimen of Solomon's House of Wisdom, which Bacon had described in the *New Atlantis*, a new education which would render obsolete many of the disciplines of the past. By this education a new, a truly scientific, humanism would be initiated. Students would turn from the works of Plato and Aristotle to examine the book of nature. Scientists and philosophers of the future would deal with things and not argue about the meaning of terms. Men generally would finally come into their original inheritance, the dominion over nature. Through this reclaimed inheritance would come relief from the miseries which beset the present ignorant, unhappy estate of mankind.

After the political revolution and the regicide (1649) which ended the reign of Charles I, Bacon's countrymen were to remember his unheeded advice to that sovereign's father, James I. Political thinkers would then recall his efforts to establish a liberal government, while upholding the King's sovereignty and confirming the privileges of Parliament and courts. Englishmen were to opine that had Bacon's principles prevailed in the mind of a stubborn Stuart, their nation might have escaped the deprivation of liberty and all the bitterness and misery which were its lot in the days of Charles I, Oliver Cromwell, and another Stuart.

On the Continent, Verulam's name and opinions were invoked in the discussions and the correspondences of scientific "agents" and founders and frequenters of the scientific "cabinets" and academies of the seventeenth century—Samuel de Fermat, Henry Justel, Marin Mersenne, Nicholas-Claude Fabri de Peiresc, members of the Cabinet Dupuy, the Academy of Montmor, and the rest. Bacon was hailed as the scientific progenitor of Robert Boyle, Walter Charleton, John Evelyn, Francis Glisson, Jonathan Goddard, John Wallis, and Thomas Willis. The Solomon's House of the *New Atlantis* (published posthumously in 1627) and the inductive inquiries described in the

Novum organum (1620) and the *De dignitate et augmentis scientiarum* (1623) were treated as models. A French correspondent of Thomas Hobbes wrote in enthusiasm, "If England had only given to science Gilbert, Harvey, and Bacon, she might have disputed the palm with France and with Italy, who have given us Galileo, Descartes, and Gassendi; but Bacon has carried it over all others in grandeur of design." In the opinion of Puffendorf, the jurist, "It was the late Chancellor Bacon who raised the standard, and urged on the march of discovery." To the inquiring Mersenne, René Descartes wrote, "You desire to know how best to make experience useful: On this point I have nothing to add to Verulam." Descartes also expressed the desire that some scientist would undertake an astronomical investigation according to Bacon's method. Pierre Gassendi hoped that the issue of Verulam's *organum* would be a replete natural philosophy.

In later years, Gottfried Wilhelm Leibniz was to say that in the matter of philosophic reach, Descartes, when compared with Bacon, "creeps on the ground." He admonished philosophers "to think highly of Verulam, for his hard sayings have in them a deep meaning," and acknowledged that the study of the *De augmentis* had set his feet on a philosophic path. While developing his own philosophic thought, Leibniz welcomed Bacon's doctrine of figure and motion as one far preferable to that of the matter, form, and change of Aristotle. Leibniz followed Bacon in asserting that "an abstract being is not a principle," and gave his monads those characteristics which Bacon had ascribed to the atom: "a true being, having matter, form, dimension, place, resistance, appetite, motion." One of Leibniz's tracts, written under a pseudonym, is called *Gulielmi Placiti 'Plus Ultra,' sive initia et specimena scientiae generalis, de instauratione et augmentis scientiarum, ac de perficiendâ mente, rerumque inventione ad publicam felicitatem.* In this title every phrase is taken from either a title or common saying of Bacon's. It had been Leibniz's intention to conclude the writing with an exhortation in the manner of Bacon, *"ad viros dignitate doctrinaque egregios de humana foelicitate exiguo tempore, si velemus modo, in immensum augenda."*

Immanuel Kant was of the opinion that the author of the *Novum organum* was "one of the greatest physicists in modern times." Arthur Schopenhauer paid a compliment when he wrote, "beautifully expressed by Verulam: The intellect is not a dry light. . . . Love and hate falsify our judgments entirely." Schopenhauer was probably repeating what he had read in Bacon when he wrote such statements as these: "That which is acted on is always matter, and thus the whole being and essence of matter consists in the orderly changes which one part of it brings about in another part." "To repeat the whole nature of the world . . . and thus to store up a reflected image of it always at the command of reason, this and nothing else is philosophy." Jean D'Alembert saluted Bacon as the most universal of all natural philosophers, and Denis Diderot gave a work a title taken from Bacon—*De interpretatione philosophiae*. They placed his name on the front page of the *Encyclopédie,* and an associate adopted Bacon's classification of the sciences. Charles Darwin wrote in his notebook that he intended, when investigating the problem of the origin of species, to proceed on "true Baconian principles."

All this, however, is but one side of the picture. On the other we see Bacon castigated for his naturalism and his materialism, his exclusion of ontology from philosophy, his refusal to accept any metaphysical account of the nature and being of God. His English contemporaries seized upon his emphasis on "works" and his designing his induction for "operative" ends. They called his philosophy a method for producing mechanics, horticulturists, and apothecaries' clerks. On the Continent, Benedict

Spinoza, too, remarked that Verulam's philosophy was only fitted to use in manufacture and trade. Indeed, from the seventeenth century to the present, contention has continued over Bacon's right to be called a systematic or significant philosopher, an original or originative thinker. Into this controversy have entered both academic prejudice and national rivalry. Frustrated inductionists, ambitious empiricists, outraged rationalists, unrealistic transcendentalists, piqued "liberal" clerics, and ethical tyros have played their several parts. Reliance has been placed on those repetitious "philosophical" causeries which find their way into the "lives" of persons whose systems of thought are never really penetrated by their biographers. There has been obvious ignorance of the author's writings and philosophical environment, misconstruction of his teachings through omission and predisposition, prejudice in the withholding of available reasons for his political and judicial attitudes, and, by no means least in influence, that serpentine venom which can issue from meandering "consciences" led hither and yon by "moral" vagaries masquerading as ethical precepts and disposed to low, and sometimes cunningly contrived, representation of the high motives of intellectually and morally articulate men. By such causes as these, within myriad treatises where his name has been invoked, a great thinker has been reduced, in endless repetition, to a minute philosopher without height, breadth, or profundity; even as, for the part he played in a massive political drama within a politically dramatic age, he has been represented not as a tragic hero but as a moral derelict.

In national rivalry, some of the French will fondly have it that their countryman in exile, Descartes, is the author of all that is modern in modern philosophy. The Germans have gravely suspected a thinker who could write a philosophy in lucid and literary prose. George William Frederick Hegel, whose transcendental habits compelled him to compose an autobiography of the Eternal *Geist*, which he supposed to be immanent within his own deep logic, saw in the case of this characteristic English philosopher no more than a scattering of observations appropriate to greengrocers' assistants. Those of Bacon's own countrymen who have been given to resting their national philosophical reputation on such epistemological writers as John Locke, David Hume, J. S. Mill, and F. H. Bradley, have seen in such of his philosophical writings as they have chosen to read merely the sections of a laboratory manual compiled by a literary man, who had never undertaken a truly scientific experiment. Members of the "Scottish School" of epistemology have been an exception. They have acknowledged Bacon's influence in Locke's elevation of common sense to science, and have found in Bacon's *Novum organum* a more workable and fruitful method for the study of the operations of the knowing mind than that contained within the logical works of Aristotle.

Those philosophers of science who consider all worthwhile speculation since the Renaissance "Galilean and Cartesian" in character condemn Bacon for his failure to discern in the theories of the "new" astronomers and physicists—Nicholaus Copernicus, Galileo Galilei, William Gilbert—the basis of a systematic philosophy. Bacon the philosopher, who rarely, if ever, made a scientific discovery, is on the one hand called the originator of modern "science," and on the other is refused even a prophetic part in the history of science for the reason seemingly that his works are not a reservoir of prior, contemporary, and postmortem discoveries! The philosopher who put Aristotelianism to rout is called a belated Peripatetic. The empirical thinker who saw Plato's induction as a vague, wandering pursuit of "abstractions" within a "divine" realm, beyond the confines of human inquiry, is represented as a proponent of the doctrine of Platonic forms. The philosopher of science who placed the induction of axioms within the province of reason, has, for his mention of "experience," been deemed the founder of modern epistemological empiricism. Because he rarely uses the term hypothesis, and prefers "axiom," Bacon's scientific thought is said to be void of this principle. Bacon's critical interpretation of causation, in which cause and effect are tried by sense (as they are in Hume's doctrine), and in which cause and effect are not sundered in time and act (while in Hume's more naive doctrine they are), is represented by Hume's disciples as an example of philosophical primitivism! Bacon's theory of induction includes J. S. Mill's Instances more critically exemplified, and rectifies, before the fact, Mill's disregard of continuity in nature and failure to describe the nature of objects except in subjective terms. Yet Bacon's scientific endeavor is regarded by those who would place Mill before him in the philosophy of induction as merely an aimless ramble into the realm of real phenomena by an intellect stuffed with traditional book lore!

More drastically yet, Bacon is put beyond the philosophic pale by historians of philosophy and critical philosophers of many sorts. Among the reasons for this are his expulsion of ontology and dialectic from the philosophy of nature, his disregard of what the Scots have sometimes named "the metaphysical," what earlier makers of university curricula have entitled "mental and moral philosophy," and what contemporary writers think epistemology to be. Philosophers of monistic disposition have been offended by Bacon's refusal, for reasons, to bring within a single set of principles the composition of nature, the nature of God, the basis of political sovereignty, the structure of knowledge, and the ethical direction of the creature man. Epistemologists have deplored his failure to cope with the foundations of and the relations between the "subjective" and the "objective," some among them regarding these two things in a Cartesian manner, as "mental and physical substances."

Bacon himself thought that the attempt to "prove" either the reality of natural things or the reality of the knowledge of them a fruitless undertaking, dialectically and not observationally motivated. Bacon's epistemology does not extend beyond a treatment of the respective functions of sense, memory, and reason in the framing and the testing of hypotheses. Human reason as such is, for him, the Image of God and therefore lies within a realm enlightened through Divine Revelation, while the other functions of knowing man belong to the area of experimental physiology. This science, like other natural sciences, requires something more than common sense, hasty abstraction, and verbal definition for its investigation. Its axioms, when established, will become part of a science of nature. They are not to be used—like Platonic forms or Aristotelian principles of analytic or logic—as instruments for the total reconstruction of the whole of reality.

Bacon's philosophical reputation has commonly been made to hang on portions of two of his thirty-odd philosophical pieces, specifically on those parts of the *Advancement of Learning* (1605) and the *Novum organum* which have to do with Idols and a new method of inquiry. Yet his doctrine of Idols extends only to a portion of the *pars destruens* of one section of his philosophic undertaking, and his method is but one of six divisions of the Great Instauration. Bacon's rule of induction is, in design, to furnish eleven "helps to the understanding in the interpretation of nature"; but of these only three are expounded by the author. One who would understand Bacon's philosophy must constantly bear in mind that this embraces much more than his inductive "helps." It includes, as well, a refutation, with reasons, of prevalent philosophies; a distinctive philosophical scheme; a realignment of metaphysics, politics, and theology; a philosophical recognition of an independent kingdom of nature; an emancipation of a "real" and "solid" experimental knowledge from the thraldom of theoretical ontology and theological metaphysics; a specification of the objects of logical demonstration; and a provision for a new regimen of learning. The calculation of the character and the place in history of Bacon's philosophy does not depend, then, on an answer to the question whether the laboratory and extra-laboratory procedures instanced in the second book of the *Novum organum* were ever employed by any investigator, by a Copernicus, say, or a Galileo, a Boyle, a Newton, or a Pasteur. Bacon said in warning that the results reached through these procedures were to be modified as the other eight "helps"—which are not exposed in his writings—were put into employment.

The more philosophically pretentious among Bacon's biographers are given to remarking on his slight knowledge of logic as something indicative of a general philosophical ignorance. Because of their author's summary disposal of deduction as a method of discovery, they surmise that he knew even less traditional logic than a modern university graduate in arts. The fact is obvious, of course, to anyone acquainted with university curricula in the sixteenth century, that a modern college textbook in logic would have seemed a primer for dullards to a disputer who had done the required reading in the complex and abstruse logics employed during Bacon's years at Cambridge. And Bacon was a diligent student with capacity for mastering details.

The same biographers assert, or assume, that their author was little read, if at all, in past and contemporary philosophy, while they themselves can speak of the "breaking down of arid, formal scholasticism" by the "new science," as if either of these were but one thing. Bacon, in fact, explicitly brings under criticism, sometimes in considerable detail—witness his treatment of Aristotle, the Peripatetics, and Telesio—the doctrines of scores of thinkers whom he names, and of varied sects and

schools. Actually, the widespread misunderstanding of what is
original and nonoriginal in Bacon's thought is in no small
measure the result of a disregard on the part of many of his
most vigorous critics of the philosophical audience to which
he addressed his writings. The Renaissance had not scores but
hundreds of philosophers and commentators who put their
thoughts into published works, commonly of eclectic sorts, with
either a Platonic, or an Aristotelian, or an Augustinian, or a
Peripatetic, or a naturalistic emphasis. These works remain
largely unread. Scholars, who find their eclecticisms tedious
and their repetitions cumbersome, turn away and leave them
unexposed. Yet these writers and their readers were the persons
to whom Bacon addressed his writings, his later works especially, as one speaking directly, even intimately to an audience.
Bacon told his contemporaries that as an author he was none
other than "the birth of Time," his philosophy the product of
Time and not of an "individual wit."

Historians of philosophy are none too regardful of this offspring of Time. Such of them as read his works fully find his
utterances too distinctive in character to suffer easy adaptation
to their continuities. Accordingly, they leave him stranded, so
to speak, on Time's shore, while giving lift and transport to his
immediate successors Hobbes and Descartes. Transcendentalists
of Hegelian or pseudo-Hegelian ilk, who until recently have
comprised the greater part of these historians, look upon this
author as a kind of stray vagrant lacking desire for settled place
or a priori haven. The inductionists who dip into history accord
their seminal forbear a polite nod of recognition—although on
occasion they can be impertinent. These descendants seem in
the main to be over-sensitively wary lest any ancient should
appear as a provider for their weak, if sometimes quite turbulent, line. Strangely enough, the naturalists, too, among historians, who could learn a good deal from Bacon's attempts to rid

philosophy of the a priori and transcendental and to purge nature of "mind," almost completely neglect his major statements in these regards.

The task confronting the historian of philosophy is not, admittedly, an easy one. He must be selective, and he will be bent on discovering continuities which are more than mere successions. Some of his authors, if only because of spatial exigence, must be treated scantily or overlooked. Thinkers receiving major recognition will be those who sustain in greater degree the historian's continuities. The most usual practice of the historian is to reduce an author to a "moment" or stage in a movement toward one culmination or another. This procedure entails the separating and weakening of the threads of an individual philosopher's design, the more thoroughly when the pattern of his thought is the more distinctive. In effect, the historic thinker's system inevitably undergoes a degree of dialectical reconstruction to accommodate anachronistic and alien principles.

To escape certain of the difficulties inherent in the writing of the story of philosophy there has been brought into use and fashion the history not of philosophers but of "ideas." However, the task of representing an author's thoughts in this sort of history is beset with special difficulties of its own. Strictly speaking, ideas never change, but only the connotations of words and the objects and topics which in denotation terms represent. When the connotation of a word changes, the term's new meaning cannot be understood without the adduction of a new context of reference. This context, in the case of a philosopher, will be found to imply a system of thought in whole or in part. Take, for example, three of Bacon's "ideas": form, matter, atom. Quite unlike Plato's and Aristotle's sorts of form, which require for their understanding two disparate sets of principles in system, Bacon's form is a materiate thing, the constituent law and active cause inherent within a sort of matter which is not recognized either by Plato or by Aristotle. Again, the "matter" of both Plato and Aristotle is unformed, indeterminate, without significant activity of its own, while Bacon's is formed, furnished, and replete with all that issues from it in action. An account of the reality, the operation, and the causation into which matter does or does not enter in the case of any one of these three thinkers necessarily entails an exposition of principles basic to a whole philosophy.

The concept atom, from the days of Leucippus in the fifth century B.C. to the first half of the seventeenth century, carries at least three independent meanings: the primary element in explanation of things whether physical or ontological, the smallest portion of a divided or a compressed body—presumably divided to "infinity" or utterly compressed, and an entity with structural pattern which enters into the composition of bodies. These three meanings cannot be presented in a philosophical succession without a major exposition of metaphysical, physical, and methodological doctrines which involve major parts of three quite different philosophies.

Baconian exposition, in summation, fails to state and to place in perspective those results of the author's thinking which render him a distinctive and original systematic philosopher, and not merely a proponent of a new method of scientific inquiry. These results include a complete reclassification of the sciences; the expulsion of theological ontology, in any guise, from natural philosophy; the removal of ethics and politics from the area of sciences discovered and established by human inquiry; the placing of human ethics under the rule of the placets of Divine Revelation; an all-embracing materialistic naturalism; the disregard in logical and metaphysical inquiry of all that is either a priori or transcendental, including the transcendental "reason"; the removal of "mind," even as "logical" structure or as rationale, from nature; the interpretation of metaphysics as generalized physics; the making of mechanics the operative counterpart of theoretical physics; the regarding of "magic" as generalized mechanics and the operative counterpart of metaphysics; the description of the nature and the place of "axioms," as principles and hypotheses, in inquiry; and, what is most necessary of all for an understanding of Bacon's way of regarding the natural, the religious, and the political events which confronted him as philosopher and statesman, the recognition of three separate kingdoms with three independent jurisdictions, viz., the kingdom of nature under the dominion of man, the Kingdom of God within the disposing of Divine Grace, and the kingdom of politics divinely endowed with a certain judicial and legislative initiative.

II

THE COURT AND LEARNING

Eɴɢʟᴀɴᴅ ɪɴ ᴛʜᴇ 1560's ᴘʀᴏᴅᴜᴄᴇᴅ ᴛᴡᴏ ɢᴇɴɪᴜsᴇs, William Shakespeare and Francis Bacon. The habitat of the first, by chance
and inclination, was the theatre; the habitat of the second,
through circumstances of birth and by design, was the Court.
The father of the one was uneducated and possessed modest
means, and his son went to the grammar school in his native
town; the father of the other was learned and wealthy, and his
son was sent to Cambridge. The youth who attended the grammar school was taught a little Greek and some more Latin, was
exercised in the grammar, rhetoric, and logic which constituted
the trivium, and was encouraged to compose pieces by following models taken from great writers. Because genius will out,
he was to have sufficient precision in the use of words, feeling
for rhythm in verse, awareness of the wisdom contained in historic lore, and sensitive discernment of the humors and motives,
comedies, and tragedies of men to write plays such as the world
had never before seen. The other youth, after private and
thorough schooling in languages and authors, was in his early
teens critically to assess academic exercises and the content of
university learning. In his early twenties he was to pronounce
a judgment against past and present philosophies, a judgment

which was an outpouring of gifted precocity. Soon thereafter he would be initiating plans for the supplanting of those philosophies by another, and confronting his political sovereign with a novel philosophical regimen for the promotion of man's rule over nature. If some of the ingredients of his philosophy had been entertained by others before him, even as had the plots of Shakespeare's plays before Shakespeare, their new placing and arrangement, and their amplification and modification in light of a new aim and a new method would mark a departure from all the philosophies that had gone before.

Francis Bacon was born in 1561 and died in 1626. He was junior by almost a century to Copernicus and by half a century to Paracelsus and Telesio; he was senior to Descartes by thirty-five years, and was a contemporary of Bruno, Campanella, Galilei, Gilbert, and Kepler. The circumstances of time, blood, family, and Court which determined Bacon's literary, philosophical, political, and juridical careers were as capacious as the Elizabethan Renaissance itself. Bacon, the product of this Renaissance, was to show the imaginative daring and literary power which characterized the other "great Elizabethans." He was born an Elizabethan and an Elizabethan he remained. If in the days of James I bickering and trading on the part of the king had superseded the majestic acts of a truly regal sovereign, if there was no longer a Drake to voyage round the world and English ships were rotting in untidy ports while Raleigh languished in the Tower for the appeasement of the Spaniards, Bacon could still storm the strongholds of learning and with intellectual daring circumnavigate the realm of nature. When necessary, too, he could call upon the foolish King of England to display the majesty becoming a sovereign and not to bargain with his Commons in the manner of a huckster.

As the "offspring of Time," Bacon's days overlapped those of Edmund Spenser, the "poet's poet"; of Richard Hooker, who in cogent prose set down the basis of a liberal ecclesiastical policy; of Christopher Marlowe, the "wild genius" who died in a brawl; of Philip Sidney, the defender of poetry against contemporary philistines; of Sir Francis Drake, the privateer who swept the Spanish Main and afterwards became Vice-Admiral of the fleet; of Sir Walter Raleigh, adventurer, buccaneer, and literary historian, who was to suffer execution at the dictate of the Spanish ambassador, who under James had for a time become the director of England's foreign policy; and of Shakespeare, the restless forsaker of his hearth for a life with strolling players, who alone among his contemporaries was equal to Bacon in perception of the motives and designs which underlie the actions and promote the prosperities and tragedies of mankind. These—Bacon and the others—were capacious persons in spacious times, whose acts resist computation by measures appropriate to commonplace men. All things, whether real or imaginary, are forgiven all of them save one—Francis Bacon!

Bacon was born within the shadow of the English Court and until his relinquishment of public office, in 1621, five years before his death, never lived beyond the range of its activity and influence. This Court was characterized by magnificence, by learning, by the ambition and intrigue of courtiers, and by belief of sovereigns in their divine right. Bacon's father, Sir Nicholas Bacon (1509-1579), held political posts during three reigns, first during the reign of Edward VI (1547-1553). Although Protestant in outlook and sympathy, he was permitted to continue in office under Mary Tudor (1553-1558), but as one suspect of seeking a closer union between English churchmen and Continental Protestants, he was denied permission to leave England. On Elizabeth's accession (1558) he became Lord Keeper of the Great Seal, receiving the full jurisdiction of Lord Chancellor in 1559. Sir Nicholas presided in the House of Lords at Elizabeth's first meeting with Parliament. For a period he had

suffered Elizabeth's disfavor because of her unfounded suspicion
that her Lord Keeper was the author of a pamphlet, *A Declaration on the Succession of the Imperial Crown of England,*
written in support of the claims of Catherine Grey. She later
sought his companionship, listened to his advice, and sometimes
visited his estate in Redgrave, where he had, with characteristic
generosity, founded a free grammar school. As one who remained aloof from court intrigue, Sir Nicholas was able to
tender respected counsel to Elizabeth and her Lord Treasurer
—his brother-in-law, William Cecil (1520-1598), Lord Burghley. The Lord Keeper had his friend Matthew Parker made
Archbishop of Canterbury (1559). He advised successfully
against the taking up of arms against Continental powers. He
advocated unsuccessfully a moderating of severe measures
against the Nonconformists respecting church discipline and
forms of worship.

Francis Bacon's father was a well-informed and greatly respected jurist and it became the ambition of the son to emulate
the father. For his formal education the son followed in his
father's footsteps. He studied at Cambridge and Gray's Inn.
Like his father, he became learned in the law and occupied the
offices of Treasurer of this Inn and Lord Keeper of the Great
Seal. He enjoyed until the end, despite his removal from office
(1621), the reputation of a just judge.

Sir Nicholas had married twice. Three sons by his first wife
held political offices, and the oldest, Nicholas, was created
premier baronet of England. His second wife was Anne Cooke,
who became the mother of two sons, Anthony and Francis.
Anthony (1558-1601) was elected a member of Parliament and
became an unofficial diplomat in the service of Elizabeth and
her favorite Essex. He had entrée to the household of the Queen
and communicated to her intelligence on personages and
affairs at home and abroad. He was associated with Essex in

illegal discussions with James VI of Scotland concerning the succession to the English throne. Anthony Bacon's confidential reporting to Elizabeth, his friendship with Essex, his enjoyment of the high regard of James of Scotland, and his opposition to a bill against Roman Catholic Recusants brought him into the disfavor of Elizabeth's Lord Treasurer, Lord Burghley, and worked to retard the granting of political office to his brother.

Bacon was the nephew by marriage of Lord Burghley. The Cecil family had been associated with royal courts from the days of Henry VII (1485-1509). William Cecil had gone to Cambridge, where he came under the influence of Roger Ascham and John Cheke and acquired skill in Greek learning. On graduation he went to Gray's Inn. He became a member of Parliament and obtained sundry legal and judicial offices. For a short time he was committed to the Tower. He was in a measure responsible for Edward VI's accession to the throne. During Mary's reign, William Cecil overtly acquiesced in her schemes and secretly corresponded with her rival, Elizabeth. After Elizabeth's accession to the throne, he became the most continuously powerful member of her Privy Council. He acted as the Queen's Lord Treasurer, Secretary of State, and first minister. He controlled Elizabeth's caprices, outmaneuvered cabals, was largely responsible for the restoration of the Reformation in its Anglican form, the Queen's foreign policy, and most of the measures instituted by Elizabeth and her Council during the latter part of her reign. Both Burghley and his son Robert (1563-1612), Lord Salisbury, were to have considerable influence on the life of Francis Bacon.

Bacon's mother, Anne Cooke, was a sister of Lady Burghley, and a daughter of Sir Anthony Cooke, the tutor of Edward VI. The two Cooke daughters were extraordinarily well-informed. Roger Ascham described Mildred, Lady Burghley, as one of the two most learned women in the kingdom—the other being Lady Jane Grey. Anne was proficient in Greek, Latin, French, and Italian learning. It was "known" that her father had entrusted her with the tutoring of Edward VI. When twenty-one she translated and published the Italian sermons of Bernardino Ochino (1487-1564), who had become a Reformer, escaped the Inquisition, joined John Calvin (1509-1564) in Geneva, and later became a prebendary of Canterbury under pension from the privy purse of Edward VI. Ochino instructed Elizabeth, to whom he dedicated a written work. Another Continental Reformer, Theodore Beza (1519-1608), a friend of her son Anthony, dedicated to Lady Bacon his *Meditations*. Beza had joined Calvin's church in Geneva. He became professor of Greek at Lausanne, Calvin's assistant in publication, professor in the Geneva Academy, and on Calvin's death his biographer and administrative successor.

From the Latin, Lady Bacon translated and published *An Apology for the Church of England* by Bishop Jewel. John Jewel (1522-1571) was a Zwinglian Reformer, who in a sermon at St. Paul's Cross had challenged "all comers" to prove the Roman case "out of the Scriptures, or the councils or Fathers for the first six hundred years after Christ." His *Apology* was regarded by many as "the first methodical statement of the position of the Church of England against the Church of Rome." In James' reign Richard Bancroft, Archbishop of Canterbury, declared the theology it contained the official statement of the Anglican position.

Anne Bacon was in theology a Calvinist, in disposition a Puritan—more than a little impressed by the writings of Thomas Cartwright (1535-1603) and other "saints"—in temperament a "fanatic," a thinker acquainted with the doctrines of the philosophico-theologians of various schools, and somewhat less than an impartial observer of the contemporary political struggles born of theological disputes. It was she who gave educational direction and dogmas to her mentally robust and physically delicate sons Anthony and Francis before and after they entered the University.

Lady Bacon did not hesitate to berate her brother-in-law, Lord Burghley, for his part in the political measures instituted by John Whitgift, Archbishop of Canterbury (d. 1604), at Burghley's and Elizabeth's bidding, against those who, in conscience, could not subscribe to practices required by the Anglican rule. If this learned and "fanatical" mother would find occasion to remind her son Francis through his brother Anthony that he was holding prayers with his servants less often than he ought, she was also to observe with some satisfaction that the same son, in agreement with the Calvinists, was contending that the forms of worship required by the rulers of the Established Church were not of the essence of religion; in statements replete with learning was separating the placets of revealed truth from man-made ethics, metaphysics, and theology; and was acknowledging in carnal human learning only enough knowledge to confound the atheist and not enough wisdom to redeem the sinner. If her son Francis was to expend a disproportionate amount of effort in the pursuit of political place, to the neglect of "godly offices," he was also to separate explicitly the Kingdom of Saving Grace from both the political kingdoms of this world (under rulers bestowed with initiative and sovereignty by the all-sufficient God) and the realm of nature, whose dominion had been granted unto man by the same Divine Creator.

Bacon's father, his uncle Lord Burghley, his cousin Lord Salisbury, and his own patron and the favorite of Elizabeth, Lord Essex, were all graduates of Cambridge. Attending university was then a relatively new practice among lay members of the Court; colleges were still commonly regarded as hostels for impecunious students destined to be clerics. Members of the families of the minor gentry (of which the English Court was for the greater part composed) who were graduates of Oxford and Cambridge had gone there in a serious pursuit of learning. At Cambridge Sir Nicholas Bacon acquired a desire for learning in the law. Burghley became well-read in Greek; his *Execution of Justice in England for maintenance of Public and Christian Peace* was recognized as a cogent explanation of Elizabeth's religious policy. His son Lord Salisbury composed treatises on politics. George Villiers (1592-1628), James' favorite and chief political agent after Salisbury's death, had not attended Cambridge but had studied in France (where he had gone for training as a courtier) under the tutorship of an Oxford man, Sir John Eliot. He was the author of verses, satires, plays, and a lost work called by Anthony à Wood a *Demonstration of the Deity*.

Queen Elizabeth herself was a woman of unusual learning. She could address the Universities in Greek and in Latin of her own composing and converse fluently with the Italian ambassador in his own tongue. Elizabeth had received instruction from Ascham. He took occasion to remark on her "wisdom and industry," and wrote to the German schoolmaster Sturm:

> She talks French and Italian as well as English: she has often talked to me readily and well in Latin and moderately so in Greek . . . she read with me all of Cicero and the great part of Titus Livius . . . She used to give the morning to the Greek Testament and afterwards read select orations of Isocrates and the tragedies of Sophocles. To these I added St. Cyprian and Melanchthon's Commonplaces.

After Elizabeth's death (1603), when Bacon found reason to write about the attitudes of politicians and monarchs towards learning, he could remind James I that "this lady was endued with learning in her sex singular, and rare even among masculine princes. . . . And unto the very last year of her life she accustomed to appoint set hours for reading, scarcely any young student in a university more daily or more duly."

As for James, who, as Bacon said, spoke "Latin like a scholar," few monarchs had ever been given more severe training in ancient and modern authors. His Scottish guardians had placed him under the instruction of George Buchanan, an accomplished scholar, a great Latinist, and a demanding teacher. Following his preceptor's example, James wrote verses. His first publication was *Essays of a Prentice in the Divine Art of Poesy*. Many others followed: two volumes of *Meditations*, translations from Du Bartas, Lucan, and the Book of Psalms, a book of poems which shows the influence of Buchanan's annotations on Vives, a work on demonology, and several political treatises in exposition and defence of the divine right of kings. His political writings contained doctrines utterly at variance with the principles of his tutor, who published a treatise under the title *De jure regni apud scotos* (1579). So scandalous was this work, ascribing as it did political initiative, even sovereignty, to the sovereign's subjects, that it was twice condemned by acts of Parliament and burned in 1683 by the University of Oxford. Bacon did not exceed the truth when he addressed James I as a sovereign in whom there was "a rare conjunction as well of divine and sacred literature as of profane and human." Nor, again, was he outdoing the ecclesiastical experts when in his *Advancement of Learning* (1605) he contrived the statement, "your Majesty standeth invested of that triplicity which in great veneration was ascribed to the ancient Hermes; the power and fortune of a King, the knowledge and illumination of a Priest, and the learning and universality of a Philosopher." For was not James assured at the Hampton Court Conference (1604) by Bacon's own former Cambridge tutor, Archbishop Whitgift— and Whitgift was no "fanatic"—that "he spoke by the special assistance of God's Spirit"?

These facts considered, there was propriety in Bacon's addressing in his early "devices" praises of learned monarchs to

Elizabeth, along with pleas that the Queen might place at her
subject's disposal means for learning's advancement. There was
literary aptness in his dedicating to Salisbury *De sapientia
veterum* (*Of the Wisdom of the Ancients*, 1609) and to George
Villiers, Duke of Buckingham, the third edition of his *Essays*
(1625). There was fitness in his addressing to James those writings in which he announced his designs for future learning,
The Proficience and Advancement of Learning (1605), *Novum
organum* (*New Organon*, 1620), and *De dignitate et augmentis
scientiarium* (*Of the Dignity and Advancement of Learning*,
1623). Of Bacon's respect for James' erudition there can be no
question. He did not hesitate to cite James' writings, including
Basilicon Doron (1599) and his *True Law of Free Monarchies*
(1598), works which became classical expositions of the doctrine of divine right.

In the year of James' accession (1603) to the English throne,
Bacon began a work which he entitled *Valerius Terminus of
the Interpretation of Nature: with the Annotations of Hermes
Stella*. In the name Hermes Stella was conjoined the powerful,
learned Hermes and a guiding star (*stella*). Both were desig-
nations which Bacon gave elsewhere to his sovereign, and here
he meant none other than King James. It was the author's hope,
in an enthusiasm soon to be dispelled, that the learned Ruler of
the political realm, the Head of the Established Church, and
the Visitor of the Universities, could be prevailed upon to co-
operate with a subject in a publication designed to implement
a new humanism. The way for this humanism would be prepared by Bacon's exposure of certain "false phantoms" of the
human mind and several past and present "impediments of
knowledge," including the traditional methods of inquiry, the
attitudes of politicians and prelates, the "superstitions and errors
of religion," and the manner of the "delivery of knowledge"
within the universities. If Bacon was to decide against the wis-

dom of inviting James in 1603—or 1605—to become a party to this undertaking, seventeen years later he was to find encouragement in the King's writing, on receiving a copy of the *Novum organum*, that he purposed to "read it through with care and attention" and then "give a due commendation to such places as in my opinion shall deserve it." In James' letter to Bacon on this occasion there is the nearest approach on the part of the King to a recognition of Bacon's philosophical enterprise. The *New Organon* probably caused James mild dismay, for it confronted a King with a Lord Chancellor's claim to full authority over a kingdom called Nature and, what was more, with this deputy's request for large financial aid for the inauguration of his philosophic rule from a hard-pressed monarch, who—as Bacon well knew—was finding it increasingly difficult to obtain means to replenish his purse from the Commons with its Puritan burghers, ambitious lawyers, and other sorts of nonconformists, all stubbornly demanding the grants of "privilege" and "right." James, who liked theological jests, indulged himself on this occasion with the remark that the *Novum organum* was "like the peace of God which passeth all understanding!"

Elizabeth, James, and their courtiers were among the learned personages to whom first the youth and then the man Francis Bacon vouchsafed, even while hoping for their support of his philosophical projects, such opinions as the following: The Greek philosophers are prattling schoolboys and their philosophical successors authors of stage plays. All theologies, those of a Calvinistic sort excepted, are heresies through their intertwining the placets of Christian Revelation with the doctrines of the pagan Plato and Aristotle. Learning both within and without the Universities is full of malignancies. The talk of learned men consists of meaningless words about false phantoms. The administrators, professors, fellows, and curricula of the Universities are impediments in the way of learning. And—

here was the important point—a college or school or other
foundation supported by public funds should be placed at
Francis Bacon's disposal for an instauration of learning on an
experimental basis under secular auspices; and, as a consequence
of their moral obligation to supply this, sovereigns, personages
at Court, and reigns of kings could be esteemed according to a
scale of contribution to the reform of learning in prospect.

Bacon's pleas fell on deaf ears. Those of the Court who took
note of them undoubtedly reflected, like Bishop (John) Bram-
hall a generation after Bacon's death, "It is strange to see with
what confidence nowadays particular men slight all the Schoolmen, and Philosophers, and Classick Authors of former ages, as
if they were not worthy to unloose the shoestrings of some
modern Authors." The very learning of the Court itself stood
in the way of Bacon's philosophical enterprise. Its clerical and
lay members were products of Oxford and Cambridge. Burghley and Salisbury were, in turn, university chancellors. All of
them by education, if not by profession, were Platonists and
Augustinians or Aristotelians and Peripatetics, or a mixture of
these four sorts of philosopher. Elizabeth and James had been
schooled in the classics. Elizabeth knew, and no doubt respected,
both the Platonic Cicero and the Reformer Philip Melanchthon
(1497-1560) who had kept Aristotelianism intact in the theology and the schools of Protestant Germany. She was, as
Bacon himself acknowledged, "a great reader" of the "writings
of the Fathers, especially those of St. Augustine." James was
conversant with traditional doctrines in the fields of logic,
physics, ethics, politics, and metaphysics.

Bacon's disciples of a later generation were to have more
success than he with a Court far less erudite and literary. Charles
II would consort with the virtuosi, look through their telescopes, watch their experiments, become their supporting
patron, and grant them a Charter as members of a "philosophical college," now elevated in status to a Royal Society.

III

BACON'S
STUDIES AND AMBITIONS:
HIS EARLY DAYS
IN PARLIAMENT

AFTER RECEIVING INSTRUCTION IN LANGUAGES and authors, and in biblical theology as well, Bacon entered Cambridge at the age of thirteen. His tutor was John Whitgift, later chosen by Elizabeth for the archbishopric of Canterbury because of his opposition to any reduction of episcopal authority in church administration, a thing much desired and advocated by those under the influence of "Genevan reform." Bacon completed his undergraduate studies in less than three years and earned a reputation for diligence and proficiency in "the several arts and sciences."

A major requirement of Cambridge students was *dialectica*: advanced grammar, rhetoric, and logic. University tutors required the study of books on rhetoric and encouraged the reading of the ethical and other writings of Aristotle, as well as scholastic commentaries abounding in Platonic, Aristotelian, Patristic, and Peripatetic references. Public exercises comprised declamations and formal disputations in Greek and Latin before university officers. Initial disputations, sometimes called "soph-

isms," were exercises in dialectic preparatory to later "demonstrations of truth." "Truth" in these instances consisted mainly
of theses taken, often out of context, from the ethical, political,
and metaphysical works of Aristotle. Theses were defended by
a respondent arguing in deductive fashion against two or more
opponents. This syllogistic method of demonstration, which
required definition at every stage and turn of argument, was
presumed by university authorities to be the quickest sharpener
of the students' wits and the best way to acquire skill in aligning grounds and consequents within systematic discourse. Contrary to a common assumption by historians, Bacon did not have
opportunity to study mathematics at Cambridge. The subject,
although it was a part of the traditional quadrivium, was not to
be taught there for decades because Peripatetic influence was
against it. During the first third of the seventeenth century
Cambridge was still without tutors who knew mathematics.
John Wallis (1616-1703) and Seth Ward (1617-1689), who
studied there and later became professors of mathematics and
astronomy respectively at Oxford, where they revived these
long defunct studies, could get no tutorial aid in either of these
subjects while undergraduates. Another supposition, incidentally, that soon the fellows and authorities at Cambridge
would be showing themselves receptive of what was to be called
the "new experimental philosophy," is also an error. The main
academic support of the extramural "philosophical college"
which was to become the founding body of the Royal Society,
came from certain men at Oxford, not from their confreres at
Cambridge. Neither university was officially to show any disposition whatever to acknowledge the academic value of this
society's undertakings until very late in the seventeenth century.
Cambridge did not hesitate to elect Bacon as its representative
in the House of Commons and to make him their standing legal
counsel, but its fellows persistently refused to countenance his
philosophy.

When at Cambridge, Bacon seems to have read a considerable part of Aristotle, including his ethics, politics, and rhetoric, and also some of Plato. It was there presumably that he first became aware, through the Stagirite's writings and those of his commentators, of the opinions of Pre-Socratic thinkers. Certainly, he was to find before long in these earliest philosophers what seemed to him a close contact with particulars and operation and, what was even more to his liking, an identification of philosophy with the science of nature and a merging of metaphysical being with formed, furnished, and active matter—not the indeterminate, inert, and deprived thing which Aristotle called by this name. By the time Bacon left the University he had rejected Aristotelianism as a method of demonstration and a system of doctrine. He found it too theoretical in definition and too remote from particulars for science, too contentious for a profession of truth, too speculative for practice and operation. Dr. William Rawley, Bacon's chaplain, early biographer, and editor, tells us that "whilst he was commorant in the university, about sixteen years of age (as his lordship hath been pleased to impart unto myself), he fell into the dislike of the philosophy of Aristotle; not for the worthlessness of the author, to whom he would ever ascribe all high attributes, but for the unfruitfulness of the way; being a philosophy (as his lordship used to say) only strong for disputations and contentions, but barren of the production of works for the benefit of the life of man; in which mind he continued to his dying day."

Bacon, however, learned many things from Aristotle. He saw in the Stagirite an investigator who, during a stay at the Court of Macedon where he was tutor to Alexander the Great, was able to collect, by the help of fowlers, fishermen, and the like, materials for a natural history—even if afterwards this great "wit" was to let the fruits of his early inquiry escape by turning to "abstractions." Aristotle also provided Bacon with the example of a thinker who had the courage to reconstruct philoso-

phy. From the same thinker Bacon learned too that human
knowledge can be organized according to a hierarchy of sciences; that logic, as an instrument of all demonstrable proof, is
not among the divisions of the sciences; and that there is such a
thing as a demonstrated metaphysics. He thought Aristotle
wrong in establishing this universal science on the single Principle of Identity—What is, is—and in supposing, in opposition to
Plato, that its subject matter could be approached directly
rather than through a lesser science. Like the Platonists, who in
another regard had identified Plato's Good with the Christian
God, Aristotle was mistaken in equating his metaphysics with
the natural theology of a First Cause. Aristotle had wisely professed a philosophy of nature and assigned it a method of
demonstration, and then had properly concluded that this
method was one which could not fully establish knowledge in
ethics and politics. If he was to bring confusion into natural
science through a division of its subject matter according to
basic axioms and by the employment of terms theoretically and
not inductively defined, he on principle did at least segregate
his physics from theology, ethics, and politics. In addition, he
issued something more than a caution against the ambitious
schemes of mathematicians, after members of the Academy
founded by Plato had interposed nonexistential mathematical
entities between particulars and their forms.

On leaving Cambridge Bacon enrolled as a student in the law
at Gray's Inn. In 1586 he became a bencher. Twenty years later
he was to become, like his father before him, the Inn's Treasurer
—equivalent to President; and after his political downfall he was
to retire to Gray's Inn and live there "by turns" until his death.
Bacon's legal studies were interrupted in 1577, when he joined
the staff of Sir Amias Paulet, Ambassador to France. He remained in the Ambassador's service for some three years. On
one occasion at least he was entrusted with a diplomatic mes-

sage to Queen Elizabeth. He also received a commendation to her Majesty. At this period Bacon showed inquisitiveness about "phenomena," including the relations between vibrations and sound, and inventiveness, as evidenced by his new method for diplomatic writing in cipher. His stay in France gave him training in diplomacy and protocol and an opportunity to observe French civil conflicts as well as intrigues against his own country by Portuguese, Spaniards, and papal agents. It was brought to an abrupt end by the death of his father in 1579. Bacon was now left with small financial means. His father, who had already provided for his other children, had been setting aside money for the purchase of considerable land for his youngest and favorite heir—"his father's first choice," as his mother said. When death intervened, the young man inherited only about one-fifth of his father's personal property. At the age of nineteen, Francis Bacon found himself facing the world with great capacities, large ambitions, and little estate.

Bacon's intellectual capacity had become evident at an early age. During his stay in France a painter inscribed on his portrait *Si tabula daretur digna, animum mallem*—"if only I had a canvas worthy to paint his mind." Those who conversed with him were struck by his discernment of principle in circumstance and the aptness of his words. Bacon's way of speaking betokened skill in writing, power in politics, and wisdom on the bench. It impressed and often delighted Elizabeth, and disquieted the Cecils. His manner of writing, like the styles of Shakespeare and Chaucer, had been shaped in the precisions of rhetoric and yet was to soar beyond rhetoric's dimensions. Bacon would become a very learned and, besides, a very observant and reflective man, and would show, as his friend Tobie Matthew said, a "facility and felicity of expressing it all in so elegant, significant, and abundant, and yet so choice . . . a way of words, of metaphors, and allusions, as perhaps the world hath not seen, since it was a world." Soon every word, phrase, and sentence which came from Bacon's pen began to tell. His constructions, now compressed and terse, now open, now pro- lix, responded in apt rhythm to each nuance of his moving thought. His precise nouns, verbs, and adjectives came in a suc- cession like the inevitable notes of a musical fugue. His prose never weakened into mere rhythmic melody, yet its sentences were to prove as resistant to paraphrase as the songs of a lyrical poet, for no word may be added, changed, or removed without weakening the part and the whole. So original are the springs of Bacon's utterance that his attempted renderings of the language of others, the Psalms of David for example, rise feebly without inspiration. Literary genius does not often, if indeed ever, abide the resaying of what is not its own.

Bacon would become a great speaker in the Commons and courts of law. Ben Jonson would be able to pay him this tribute: "There happened in my time one noble speaker, who was full of gravity in his speaking. . . . No man ever spake more neatly, more pressedly, more weightily, or suffered less empti- ness, less idleness, in what he uttered. No member of his speech, but consisted of his own graces. His hearers could not cough, or look aside from him, without loss. He commanded where he spake; and had his judges angry and pleased at his devotion. No man had their affections more in his power. The fear of every man that heard him was, lest he should make an end."

Bacon's tastes—to change the theme—were those befitting one accustomed from birth to houses of splendor and courts of mag- nificence. His "luxuries" were none other than the necessities of Aristotle's magnanimous citizen who, as a fully actualized and wholly virtuous man, was both a philosopher and a states- man. Aristotle had taught that this virtuous citizen would have at his disposal the products of husbandmen, mechanics, artisans, and artists. Bacon regarded such things as proper means for the

elevation of man from savagery to civility and as goods of the
kingdom of nature granted to man by God. Bacon would have
thought strange indeed an educated biographer's finding signs
of moral depravity in the spacious scale of his living. In the
Advancement of Learning Bacon took note that there were
monks who chose poverty for good purposes; but he also deplored those "derogations . . . which grow to learning from the
fortune or condition of learned men in respect of scarcity of
means." Some years before, he had told Essex in a letter that he
"partly" leaned "to Thales' opinion, that a philosopher may be
rich if he will." This was an opinion for which Bacon had found
specific support in Aristotle, who had used the rich Thales as a
model for such householders as had been deprived, by small
means, of magnanimous living. Bacon did not associate the ac-
quisition of goods with loose living, idleness, intellectual weakness, or corruption of morals and manners. While he affirmed
the necessity of the priceless things of the mind, and while he
understood the choice of poverty by monks for religious ends,
it was not Bacon's opinion that penurious living as such makes
for fuller understanding or greater virtue. He always thought
that men of learning were more deserving of financial reward
than mechanics, manufacturers, amusement-makers, importers,
exporters, and money-changers.

Bacon earned a great deal of money, but his tastes, like his
ambitions for science, succeeded always in outstripping his
means. He lived lavishly, and the arrangements of his household,
which was not well managed, were always in full keeping with
what he considered his rôle at Court. On the expectation of a
new public appointment he would take the precaution of putting his servants into new cloaks. As he took his seat in Chancery
he surpassed all "within living memory" by "the bravery and
multitude" of his attendants. While Chancellor (1618-1621) he
employed in his household some forty gentleman-waiters, and

other servants in proportion. In 1608 his income was nearly
£5,000 and some ten years later about £16,000. Yet he was still
in debt, paying ten per cent to the money-lenders. At the time
of his death (1626), his debts amounted to over £22,000 and his
estate to some £7,000. Bacon's thoughts about finance had ever
been dominated by the hope, which continued even to the days
when he wrote his final will and testament, that financial habili-
tation would eventually come through James' placing large
means at his disposal, as the magnanimous director of an enterprise of experimental inquiry. These grants, he anticipated,
might be comparable at least to those bestowed on James'
favorite, Robert Carr, Earl of Somerset. They were never
forthcoming.

Bacon's career was determined by two ambitions, one political, the other philosophical. From his teens he was sure of
his philosophic mission and sanguine about its courtly support.
In his scheme of appraisal he placed the attainment and perpetu-
ation of learning above political success. The works on which he
relied "to maintain memory and merit of the times succeeding"
were not his "advices" to sovereigns, speeches in Parliament,
judgments in courts, literary essays, or histories of reigns. They
were writings and other efforts on behalf of the advancement
of learning. In 1592 Bacon was affirming that "the sovereignty
of man lieth hid in knowledge." In 1595, he was reflecting that
"the monuments of wit survive the monuments of power." Ten
years afterwards, in a temporary despair, he was lamenting to
his friend Sir Thomas Bodley his greatest "error": "knowing
myself by inward calling to be fitter to hold a book than to
play a part, I have led my life in civil causes, for which I was
not very fit by nature, and more unfit by the preoccupation of
my mind." Two years later, in 1607, after receiving the considerable public appointment of Solicitor-General—earlier he
had been made King's Counsel with Patent—he was repining:

"I have found now twice, upon amendment of my fortune, disposition to distaste." In 1617, on taking his seat in Chancery, Bacon told the assembled members of the court that it was his intention to reserve "the depth of the three long vacations . . . in some measure free from business of estate, and for studies, arts and sciences, to which in my nature I am most inclined." In 1620 he wrote in the proem to his *New Organon* that, compared with the instituting of a new philosophy, a new science, and a new learning all other ambitions seemed poor in his eyes. In 1623, now trying desperately to provide written content for some of the six parts of his instauration of the sciences, the author was to reflect on his carriage by destiny, against the inclination of his genius, into political affairs. When overwhelmed politically (1621), deserted by Commons, Lords, and King, the man who still held firm to his philosophy addressed his Maker with a prayer of penitence, worded in keeping with his literary disposition—that prayer which some critics have carpingly called "a public address":

Besides my innumerable sins, I confess before thee, that I am debtor to thee for the gracious talent of thy gifts and graces, which I have neither put into a napkin, nor put it (as I ought) to exchangers, where it might have made best profit; but misspent it in things for which I was least fit; so as I may truly say, my soul hath been a stranger in the course of my pilgrimage.

Never once, however, in any of these statements does Bacon deny, even implicitly, the suitability of political office for a philosopher. In his early *Valerius Terminus* he raised precisely this question, only to give a noncommittal answer. "It is hard to say," he wrote, "whether mixture of contemplations with an active life, or retiring wholly to contemplations, do disable and hinder the mind more." But at the same time he was bringing under censure the "tenderness and want of compliance of some of the most ancient and revered philosophers, who retired too early from civil business that they might avoid indignities and perturbations, and live (as they thought) more pure and saint-like." In his formative years Bacon had been taught by Aristotle, and by Plato too, that philosophers should spend part of their lives in the service of the state. He had found in Aristotle's *Politics* and in Plato's *Republic* portrayals of the most virtuous man as the most fully functioning citizen. The ethical man, according to both these philosophers, would possess both goodness and "universal and methodick knowledge"—something which James I was to acknowledge in Bacon on the occasion of his accepting a copy of the *Novum organum*—and would endure the arduous duties of politics. This conception of the duty of a philosopher became so much a part of Bacon's thinking that he was given to representing threatened retirements from politics, when advancement did not come, as a departure from what was proper and becoming to a full man.

It is hardly appropriate, or even sensible, to call Bacon the politician a "truant from the academy." Bacon never was an academic, and in the scholastic circumstances of his time he could neither have become nor remained one. His views on learning were anathema in the Universities from the beginning, and were to remain so for nearly a century. More than fifty years after his death and a generation after mathematics and astronomy had been revived at Oxford, his philosophy and his disciples in the Royal Society were publicly condemned in the Theatre of the same University, along with "fanatics" and "conventicles," *ad inferos, ad gehennam*. What Bacon proposed for learning could no more have been put into effect by a rebel in academic place than by a seer in solitude. His project entailed the collection of observations and the results of experiments on an enormous scale, in range as vast as "the universe." The natural history on which his philosophy was to rest would have the scope of nature itself. His design could be implemented only at great expense and under great patronage. If, despite these circumstances, Bacon is perforce to be regarded as a truant from the academy—in some strained sense of that phrase—it must be conceded that his truancy took the form of very notable endeavor. Without a nod of encouragement from any learned body—his name was even rejected for enrolment in the Lincei Academy of Florence—and without sympathy on the part of more than a few of his closest friends, this lone thinker prepared a map of the whole territory of human knowledge and then designed in detail a new scheme for its cultivation. He then, as both he and his editor, William Rawley, were to remark, became laborer and workman, dug the clay singlehanded, collected the stubble, and burned the bricks for the philosophical edifice of which he was the architect. The same alleged truant managed to write thirty-odd philosophical pieces. If most of these were composed during vacations between sessions of Parliament, sittings of law courts, and consultations with ministers and monarchs, if many of them were to remain incomplete in pattern and truncated in structure, they proved sufficient to start learning on a new road. It was a road taken at first by only a small band of his countrymen in their "philosophical college," then by an ever-increasing host of inquirers within and without scientific academies at home and abroad, and finally, after a long period of ridicule, doubt, and hesitancy, by fellows and lecturers within the Universities. Bacon, who never was an academician, was to become the propagator of all that is distinctly modern in modern academies. A learning identified with natural philosophy and a natural philosophy identified with experimentally established knowledge were to be his "merit" if not always his "memory" in "times succeeding."

At the age of eighteen Bacon found himself dependent for employment on the influence and goodwill of relatives and friends of his father at Court. As the son of a former Lord Keeper and the nephew of Queen Elizabeth's present Lord Treasurer, Bacon expected that, once he had prepared himself in the law, political office would be his for the asking. Already, he had "by birth and education . . . been absorbed with affairs of state." He had been reared in a politically and juristically minded family. He was well known to the Queen, who had paid visits to his father's house, and on one occasion, after receiving his apt replies to her questions, had jokingly dubbed him her "young Lord Keeper." Bacon's first request for office seems to have been addressed in letters to his aunt, Lady Burghley, who did not look with favor on his suit. For some years she had thought her nephew too sure of himself. When he was twenty she told him so, only to become more confirmed in her opinion. Francis Bacon then assured her, in reply, "My thankful and serviceable mind shall always be like itself, howsoever it vary from the common disguising." The nephew next addressed entreaties to his uncle. Burghley, aware of Bacon's capacities of mind and speech and having at the same time the political future of his physically deformed son, Robert Cecil, in mind, was not eager to advance a prospective rival to his heir. Besides, the uncle considered Bacon presumptuous in his dealings and arrogant in his nature. Burghley found occasion to tell the nephew that others had remarked on his arrogancy. Bacon asked his uncle to believe that "arrogancy and overweening" were "far" from his nature, explaining that "such persons as are of a nature bashful (as myself is), whereby they want that plausible familiarity which others have, are often mistaken for proud."

In 1584, partly through Burghley's influence, Bacon, at the age of twenty-three, obtained a seat in the House of Commons. There he remained, a member of all the ensuing sittings of Parliament under Elizabeth and James I, until he went to the

House of Lords. In one Parliament he represented two constituencies and in another, three. Five years after his first election, he was made Clerk or Registrar of the Star Chamber, a court of the Queen in Council. But the clerkship, which carried a large stipend, was given by reversion, and Bacon was not to take office until 1608, some nineteen years after its award. A few years after his nomination to the office, its occupant engaged in irregular practice which could have resulted in his dismissal, and some of Bacon's friends suggested punitive action. Bacon informed the Lord Keeper, Sir John Puckering—whose advancement at Court had been dependent on Sir Nicholas Bacon's influence—that while he had been "incited" to do so he would not consider "coming in upon a lease by way of forfeiture" and "would not be thought to supplant any man for great gain."

In 1592, three years after he had obtained the clerkship in reversion, Bacon sent a striking letter to Burghley. The outlook revealed in this communication made it evident that the law, which he was now practising, had been, in the words of Rawley, "but as an accessary, and not his principal study." Bacon reminded his uncle of the "meanness" of his estate, professed "moderate civil ends," and asked for a place to "carry" him. He wrote:

I have taken all knowledge to be my province; and if I could purge it of two sorts of rovers (whereof the one with frivolous disputations, confutations, and verbosities, the other with blind experiments and auricular traditions and impostures, hath committed so many spoils) I hope I should bring in industrious observations, grounded conclusions, and profitable inventions and discoveries—the best state of that province. This, whether it be curiosity, or vainglory, or nature, or (if one take it favourably) *philanthropia*, is so fixed in my mind as it cannot be removed. And I do easily see that place of any reasonable countenance doth bring commandment of more wits than of a man's own which is the thing I greatly affect. . . .

And if your Lordship will not carry me on, I will not do as Anaxagoras did, who reduced himself with contemplation into voluntary poverty. But this will I do. I will sell the inheritance that I have, and purchase some lease of quick revenue, or some office of gain that shall be executed by deputy, and so give over all care of service, and become some sorry book-maker, or a true pioneer in that mine of truth which (he said) lay so deep.

In this message Bacon was communicating, somewhat like a prophet, to Elizabeth's Lord Treasurer his twofold ambition: to occupy high office in the manner of Aristotle's virtuous man and, after the example of Aristotle but in his own way, to reconstruct human learning. It was his expectation that if the first of two ambitions were realized, the second would, as a consequence, be attained. But his letter did little more than confirm his uncle in the view that Francis Bacon was highly opinionated, very ambitious, and, by nature, inclined to innovation, which could prove disturbing to settled institutions. How highly opinionated the nephew was, Burghley did not in fact then know. Eight years before (1584), at the age of twenty-three, Bacon had written an unfinished work which he called by no less a title than *Temporis partus maximus* (*The Greatest Birth of Time*). Later, by a change of adjective, this became *Temporis partus masculus* (*The Fertilizing Birth of Time*). In it Bacon had brought under judgment and condemnation, after the manner of a judge in court, all philosophers and all philosophies of the past and the present.

Burghley's earlier opinion of his nephew received further confirmation in a political regard when in 1593 Bacon, who had been granted the privilege of pleading in the courts only some seven years before, assumed that he should be given the Attorney-Generalship. The nephew was not unmindful of his own legal talents or of the fact that his father had been appointed "Solicitor of the Augmentation, (a court of much business) when he had never practised, and was but twenty-seven

years old." Bacon's suit for the place now vacant was supported
by entreaties on the part of Essex; by Bacon's own letters to
the Queen, to the Lord Keeper, and to the Lord Treasurer; and
by his mother's importunity of Burghley. Elizabeth, Burghley,
and others at Court thought Bacon too young and inexperienced for the office. But there was a more personal reason for
Elizabeth's and Burghley's refusing him the Attorneyship.
Earlier in the year the Queen had requested large funds to meet
the danger of Spanish undertakings in prospect against England.
Burghley asked the House of Commons for three subsidies pay-
able at an increased rate; and, because of the largeness of the
sums involved, made the request that the Lower House consult
with the Lords. This procedure was strenuously opposed in
speeches by Bacon, because it violated a "privilege" of the Commons which prevented consultation with the Upper House on
a question of supply. When Bacon's objection was sustained by
the Lower House he was not yet satisfied, and argued against
the proposed rate of collection. "The poor men's rent," he said,
"is such as they are not able to yield it, and the general com-
monalty is not able to pay so much upon the present. The
gentlemen must sell their plate and the farmers their brass pots
ere this will be paid." The Queen showed great indignation at
what she considered an affront to her person by the young man
she had smiled upon from his boyhood and with whom she had
often conversed about serious questions of state. She spoke
bitterly of those who placed the burdens of their constituents
before "the necessity of the time," and banished Bacon from
her presence.

Bacon, who refused to retract what he had said in the Commons, asked the Queen's pardon for his "boldness and plainness"
and told her, "Your Majesty's favour indeed, and access to your
royal person, I did ever, encouraged by your own speeches,
seek and desire; and I would be very glad to be reintegrate in

that." The "exquisite disgrace" he felt on being refused the
office he now sought consisted largely in the denial of access to
his sovereign. How he regarded such a denial he was to tell in
a charge to a jury twenty-odd years later, after he had obtained
the office his heart was now set on: "The fountain of honour is
the king and his aspect, and the access to his person continueth
honour in life, and to be banished from his presence is one of
the greatest eclipses of honour that can be."

Bacon told his uncle in a letter, which he hoped the Queen
would see, that he "was sorry to find . . . that my last speech in
Parliament, delivered in discharge of my conscience and duty
to God, her Majesty, and my country was offensive. . . . If my
heart be misjudged by imputation of popularity . . . I have great
wrong; and the greater, because the manner of my speech did
most evidently show that I spake simply and only to satisfy my
conscience, and not with any advantage or policy to sway the
cause; and my terms carried all signification of duty and zeal
towards her Majesty and her service. . . . And therefore I most
humbly pray your Lordship, first to continue me in your own
good opinion: and then to perform the part of an honest friend
. . . in drawing her Majesty to accept of the sincerity and simplicity of my heart, and to bear with the rest, and restore me
to her Majesty's favour."

The Queen, who was probably informed of the content of
this letter, still refused to see Bacon. To Puckering Bacon wrote
of his "grief" and "marvel" at the Queen's "hard conceit" of his
speeches in the Commons. "It mought," he told the Lord
Keeper, "please her sacred Majesty to think what my end
should be in those speeches, if it were not duty, and duty alone.
I am not so simple but I know the common beaten way to
please. And whereas popularity hath been objected, I muse
what care I should take to please many, that taketh a course of
life to deal with few."

To Lady Bacon's complaint that her son was being "robbed" through his uncle's denying him office the Lord Treasurer answered that he had "less power to do my friends good than the world thinketh." Throughout a whole year Essex pleaded vehemently with Elizabeth and even begged the Cecils to give Bacon the place that he sought. To Robert Cecil he expressed surprise, which was probably feigned, that the latter's father should prefer a "stranger"—Edward Coke—to a "kinsman," whose "parts and sufficiency" were greater "in any respect." Elizabeth was not to be moved, even after the Earl warned her against losing "the use of the ablest gentleman to do her service of any of your quality whatsoever." When of an evening the favorite talked much of the time of little else besides Bacon's talents and virtues, the Queen would order him to desist. On one occasion she sent him to bed. Finally Elizabeth told Essex that, plead as he might, Bacon would not yet be put into a place where his duties might require access to her person. She reminded the favorite that "if it had been in the King, her father's time, a less offence than that would have made a man be banished from his presence for ever."

In 1594 Sir Edward Coke, Bacon's senior by nine years, an experienced lawyer of considerable repute, became Attorney-General. Bacon then made an effort to obtain the Solicitor-Generalship. Earlier, Cecil had told Essex that his protégé would have been better advised to seek this office instead of the Attorneyship. Burghley recommended the nephew's appointment, but in a half-hearted manner. Robert Cecil presented his cousin's "virtues" in such a way that suspicion of Bacon's political capabilities was spread about the Court. Bacon threatened to retire from law and politics if the office now sought was not to be his. The Queen, through Robert Cecil, who by now was Secretary of State although his appointment had not been made public, made known her decision that, if

Bacon continued to hold the view that either he got the office he now sought "in his own time" or he would regard himself as one denied all office, she would search the whole of England for another candidate rather than give the Solicitor-Generalship to the young man. In November, 1595, Sir Thomas Fleming, Bacon's senior by seventeen years, was appointed to the post.

The following spring Puckering died and Sir Thomas Egerton, Master of the Rolls, was made Lord Keeper and Lord Chancellor (1596-1617), under the title of Lord Ellesmere. Bacon now became a candidate for the Mastership. Essex having twice failed to persuade the Queen to advance his protégé, was not pressed to entreat Elizabeth in his behalf again. Egerton instead was asked to use his influence with her Majesty, who for a third time refused to appoint Bacon to a regular office of state.

The Queen, however, had been keeping an eye on the son of her former Lord Keeper. Her character being what it was, she had probably come to admire his steadfastness during more than three years, while he refused either to apologize or recant. She invited him into the Royal Presence, and made him "Queen's Counsel, Extraordinary"—as Bacon called the office in a letter to James on a later occasion—by her own edict, dispensing with the ordinary Patent. Bacon received no further appointment under Elizabeth, yet he was brought continually into her employment. In retrospect he was to tell King James: "My good old Mistress was wont to call me her watch-candle, because it pleased her to say I did continually burn (and yet she suffered me to waste almost to nothing)." Bacon's first editor, William Rawley, whose opinion in the matter was doubtlessly inspired by the candidate himself, wrote of Bacon's failure to obtain promotion from Elizabeth in his *Life of the Honourable Author*: "His birth and other capacities qualified him above others of his profession to have ordinary accesses at court and to come frequently into the queen's eye, who would often grace him with private and free communication, not only about the matters of his profession or business in law, but also about arduous affairs of estate; from whom she received from time to time great satisfaction. Nevertheless, though she cheered him much with the bounty of her confidence, yet she never cheered him with the bounty of her hand . . . which might be imputed, not so much to Her Majesty's averseness and disaffection towards him, as to the arts and policy of a great statesman then, who laboured by all industrious and secret means to suppress and keep him down; lest if he had risen, he might have obscured his glory." The statesman blamed by Rawley was Bacon's cousin, Robert Cecil, against whose guile and craftiness Lady Bacon had early warned her sons.

Bacon's political undertakings during the reign of Elizabeth were those of a Parliamentarian, a Queen's Counsel "Extraordinary," and a writer of political tracts. His grasp of constitutional questions and his skill in debate gave him a commanding place in the House of Commons. Experienced Parliamentarians, newly elected representatives from the shires, the Secretary of State, and the Queen herself were given the benefit of his advice. In the Commons Bacon's voice was heard in advocacy of the repeal of outmoded laws and in a plea, by implication, for a digest and compilation of legal statutes and precedents. The laws, he said, are "so many in number that neither common people can half practise them, nor the lawyer sufficiently understand them." Bacon asked the Lower House for a rectification of weights and measures in view of the fact that false weighing had become widespread. As the advocate of a strong agricultural population, he argued against any bill on tillage which would further the engrossing of "the wealth of the kingdom . . . in a few pasturers' hands." He opposed a repressive measure of Burghley's against Roman Catholic Recusants, and another affecting procedures in the Council's Court of Star Chamber.

In 1593 Bacon refused to permit Burghley to have the Lords discuss a question of supply, and led a Commons bent on affirming once and for all that its constitutional privileges were to be recognized and sustained. Eight years later Bacon asserted a second constitutional principle of another sort, this time to the Queen's great satisfaction. The Commons had begun to consider the repeal of certain Monopolies with Patents which had been granted by the Queen. Bacon undertook to clarify the general question of Monopolies, which members of the Commons tended to treat in gross. He distinguished among several sorts, arguing that the soundness of any one Monopoly depended on its circumstances and purpose. "If," he said, "any man out of his own wit, industry, or endeavour, find out any thing beneficial to the Commonwealth, or bring any new invention which every subject of this kingdom may use; yet, in regard of his pains and travel therein, her Majesty perhaps is pleased to grant him a privilege to use the same only, by himself or his deputies, for a certain time. This is one kind of Monopoly. Sometimes there is a glut of things, when they be in excessive quantity, as perhaps of corn; and perhaps her Majesty gives licence of transportation to one man. This is another kind of Monopoly. Sometimes there is a scarcity or a small quantity; and the like is granted also." Bacon also made it clear to the Commons that since the granting of Patents lay within the Royal Prerogative, the House could proceed in the matter only by way of petition to the Queen. His speech on this occasion included a statement which was to be recalled in later years by his political enemies: "For the prerogative of the prince, I hope I shall never hear it discussed. The queen hath both enlarging and restraining power; she may set at liberty things restrained by Statute and may restrain things which be at liberty." The Commons concurred in a proposal of petition. On being informed of this proceeding, Elizabeth suspended some of the unpopular Patents in question and revoked others. She granted in unfeigned affection for her subjects what she would have refused a demanding Commons which sought to bring within question her comprehensive Prerogative. It was at this time, near the end of her long reign, that she summoned her Parliament to Whitehall and told them in a farewell, "Though God hath raised me high, yet this I count the glory of my crown, that I have reigned with your loves."

After the defeat of the Irish armies and the rout of a supporting Spanish force in 1601 had terminated a rebellion of eight years' duration, Bacon wrote a letter to the Secretary of State, advising him how to proceed in arranging a settlement of Ireland. He asked Robert Cecil "to embrace the care of reducing that kingdom to civility . . . for . . . sound honour and merit to her majesty and this crown." He counselled his cousin against punitive measures, displanting of ancient "generations," and the opening of wounds in a recrudescence. The reduction of Ireland, he wrote, "as well to civility and justice, as to obedience and peace, which things, as affairs now stand, I hold to be inseparable, consisteth in four points: 1. The extinguishing of the relicks of the war. 2. The recovery of the hearts of the people. 3. The removing of the root and occasions of new troubles. 4. Plantations and buildings."

To further these ends Bacon advised that Irish "weakness" be supplanted by Christianity and Irish "conditions" be replaced by "graces," through such agents as justice, protection, and reward. He asked for a "toleration of religion," "the recontinuing and replenishing of the college begun at Dublin," "versions of bibles and catechisms, and other books of instruction into the Irish language," and "justice . . . as near as may be to the laws and customs of England." He counselled the "carrying of an even course between the English and Irish . . . as if they were one nation," the countenancing of the Irish nobility, the bestowal of knighthood on Irish subjects, and the care and education of their children. He argued that plantations would be better and more economical than a large military force, that persons chosen as "governors and counsellors" must have the affection and esteem of the people, that building and planting should proceed, not haphazardly, but "according to a prescript or formulary," and that an increase of new inhabitants should be encouraged by ample liberties and charters.

Bacon was to make similar representations to James, in 1609, and to Buckingham, in 1616, on the Irish question. His advice on each occasion was the issue of a desire to make Ireland "another Britain." It was characterized by a magnanimity toward a conquered race and by sensitivity to the temperament and the customs of what were called a "wild" people, with their bards, their harps, their contentiousness, their impatience of restraint.

IV

BACON AND ESSEX

W<small>HEN</small> E<small>LIZABETH</small> <small>MADE</small> B<small>ACON</small> Q<small>UEEN'S</small> C<small>OUNSEL</small> on her own
warrant she intended that his duties should be of an extraor-
dinary sort. She continuously discussed questions of state with
him. When in a pamphlet the Jesuit priest Robert Parsons
attacked the Queen and her Lord Treasurer for their measures
against Roman Catholic Recusants, Bacon was given the task of
preparing a reply. He was also called upon to compile a state
report on the treason of Robert Devereux (1566-1601), Second
Earl of Essex, at whose trial he had been assigned the role of
prosecutor, along with Attorney-General Coke. This engage-
ment in what came to be known as "the case of Essex" was to
be one of the most distressing episodes of his life. After Bacon
had become renowned and his name enduring, few subjects in
English history would be dilated upon with more dissolute
sentimentality and greater moral confusion than this. The case
has been cited, as a biographer, John Nichol, has remarked, "to
point half the morals and adorn half the tales against ingratitude
for . . . centuries." The Queen's Counsel, who performed a required duty of state, has been presented as a man devoid of "instinct of honor," "ethical sentiment," "moral instincts." Altogether, his conduct "has been the subject of more vituperation

than perhaps any other single act of any other single man." One
expositor crowns his account of the Earl's trial for treason with
this flourish: "Essex was a traitor to the laws which make possible a civilized and organized state, and by those laws he deserved death. Bacon was a traitor to higher laws than these—
the laws of honour, of pity, of love; and by those sacred laws
he stands condemned." One wonders how the man who composed this statement could ever suppose that any honorable
officer of state who loved and pitied the members of the human
race could ever prosecute any individual in a court of law. Or
should such an officer presume that there is to be one justice
for late intimates and benefactors turned political traitors and
another for strangers among malefactors? Let us review the
circumstances of the case.

About the time when Bacon was imploring his uncle Lord
Burghley for an office so that he might pursue his scientific
endeavors, he had been extended the patronage of the rising star
in the Court, the Earl of Essex. The Earl, five years Bacon's
junior, was a man with literary gifts, who had entered Cambridge at the age of ten, and would probably have chosen a
"retired course" in study, had he not been brought into the
Queen's service. After taking part in a military campaign under
the Earl of Leicester, another of Elizabeth's favorites, Esssex
was made Master of the Horse, before he was twenty-one. By
1589 he was supplanting Leicester in the affections of an in-
fatuated Queen—almost three times his age. Essex responded
with a temperament which always displayed more ardor than
caution in the presence of lovers and admirers; he took Elizabeth by storm. She was behaving, once more, like the coquette
she was, in demanding the Earl's constant attention. Queen and
courtier became jealous one of the other. Anyone who came
between Elizabeth and Essex on any matter, in any circumstance, on any business, was deemed a potential rival or enemy

by the Earl. Affection for the Queen did not, however, preclude his marrying secretly, and thereby occasioning in Elizabeth great pique and unbounded, uncontrollable rage. The indulgence of the Queen made the Earl unaware of her wariness lest any favorite should presume politically on her sentiment. Jealousy rendered Essex blind to her skill in playing one courtier against another. A romantic temperament made him oblivious to a Queen's capacity to control her affections when confronted with acts or circumstances which might infringe upon her queenly majesty or the welfare of her throne and people.

After a time the new favorite at Court was looked upon as the political rival of Burghley. Essex began to assume that his position was such that he could name the leaders of military expeditions, influence the course of justice by a note to a Lord Keeper, and assign offices of state to persons of his own choosnig. In this assumption he undertook the promotion of Bacon, a candidate to his liking because of his capacity of mind, his conversation, kindliness, reverence of the Queen, and—by no means least—his being denied office by his uncle, Lord Burghley.

Essex became Bacon's patron in the year 1591. For some four years the two men, divergent in temperament, were on very friendly terms. The patron offered "power, might, authority, and amity" to an aspirant for political place at Court, as well as the prospect of advancement for a philosopher's scientific designs. Bacon, long denied what he considered his due recognition by Burghley, became the willing protégé of the Cecils' most powerful opponent at Court. In 1592, Anthony Bacon on his return from travels on the Continent, found his brother "bound and in deep arrearages" to the new patron.

Bacon's early faith in the Earl, even to the extent of entering into the Essex-Burghley rivalry, showed itself in the firmness of his treatment of his uncle on the question of subsidies and other

matters in the House of Commons. When the office of Attorney-General fell vacant Essex was given opportunity to
effect the patronage he had undertaken. The Attorneyship was
a place to which a legally inexperienced man could hardly have
expected promotion. Essex, who had been rapidly advanced at
Court in his twenties, saw no reason why a man of thirty-two
should not be given the post. He had, however, miscalculated
the Queen's character and the influence of her trusted Lord
Treasurer. Bacon's suit, advanced through Essex, failed, despite
the vehemence of his patron's entreaty. In a second suing, for
the Solicitor-Generalship, history repeated itself. Elizabeth may
have secretly admired the young Parliamentarian's standing up
to her "solid" Burghley and his refusal to retreat. Probably, too,
she was unconsciously jealous, as only a coquette could have
been, of the warmth and zeal of her favorite's support of Bacon
in which, as Lady Bacon remarked, "the Earl showed great
affection" and "violent courses." Before many years had gone
by Bacon was to have occasion to remark, when he was entreating the Queen in behalf of the disobedient Essex, "that there are
not only jealousies, but certain revolutions in princes' minds."

    While Bacon's political promotion and reconciliation with
the Queen were being pursued, Essex had Bacon prepare devices or masques for Elizabeth's entertainment. In these the
Queen was complimented and praised, Essex was portrayed as
a faithful suitor, and the founding of a new experimental learning under the direction of the author was represented as an
undertaking worthy of a great sovereign. When nothing came
of his efforts to promote Bacon's cause, Essex decided, in 1595,
that he would yet prove himself a worthy patron of an impoverished suitor, gifted beyond any inhabitant of the Court
and denied place because he refused to recant what he had a
right to say in the Commons and because Burghley was intent
on impeding the advancement of any potential rival to his heir.
The Earl presented his protégé with an estate at Twickenham

worth £1,800—the amount obtained by Bacon when he sold the land to pay creditors. "You fare ill," Essex wrote, "because you have chosen me for your mean and dependence; you have spent your times and thoughts in my matter. I die if I do not somewhat towards your fortune. You shall not deny to accept a piece of land I will bestow on you." Bacon accepted the land as the gift of a generous patron and friend. On receipt of the benefaction, which he did not specifically mention in his letter, because this was intended for the Queen's reading, Bacon wrote:

TO MY LORD OF ESSEX, it may please your good lordship:
I pray God her Majesty's weighing be not like the weight of a balance: *gravia deorsum, levia sursum*. But I am as far from being altered in devotion towards her as I am from distrust that she will be altered in opinion towards me, when she knoweth me better. For myself, I have lost some opinion, some time, and some means. This is my account. But then, for opinion, it is a blast that cometh and goeth; for time, it is true it goeth and cometh not; but yet I have learned that it may be redeemed.

For means, I value that most, and the rather because I am purposed not to follow the practice of the law (if her Majesty command me in any particular I shall be ready to do her willing service), and my reason is, only because it drinketh too much time, which I have dedicated to better purpose. But even for the point of estate and means, I partly lean to Thales' opinion, that a philosopher may be rich if he will. Thus your lordship seeth how I comfort myself; to the increase whereof I would fain please myself to believe that to be true which my Lord Treasurer writeth, which is, that it is more than a philosopher morally can digest. But without any such high conceit, I esteem it like the pulling out of an aching tooth, which I remember when I was a child and had little philosophy, I was glad of it when it was done.

For your Lordship, I do think myself more beholding to you than to any man. And I say I reckon myself as a *common* (not popular, but *common*); and as much as is lawful to be enclosed of a common so much your Lordship shall be sure to have.
Your Lordship's to obey your honourable commands,
More settled than ever.

This letter, veiled in its wording because intended for the Queen's reading, invites a comment. Bacon now compares himself to a "common," something which, as such, cannot be "enclosed," however much liked, loved, desired, or coveted, with however generous intentions by an individual. His statement in effect amounts to this: he accepts the Earl's gift as one eager to serve the Queen and also to engage in a philosophical enterprise for the common good, and not as one at the disposal of any individual, even an individual to whom, for his efforts to promote a friend and for his financial aid, he is "more beholding . . . than to any man."

The following year, when a vacancy in the Mastership of the Wards occurred, Bacon's candidature for the office was proposed to the Queen and supported by other persons than Essex. The dependence of Bacon on the patronage of the impulsive Essex was about to come to an end. By 1595 Bacon had come to see in clearer perspective, and with more objectivity than before, certain dominant elements in the Earl's mentality and character, and, by way of consequence from these, the Earl's place in the emotions and the thoughts of the Queen. A year later Bacon, having discerned that certain difficulties of his own making were accumulating about the headstrong and temperamental favorite and unable to approve of much of his behavior in the dealings with the Queen, offered the frank advice of a friend to the man who for four years had been his enthusiastic patron.

Bacon and Essex were friends, but there has been a too extravagant playing by biographers upon the "sacred word friend" in their treatment of the Bacon-Essex relationship. By the romanticizing of some of these writers one could be led to suppose that until the time of the trial of Essex for treason, this attachment had been of a Damon and Pythias kind. There had never, in fact, at any time been anything of the sort. Essex was a vehement, if fond, patron, conscious of his power, his high estate, and his place in the Court. In keeping with a nature which could be imperious, the Earl as a patron expected from his protégé not mere gratitude but submission to "enclosure" within his personal political service. Bacon's brother Anthony was at times in this service. A grateful Bacon had to make his own position clear in this regard and, after he had done so, a cooling in relations became manifest. It was at this juncture that Bacon thought it his friendly duty to address some pointed admonitions to the Earl. In 1596 Essex stood in need of advice, not because of a failure but because of a success. As the leader of an expedition, he had made a dashing assault on Cadiz and destroyed what had remained of the Spanish fleet after the rout of the great Armada. Overnight Essex became a nation's hero, and began to behave like a popular figure much aware of the fact. Elizabeth, who never desired that any person in her service should hold the centre of the public stage for long, was displeased, the more now because in this instance, the manners and the mien of a favorite were being affected. For some time the Queen had been troubled by the Earl's heady and uncontrollable behavior. Never fully submissive to the Royal will, and long given to presuming on the Queen's affection, Essex was becoming increasingly demanding, even sullen and truculent, when not given his own way.

The burden of the advice which Bacon now tendered the Earl was: "Win the Queen; if this be not the beginning, of any other course I see no end." Bacon, as a friend, told his former patron that, as the Queen's favorite, he could no longer rely on the mere "favour of affection" but must in the future cultivate "correspondence and agreeableness" with her wishes. He should dissipate certain impressions which were fast becoming fixed opinions in the Queen's mind: that he is "opinionastre and not rulable," is "of a militar independence," is desirous of a "popular reputation," is lax in financial matters, and is given to making use of the Queen's sentiment to further his own financial ends. The aptness of the last of these several cautions was later to be confirmed, when Essex had been put under detention for disobeying the Queen's orders. Then Elizabeth was to tell Bacon, in so many words, that the Earl's professions of affection in his letters of entreaty were motivated by the desire to have his Monopoly on sweet wines renewed. None of the warnings of the protégé of earlier years was acted upon by Essex.

The Earl's relationship with the Queen deteriorated the following year. An expedition which he led against the Azores (1597-1598) proved a failure. Its only success was the capture of Fayal, and this minor achievement Essex refused to have recorded because it was the work of Raleigh. In a compounded jealousy the Earl showed so great vexation at the promotion during his absence of Robert Cecil and the raising of the Lord Admiral, Charles Howard of Effingham, to the rank of Earl of Nottingham, that he left the Court and refused to return until he had been made Earl Marshal. This was a position against the seeking or acceptance of which Bacon had cautioned Essex. Never thereafter, until the time of the Earl's detention for disobedience, did Bacon offer Essex specific personal advice. Many letters requested of Bacon by Essex were not written; those sent contained little but polite compliment and general comment on circumstances. To Bacon it had become clear that the man whose place at Court rested on the Queen's affection, was incapable of taking to heart any reasonable advice, no matter how sincerely he might request it. The two men drifted apart. The days of patronage had ended in 1595 when Bacon had declared himself against "enclosure" as a patron's bondsman. The patron's interest in philosophic and scientific causes had evaporated on the presentation of the masques for Elizabeth's entertainment and her favorite's advancement. The independent and irresponsible attitude of Essex to the Queen, seemingly devoid of any discernment of the monarch's circumstances, was not pleasing to the man who in his youth had himself been content to "bear the yoke," as he said, of his Queen's displeasure. So wide had the cleavage between Bacon and his former patron become by 1597 that Bacon dedicated the first edition of his *Essays* not to Essex but to his brother Anthony, a political servant of the Earl. The brother became so perturbed over this act that he begged of Essex "leave to transfer my interest unto your Lordship." Despite the implied reproof in this pointed dedication, the Earl, in the following year, again wrote Bacon, seeking advice. The occasion was an uprising under Hugh O'Neill, Earl of Tyrone in Ireland. Essex was assuming that if forces were sent to quell this rebellion either he himself would be put in command, or, if he decided not to go, the choice of a leader would be his. Bacon withheld detailed advice. Thinking that an admonition to the Earl to remain in England, near the Queen, was best in the circumstances, he gave this, in March, 1598, and added a warning:

But that your Lordship is too easy in such cases to pass from dissimulation to verity, I think if your Lordship lent your reputation in this case—that is to pretend that, if peace go not on, and the Queen mean not to make a defensive war, as in times past, but a full reconquest of those parts of the country, you would accept the charge—I think it would help to settle Tyrone in his seeking accord, and win you a great deal of honour *gratis*.

The Queen and her Council decided that an expedition should be undertaken. Members of the Privy Council were aware that the man who led the English forces would probably suffer in reputation, for already a soldier of much skill, Sir John Norris, had failed to subdue the rebels. Tyrone was a resourceful leader in guerilla warfare. Essex now began to suspect that the Cecils were bent on sending him to Ireland in order to accomplish his ruin. His reputation had already been damaged by the failure of the expedition to the Azores; it might not survive another defeat. Essex named Sir George Carew, a friend of the Cecils, as the person fitted for the command. The nominee of the Cecils was Sir William Knollys, uncle of Essex. At a stormy meeting of the Council, when Essex acted imperiously, the Queen interposed some observations. These Essex received with a show of contempt—the accumulated contempt of a young man for an old mistress who was in turn demanding, teasing, physically withholding, and irritable. Elizabeth gave Essex a slap on the face and had him removed from the Council-Chamber. The Earl stayed away from the Court, expecting that the Queen would soon show contrition. Had he been a wiser lover, he would have known that one show of public scorn could seal a favorite's fate with a coquette who was still the daughter of Henry VIII. Egerton, the Lord Keeper and Lord Chancellor, who had witnessed the scene in the Council, and was a friend of Essex who had continued on good terms with him even after the favorite had interfered in cases before the courts, wrote the Earl. "Yield," he said, "let policy, duty, and religion enforce you to yield; submit to your sovereign, *between whom and you there can be no proportion of duty*." Essex replied, "In such a case I must appeal from all earthly judges . . . I keep my heart from baseness, although I cannot keep my fortune from declining."

Before long, the Earl gave the impression that he himself was ready to lead an expedition into Ireland. Whether he intended to go remained a question; the odds were that he did not. Once more he would act contrary to Bacon's advice; he was about "to pass from dissimulation to verity." Within months he would be disobeying the Queen's orders and then setting out with an armed force to seize her person. If the first of these deeds could ever be excused, the last could never in Bacon's view be condoned. It was the outrageous and treasonable act of an outlaw. If let pass without resort to a court of justice, neither sovereign, constitution, government, nor minister of state could ever be secure in rightful authority.

Meanwhile the Earl's friend Henry Wriothesley, Earl of Southampton—who was to be one of the cooperators in his rebellion—begged him to retrace his steps and not to undertake the Irish assignment. Essex replied: "I am tied in my own reputation to use no tergiversation; the Queen hath irrevocably decreed it, the Council do passionately urge it." Before the expedition had departed Bacon wrote a letter of encouragement to the Earl, whose mind by now was becoming apprehensive and confused. He mentioned the honor and other desirable ends which could be attained by success in the campaign and begged of Essex, now that an opportunity was his for mending his relationship with the Queen, "that your lordship in this whole action, looking forward, would set down this position, that merit is worthier than fame; and looking back hither, would remember this text, that obedience is better than sacrifice."

The Irish campaign was doomed to failure from the start. At the outset Essex declared: "I am defeated in England." The Earl now realized that he had already played into his enemies' hands. To his mortification, Sir Christopher Blount—his stepfather and the third husband of his mother, Letitia Knollys—was refused a seat on the Irish Council. Blount had served under the Earl at Cadiz and in the Azores; he would be going with him to Ireland and would be a fellow conspirator. Essex became more convinced than ever that the Cecil faction was plotting his downfall. The Queen's attitude was uncertain. He refused to embark for Ireland until Elizabeth had granted him permission under seal to return when he so desired.

Essex on setting out in March, 1599, had under his command 16,000 infantry and 1,500 cavalry. By the end of two months' campaigning his forces had been reduced to 4,000. In September he arranged to meet Tyrone, and agreed to a truce whose terms amounted to an English capitulation. The Queen sent two dispatches to the Earl, demanding a written explanation of his conduct. She retracted her former permission for his return, and forbade him to leave Ireland without her express command. Contrary to this order, the Earl landed in England and threw himself at the Queen's feet on the 28th of September, six months and one day after he had embarked on his ill-fated undertaking. So fearful was the Earl's state of mind, and so far had he already gone in contemplating open warfare against real or supposed intriguers at home while he had been in Ireland, that he had intended initially "to carry with him as much of the army as he could conveniently transport." However, he brought only "the main part of his household and a great part of captains and gentlemen."

Essex was put under detention by the Queen's orders and so kept until the following March. After his release he remained under the Queen's "displeasure." This, as the Secretary of State, Robert Cecil, explained, prevented persons from resorting to him, except a few on business and those "that were of his own blood." While Essex was under detention two commissions, one in November, 1599, and another in the following June, had considered two charges against him, disobedience to the Queen and disregard of military orders in the moving of his troops from place to place. Before the second hearing took place, Bacon, in order to present the Earl's acts in as favorable a light as possible, arranged for his employment as one of the Queen's Counsel. Bacon also, when he found himself in the presence of Elizabeth, tried, time after time, to assuage her feelings and moderate her displeasure with the Earl's conduct. The Queen proved unyielding, and finally, having grown weary of Bacon's incessant pleading, told him to cease from speaking on the subject of the Earl.

When Bacon's discussion of Essex with the Queen became

known, it gave rise to ugly rumors. Robert Cecil thought it well to send a caution: "Cousin, I hear it, but I believe it not, that you should do some ill service to my Lord of Essex; for my part I am merely passive and not active in this action, and I follow the Queen, and that heavily, I lead her not . . . and the same course I would wish you to take." Fearing that Essex might have heard and been misled by the rumors, Bacon sent the Earl a letter offering his support and stating the conditions under which this could be given. He now affirmed the principle of the order of his duty, as a loyal subject of the Queen, the same principle he had enunciated in correspondence with Burghley twenty years before. In 1580 Bacon had written: "To your lordship . . . I can be but a bounden servant. *So much may I safely promise and purpose to be, seeing public and private bonds vary not, but that my service to God, her Majesty, and your Lordship draw in a line.*" Loyalty to God came first, then loyalty to the Queen, then loyalty to minister of state or friend, as Bacon was more than once to tell Essex. Bacon wrote Essex as follows:

No man can better expound my doings than your Lordship, which maketh me say the less. Only I humbly pray you to believe that I aspire to the conscience and commendation of first, *bonus civis*, which with us is a good and true servant to the Queen, and next of *bonus vir*, that is an honest man. I desire your Lordship also to think that, though I confess I love some things much better than I love your Lordship, as the Queen's service, her quiet and contentment, her honour, her favour, the good of my country and the like, yet I love few persons better than yourself, both for gratitude's sake and for your own virtues, which cannot hurt but by accident or abuse. Of which my good affection I was ever and am ready to yield testimony by any good offices, but with such reservations as yourself cannot but allow. For as I was ever sorry that your Lordship should fly with waxen wings, doubting Icarus' fortune, so for the growing up of your own feathers—especially ostrich's or any other save of a bird of prey—no man shall be more glad. And this is the axle-tree whereupon I have turned and shall turn. Which to signify to you, though I think you are of yourself persuaded as much, is the cause of my writing. And so I commend your Lordship to God's goodness. From Gray's Inn, this 20th day of July, 1600.

It was not a mere afterthought, then, which Bacon stated in the year 1604 in an *Apology . . . in certain imputations concerning the late Earl of Essex,* where he wrote: "For every honest man that hath his heart well planted, will forsake his king rather than forsake God, and forsake his friend rather than forsake his king; and yet will forsake any earthly commodity, yea, and his own life in some cases, rather than forsake his friend. I hope the world hath not forgotten these degrees, else the heathen saying, '*Amicus usque ad aras,*' shall judge them."

So far was Bacon prepared to go in risking his reputation with the Queen, Privy Council, and public on behalf of the Earl, he even composed pretended letters between his brother Anthony and Essex, writing these in the different styles of the two, for presenting to the Queen as evidence, first, of the Earl's devotion and allegiance to her person and, second, of the common public belief that her displeasure with Essex was the result of the representations of his enemies at Court. To these secret letters Essex was to make allusion at his trial in an attempted defence. There can be no doubt, then, that up to the time of the Earl's engaging in a treasonable act, Bacon still felt "much bound unto him" as a former friend and generous benefactor. Bacon could write excusably to Lord Henry Howard (Northampton) respecting his attitude to Essex, "I have spent more time and more thoughts about his well-doing than ever I did about mine own."

While on campaign in Ireland Essex had become fully convinced that his enemies at home had determined on his destruction. He was of the opinion, too, that Robert Cecil was bent on making the Infanta of Spain the next ruler of England. The Earl began a treasonable correspondence with James VI of Scotland about his assuming the throne of England in succession to Elizabeth. Essex, while still in Ireland, seems to have discussed with his fellow-intriguers the question of obtaining the support of the Roman Catholics in a national uprising, on the promise of their political toleration.

In September, 1600, while the Earl was under the Queen's displeasure, his Monopoly on sweet wines came up for renewal. This was refused by the Queen. Essex, already heavily in debt, faced financial ruin. Thoroughly distraught by now, with a mind inflamed by frightful imaginings, the Earl railed against Elizabeth for her inconstancy, against Cecil for a supposed design to put the Infanta on the throne, and against members of the Privy Council as enemies seeking his life. He determined on the physical seizure of Elizabeth and her segregation from her ministers. Plans to this end had been discussed in a vague manner by Essex and his military intimates while he was still in Ireland. As early as August, the Earl's followers began to hold secret meetings in Essex House. A plot was taking definite shape. First the Queen was to be taken captive, and then the City was to be aroused to the support of the rebels. Elizabeth would be held under restraint until new officers of government, of the Earl's own choosing, were appointed. The uprising was to be much more than part of a "private quarrel." The conspirators had political designs and meant business. "Now I see too late," confessed the convicted Blount on the scaffold, "that rather we should have failed of our purpose, it would have cost much blood, and perhaps drawn some from her Majesty's own person."

On February 7th, 1601, some eight months after Bacon had joined a commission in order to promote the Earl's defence on a charge of disobedience—still knowing nothing of the former patron's treasonable intent—Essex was summoned to appear before the Privy Council and provide an explanation of meetings in his residence. He declined to attend, pleading illness. That night some three hundred armed followers gathered at his house. The next day the Lord Keeper, Egerton, accompanied by three other peers, came officially to demand an explanation of the assembly. They were confronted with a blustering crew. Of those surrounding the Earl some shouted, "Kill them"; others, "Nay, but shop them up, keep them as pledges, cast the Great Seal out of the window." The general cry was, "To the Court! To the Court!" The Lord Keeper and his company were held as hostages. Essex was sure that the inhabitants of the City would respond in support, once an uprising had begun. The Earl was thinking of himself as a romantically popular hero. Many influential persons in the City had displayed great anger and indignation at the findings of the Queen's ecclesiastical commissions and her grants of Monopolies. There was precedent for the success of the present undertaking—precedent to which Bacon was to point, when as Queen's Counsel he addressed Essex at his trial for treason. "It was not," Bacon was then to say to Essex, "the company you carried with you, but the assistance which you hoped for in the City, which you trusted unto. The Duke of Guise thrust himself into the streets of Paris on the day of the Barricadoes, in his doublet and hose, attended only with eight gentlemen, and found that help in the City which (thanks be to God) you failed of here. And what followed? The King was forced to put himself into a pilgrim's weeds, and in that disguise to steal away to scape their fury. Even such was my Lord's confidence too; and his pretence the same—an all-hail and a kiss to the City. But the end was treason, as hath been sufficiently proved."

The armed conspirators set out on their undertaking. Word was brought them that the Queen's guard had already been doubled and made ready for action. Essex thereupon directed his men towards the City to sound an alarm. This alarm fell on deaf ears. The revolt was over before it had begun. After a brief skirmish with some loyal troops, the rebels retreated. The Earl managed to make his way back to his house to destroy incriminating papers. That night he was a prisoner in the Tower.

Essex was brought to trial before twenty-five of his peers—

"a greater number than hath been called in any former precedent." Bacon was required to take part in the proceedings as Queen's Counsel, as one of a commission earlier involved in the examination of the Earl's disobedience, and as assistant to the Crown-Attorney, Edward Coke, whose competence in handling constitutional cases was not great. In this trial, as in many others, Coke let questions become confused by unessentials, and the proceeding returned to the main charges only after Bacon had intervened. Whether Bacon would have withdrawn from the case, had he been permitted, is impossible to say. "The precedence of personal over political ties," as a historian has observed, was "hardly applicable to a state of affairs in which anarchy, with its attendant miseries, would inevitably follow on the violent overthrow of the Queen's right to select her ministers, even if her person for a time continued to be outwardly respected; and it is, at all events, one which Bacon studiously renounced from the very beginning of his connection with Essex."

Bacon thought Essex guilty of treason with intent. He discovered that the Earl's conspiracy against the Queen was being hatched even while he had been making representations to the Queen of the Earl's affectionate and loyal devotion. After the trial had begun he was informed of some of the Earl's treasonable acts and intentions while in Ireland. Bacon could not in honesty entertain the Earl's defence that his actions were part of a "private quarrel," and that he was intent only on supplication to the Queen by way of petition. Said Bacon to the court, "Now put the case that the Earl of Essex's intent were, as he would have it believed, to go only as a suppliant to her Majesty. Shall their petitions be presented by armed petitioners? This must needs bring loss of liberty to the prince. Neither is it any point of law, as my Lord of Southampton would have it believed, that condemns them of treason, but it is apparent in common sense. To take secret counsel, to execute it, to run together in numbers armed with weapons—what can be the excuse?

Warned by the Lord Keeper, by a herald, and yet persist. Will
any simple man take this to be less than treason?"

Essex was found guilty, and seventeen days after his abortive
rebellion was executed for the crime. During the trial Bacon
had performed a public duty in defence of the Queen's honor
and person, with temperance, courage, wisdom, and justice. He
had acted in accordance with his own studied views respecting
honor and morality. To contend that these were overlooked or
repudiated by him in or out of court is nonsense. Certainly, he
would have considered the invoking of the word "honor" in
criticism of his taking part in the trial as a perversity. It was
Bacon's definite and explicit opinion, as he told a jury in a later
case respecting duelling, that "the fountain of honour is the king
and his aspect." Those who upheld the aspect of the sovereign
could be deemed men of honor; those who defaced it must be
treated as dishonorable. The sort of "honor" which promoters
of "moral sentiment" were to invoke was regarded by Bacon,
in explicit statements before courts of law, as something "no
better than a sorcery, that enchanteth the spirits of young men,
that bear great minds, with a false shew, *species falsa;* and a kind
of satanical illusion and apparition of honour against religion,
against law, against moral virtue, and against the precedents and
examples of the best times and valiantest nations."

The trial of Essex, as Bacon saw it, was a proceeding within
justice. Justice, in Bacon's view, was a "royal" virtue, "which
doth employ the other three cardinal virtues in her service: wisdom to discover, and discern nocent and innocent; fortitude to
prosecute and execute; temperance, so as to carry justice as it be
not passionate in the pursuit, nor confused in involving persons
upon light suspicion, nor precipitate in time."

V

BACON'S RELIGIOUS WRITINGS IN THE REIGN OF ELIZABETH

Dᴜʀɪɴɢ ᴛʜᴇ ʀᴇɪɢɴ ᴏꜰ Eʟɪᴢᴀʙᴇᴛʜ, Bacon composed three political pieces: first, a *Letter of Advice* in 1584, the year in which Bacon was first elected to Parliament; second, *On the Controversies of the Church of England* in 1589; and third, *Observations Upon a Libel Published This Present Year, 1592* (1593 according to the modern calendar). The first and second were addressed to the Queen; the third was written in defence of her policies. The first dealt with the Puritans and Roman Catholics, the second with the Puritans and the Anglican episcopate, the third mainly with the Roman Catholics and incidentally with the Puritans generally and lesser religious sects. In order to comprehend the tenor, purpose, and implications of these three writings of Bacon, his later *Pacification and Edification of the Church of England*, written for James, and his still later *Advice to Villiers*, certain aspects of the earlier stages of the Puritan movement in England must be kept in mind. These entered into the author's thought while his opinions on questions of religion and politics were in process of formation. They were among the immediate concerns of Bacon's father, as Lord Keeper; of his

mother, as a politico-religious contender; of his uncle, as the
Queen's chief advisor; of Whitgift, his tutor at Cambridge, and
later Archbishop of Canterbury; of his University, where two
of the chief Puritan contenders were, for a time, respectively a
professor and a fellow.

Some of Bacon's commentators seem to be under the impression that the Puritans in the reigns of Elizabeth and James were
gentle, quiet, tolerant, and charitable individuals who sought
only freedom to engage in a private and personal worship required by their biblically informed consciences. Few opinions,
of course, could be more opposed to the facts. The Puritans
were a severe, clamorous, intolerant, uncharitable band, ever
bent on putting out of countenance and sometimes given to
consigning to punishment in this world and to Hell in the next
those who refused to accept their tenets. Members of the English
clergy who had fled to the Continent during the persecutions of
the Protestants under Mary Tudor (1553-1558) acquired in
Geneva a doctrine of salvation, and saw in operation a fully
regimented "godly discipline" under the rule of a Consistory.
They returned home with very definite opinions on Saving Faith
and church discipline. It was their belief that the Church in
England had never really undergone reformation; that its prescribed ritual, clerical orders, and canonic laws were still Roman
in character. Now that England had a Protestant sovereign, the
time had come, they believed, for the bringing of the Church of
England—or rather the Church *in* England—within the true Reformation; they would provide this Church with a new rule and
a new theology, both founded on Scripture and on Scripture
alone. The Church of Geneva would be their model. These
English Calvinists found encouragement in the success of John
Knox (1505-1572) with the Scots to the north. The Church in
Scotland had accepted his directions for the rule of elders, Presbytery, and a General Consistory or Assembly. One sovereign,
Mary of Scotland, had been cashiered for her ungodliness, and

another ruler, James VI, was being kept under spiritual duress by a General Assembly. The Word of the Lord, as interpreted by Geneva, was beginning to prevail. The English Calvinists, however, were confronted with three difficult obstacles: the Act of Supremacy, the Act of Uniformity, and the Court of High Commission. Through the use of these Queen Elizabeth and her Privy Council were bent on enforcing uniformity in a church far removed in organization and rule from that of Geneva. The Sovereign of England had determined on having both a unified state and a unified church. The civil organization of the nation included several estates; so did the Established Church, with its bishops, priests, deacons, and laity. In this church, as it now stood, there could be no "democratic" rule by elders and a Genevan Consistory of laymen and ministers.

In theology the Calvinists professed the doctrine of the utter efficacy of God's Free Grace for the saving and the continued redemption of fallen man, without regard to natural knowledge, the exercise of the human will, or "works." In the organization of the Church, according to the Genevan understanding, congregations were assemblages of persons elected by God unto salvation, who submitted themselves to the rule and care of men chosen for their superior "wisdom" within the area of Divine Grace. Over all was a Consistory composed of six ministers who continued in office more or less permanently and twelve laymen elected annually. In Geneva the permanent members controlled policy, and the most influential among them came to be regarded as the source of ecclesiastical wisdom. Bishop Bancroft observed that in Genevan practice the laymen of the Consistory had been "not only over-ruled by the said six ministers; but likewise all the ministers over-topped by Maister *Calvin*, as that in effect he was *Domine fac totum*." "In show," said Richard Hooker, "a marvellous indifferently composed senate ecclesiastical was to govern, but in effect only one man should."

After a study of the opinions of the English Calvinists, Archbishop Parker reported to Burghley: "All that these men tend towards is the overthrow of all honourable quality and the setting afoot a Commonwealth, or a popularity." The Queen wrote to James in Scotland: "There is risen a sect of perilous consequences, who would have no kings but a presbytery.... Suppose you I can tolerate such scandals." James, before he left Scotland to assume the throne of England, thought it well to tell his son Henry (1594-1612, Prince of Wales in 1610):

> Some fiery spirited men in the Ministry got such a guiding of the people in the time of confusion that, finding the gust of government sweet, they began to fancy a democratic form.... I was calumniated in their sermons not for any vice in me but because I was a king, which they thought the highest evil. For they told their flocks that kings ... were naturally enemies to the Church.

Bancroft in his *Dangerous Positions* (1593) warned of the peril to the Established Church in the professions and undertakings of the new sect: "Hereby," he wrote, "it shall appear to our posterity if ... mischiefs shall happen, they were suffciently warned."

Under the Act of Supremacy, the Court of High Commission was empowered "to visit, reform, redress, order, correct and amend all such heresies, errors, schisms, abuses, offences, contempts and enormities whatsoever which by any manner of spiritual or ecclesiastical power, authority or jurisdiction can or may lawfully be reformed, ordered, redressed, corrected, restrained or amended." By the Act of Uniformity, "any manner of parson, vicar or other whatsoever minister" who should wilfully "use any other rite, ceremony, order, form or manner" of service than that set forth in the Prayer Book of 1559, or who should "preach, declare or speak anything in the derogation or depraving of the said book" would render himself liable to punishment and, in case of repeated offence, to life imprisonment.

Yet these Acts were far less comprehensive in scope and far less drastic in penalty than the regimen advocated by persons under the influence of Geneva. To the Genevan Consistory, a "standing ecclesiastical court," was committed—in Hooker's words—"the care of all men's manners, power of determining all kind of ecclesiastical causes, and authority to convent, to control, to punish, as far as with excommunication, whomsoever they should think worthy, none either small or great excepted." In Genevan teaching it was the duty of the secular power to uphold the Consistory in its decisions. A Christian magistrate, as a person obedient to the "spiritual powers," could do nothing less. The Calvinist John Knox, in a reference to the Book of Deuteronomy 13: 6-10, and in full compliance with its primitive severity, found it righteous to say, "Of these words of Moses are two things appertaining to one purpose, to be noted. Former, that such as solicitate only to idolatry ought to be punished to death without favour or respect of person." "I say," he also wrote, in characteristic vein, "if any go about to erect and set up idolatry or to teach defection from God, after that the verity hath been received and approved, that then not only the Magistrates, to whom the sword is committed, but also the people are bound by that oath, which they have made to God, to revenge to the uttermost of their power the injury done against his Majesty."

Thomas Cartwright, the leader of the English Calvinists, a disputer against Whitgift, and the professor of a faith that "purifieth the heart," was not to be outdone by the Scottish Knox. He held that "the same severity of punishment that was used against false prophets then under the Mosaic law ought to be used now under the gospel against false teachers comparing one person and circumstance with another. As he that hath fallen away from God and gone about to draw others away; to be handled according to the law prescribed in that Ch. 13 of Deuteronomy. If this be bloody and extreme I am content to be so counted with the Holy Ghost." "In this case of willing sliding back and moving others to the same, and other some cases which are expressed in the law, as of open and horrid blasphemy of the Name of God, I deny that upon repentence there ought to follow any pardon of death, which the Judicial law doth require."

When Bacon intimated in his *Controversies of the Church of England* that "profane scoffing" had proceeded out of the Universities he undoubtedly had in mind Thomas Cartwright and a disciple Walter Travers. Cartwright had been Lady Margaret Professor of Divinity and Travers a fellow of Trinity College in the University of Cambridge. In Travers' eyes the Universities were "the skulking places of drones, monasteries of yawning, snoring monks, trees not only barren but baneful with their poisonous shade to all plants that grow up under them." Cartwright called the clergy of the Established Church "bastards" and "boys and senseless asses"; non-Calvinist Christians, "swine"; the Universities, "dens of many-thievish non-residents"; benefices, so many bestowals "to the greedy use of many cormorant masters of Colleges at their wicked pleasure"; bishops, "a remnant of Antichrist's brood" for their corruption, arrogance, tyranny, and "flat heresy in the sacrament." One of the writers of what came to be known as "the First Admonition to Parliament" (probably Cartwright) deemed cathedral churches "the dens ... of all loitering lubbers," the Archbishop's Court "the filthy quagmire and poisoned plash of all the abominations that do infect the whole realm," and the Court of Commission "but a petty little stinking ditch."

Those adherents of Geneva who refused to accept the Anglican rule and rite on principle, even when they yielded in passive obedience, were given the name of Puritans or Precisians about 1564—three years after Bacon's birth. "The English Bishops," Thomas Fuller (1608-1661) says, "conceiving themselves impowered by their Canons, began to show their authority in urging the Clergy ... to subscribe to the Liturgy, Ceremonies and Discipline of the Church, and such as refused the same were branded with the odious name of Puritans." "This name Puritan," said Whitgift, "is very aptly given to these men, not because they be pure no more than were the Heretics called Cathari, but because they think themselves to be *mundiores caeteris,* more pure than others, as Cathari did, and separate themselves from all other Churches and congregations as spotted and defiled. Because also they suppose the Church which they have devised, to be without all impurity."

At the beginning of their endeavor the English Puritans put their request in words like these: "That we may altogether teach and practise that true knowledge of God's Word, which we have learned in this our banishment, and by God's merciful providence seen in the best reformed Churches." Before long they made a specific entreaty for the discontinuance in the services of the Established Church of what they called "Popish remnants," such as the wearing of the surplice, the making of the Sign of the Cross in baptism, kneeling at Communion, use of the ring in marriage, proceeding according to the Prayer Book, and the regarding of the Communion table as an altar. Certain of these practices soon became more than subjects of petition; in many instances, they became rejections in fact. In 1564 Burghley compiled a list, in manuscript, of *Varieties in the Services of the Church of precisians.* In this Burghley repeatedly mentions the failure on the part of clergy to wear the surplice. He notes discrepancies in the saying of service and prayers, in the position of the Communion table, in the administration and receiving of Communion, and in baptizing. "Some," he records, "say the service and prayers in the chancel; others in the body of the Church." The Communion table "standeth in the body of the Church in some places; in others it standeth in the chancel. In some places the Table standeth Altarlike, distant from the wall a yard." Some administer the Communion "with chalice, some with a Communion Cup, others with a Common Cup. Some with unleavened bread, some with leavened. . . . Some receive kneeling, others standing, others sitting." "Some baptize in a Font, some in a Basin. Some signed with the sign of the Cross; others not signed."

Burghley asked the Queen to bring these discrepancies to Archbishop Parker's attention. Parker summoned two Nonconformists, Thomas Sampson and Lawrence Humphrey, from Oxford and commanded them "to wear the cap appointed by Injunction, to wear no hats in their long gowns, to wear a surplice with a non-regent hood in their quires at their Colleges, according to the ancient manner there, to communicate kneeling in wafer-bread." Sampson, Dean of Christ Church, could not agree in "conscience" and was removed from his place. Humphrey, Regius Professor of Divinity and President of Magdalen, "for his usefulness in the University" was treated with leniency. Later he complied. At Cambridge the situation had become equally irregular. One George Withers, who refused to wear the square cap, had "stirred up a racket for the reformation of the University Windows" on the ground that their subjects smacked of superstition; "whereupon followed a great destruction of them." On a festival day, when the master of St. John's College was conveniently absent, "the most part of the College-Company," about three hundred in number, came to chapel without their surplices. Burghley, the Chancellor of the University, was shocked. Comparable happenings were becoming frequent in London.

Early in 1566, the Queen found it necessary to promulgate *Advertisements* for the bringing of order into the service of the Church. From that time the Puritan struggle entered upon a new phase. Some of the deprived clergy decided that "since they could not have the word of God preached, nor the Sacraments administered without idolatrous gear . . . it was their duty . . . to break off from the publick Churches, and to assemble, as they had opportunity, in private houses, or elsewhere, to worship God in a manner that might not offend against the light of their consciences." There was to be secrecy in meeting.

Edmund Grindal, Bishop of London, wrote to Henry Bullinger, in 1568:

Some London citizens of the lowest order, together with four or five ministers, remarkable neither for their judgment nor learning, have openly separated from us; and sometimes in private houses, sometimes in the fields, and occasionally even in ships, they have held their meetings and administered the Sacraments. Besides this, they have ordained ministers, elders, and deacons, after their own way, and have even excommunicated some who had seceded from their Church. And because masters Lawrence Humphrey, Sampson, Lever, and others, who have suffered so much to obtain liberty in respect of things indifferent, will not unite with them, they now regard them as semi-papists, and will not allow their followers to attend their preaching.

Within eight years after the publishing of the *Advertisements*, there appeared signs of the politico-religious revolution that was to become openly manifest in England after the Civil War in the reign of Charles I. In 1573 a number of Puritan leaders resolved on the secret formation of a Presbytery at Wandsworth. Eleven elders were chosen and their offices stated in a register called "The Orders of Wandsworth." About the same time another sort of assembly, the "Protestation of the Puritans," was organized. Each member swore to "come not back again to the Preaching of them that have received . . . marks of the Romish Beast," and took the following vow: "I have now joined myself to the Church of Christ. Wherein I have yielded myself subject to the Discipline of God's Word, as I promised at my Baptism. Which if I should now again forsake, and join myself with their Traditions, I should forsake the Union, wherein I am knit to the Body of Christ, and join myself to the Discipline of Antichrist." Persons who took this vow or made a similar assent came to rely increasingly on the immediate vouchsafing to the believer of the presence and the "wisdom" of God. The more this "wisdom" was exalted and proclaimed in "prophesying," the less place was given to the "carnal" knowledge acquired from university or other secular learning as part of the training of preachers. One culmination of the belief in the immediate presence of God appeared in the "conspiracy" of William Hacket, who had been "called," through the influence of Puritan preaching, to take "a strange and extraordinary course." On July 16th, 1591, two of his followers went through the streets of London proclaiming that Jesus Christ in the person of Hacket had come to judge the earth, to separate saints from sinners, and as King of Kings to establish the Throne of God and his gospel in Europe. Hacket was hanged. One disciple starved himself to death in prison; the other repented a year later, made a submission, and turned to the writing of poetry.

Puritanism now embraced, first, those who connived at the rule of Presbytery within the Established Church and hoped that this rule would ultimately be imposed on the whole ecclesiastical system; second, those who awaited the day, in passive conformity to what the law required, when a Presbyterian body independent of the national church would be countenanced; and third, those who, placing their trust in the "wisdom of God" immediately vouchsafed to them as "prophets," disapproved of all rule in matters of religion. These last persons came to be known as Enthusiasts.

The Puritans began to have energetic spokesmen and organizers. The former prepared contentious "admonitions" for Parliament and the public, as well as "loyal petitions" to the Queen and the Commons. The organizers promoted conventions, or *classes*, throughout the nation on a provincial and a national scale. In these *classes* instructions were to be given to ministers for the purpose of spreading the New Discipline within their parishes. Sympathetic clergymen were told that "those ceremonies in the Book of Common Prayer, which being taken from popery are in controversy, ought to be omitted, if it may be done without danger of being put from the ministry; but if there be imminent danger of being deprived, then let the matter be communicated to the *classis* in which that Church is, to be determined by them." Puritan ministers were to look about parishes for prospective "elders" and "deacons." The elders were to be made church wardens for the present and the deacons assigned the task of collecting and distributing monies for the poor—their proper office according to the Puritan understanding of the practice of the Church of the Apostles. Clergymen were to encourage any who felt called to the ministry to appear for approval before *classes*. For the increase of "true religion" and progress in "true reform" there was to be continuous prophesying, in covert and open meetings, by resident clergymen and gifted laymen, by itinerant ministers, and indeed by any who could profess a "call" from the Lord. Needless to say, prophesyings became a cause of alarm among the bishops and even for the Queen herself. Archbishop Parker made attempts to suppress them. They were "put down" in 1577, two years after Parker's death; but down they would not remain.

Of the publicists, controversialists, and pamphleteers within the ranks of the Puritans, the most impressive were Thomas Cartwright and Walter Travers. The latter—one of the promoters of the Wandsworth Presbytery—had been Reader at the Temple Church. After Archbishop Whitgift appointed Hooker to the Mastership of the Temple, then, as Fuller said, "the pulpit spake pure Canterbury in the morning, and Geneva in the afternoon." Travers, who was removed from the Readership, was strong on church discipline. He contended that discipline and dogma were like the twins mentioned by Hippocrates, who always fell ill at the same time. In Travers' opinion, it was futile to reform doctrine without prescribing, at the same time, a "polity of the Church of Christ ordained and appointed by God." Cartwright, of whom Travers was a disciple, instigated one Admonition to the Parliament and was author of another.

The first of these was published in 1572 without the name of either author or publisher. So widely was it read, four printings were called for in the same year. The First Admonition brought under condemnation "Romanist" survivals within the Church of England: the regarding of the Apocrypha as Scripture, saints' days, kneeling to receive Communion, private Communion, the title "priest," private baptism, baptism by women, the Sign of the Cross, questions to sponsors in the rite of baptism, the use of the ring in marriage, confirmation, prayers for the dead, prayers that all men might be saved, "organs and curious singing," the orders of bishops, archbishops, archdeacons, and chancellors, canon law, episcopal authority, cathedral churches, and bishops' courts. Cartwright in the Second Admonition, as did Travers in his writings, argued against all of the foregoing practices as "innovations" lacking the sanction of Scripture and the approval of the Early Church. Both authors demanded that every remnant and reminder of the Roman mass be discarded, that every Romanist court and discipline be abolished; priests ordained in the reign of Mary Tudor must be removed from office. In the Church of the Apostles bishops were pastors, and these they must again become. All ministers are to be equal in status and of two sorts, pastors and teachers. The rule of the Church is to be under local Consistories, Provincial Councils and, perhaps, a National Council. These bodies will control the ceremonies of congregations and the lives of their members. Excommunication is to be exercised, but only with great care and for great offences, since the punishment of excommunication is so dreadful there is nothing like it on earth, "but only hell eternally." The Consistory, according to Cartwright, will "excommunicate the stubborn . . . yet ever so must they excommunicate, and receive the excommunicate in again, that they require the assent of their whole congregation . . . Nevertheless, what they do well, the congregation cannot alter, neither shall the congregation put them, or any of them out, but upon just cause proved, either in that Consistory or in some one of the Councils, and the cause accepted for sufficient." "The civil magistrate, the nurse and foster father of the Church, shall do well to provide some sharp punishment for those that contemn this censure and discipline of the Church." The Queen will defend in righteousness this Church government, founded as it is on Scriptural authority; for although the rule of the Church be taken from the Book of God, "yet it is her majesty that by her princely authority should see every of these things put into practice, and punish those that neglect them."

The efforts of the Puritans produced a very great effect on the English public. Their stress on the Scriptures, as God's Revealed Word and wisdom, their opposition to Rome, their professed return to the practices of the original Church, their theology, which depended utterly on God's grace without the interposition of "sinful priests," the strictness of their self-sacrificing lives, their endurance of suffering at the hands of prelates and magistrates, all these things won them compassion and support throughout the kingdom. Complementary to this general sympathy was the common knowledge that nearly all of the ablest clergy in the Established Church were Calvinist in dogmatic theology at least—a fact that Elizabeth had to bear in mind when seeking appointees for archbishoprics. If in 1598 George Cranmer, a friend of Hooker, could discern some subsidence in public sympathy for the Genevan discipline, a few years before he had found that "the greatest part of the learned in the land were either eagerly affected, or favorably inclined. Many which impugned the Discipline yet so impugned it, not as not being the better form of government, but as not so convenient for our state." As time went on, the House of Commons included among its popularly elected representatives an increasingly large number of Puritans, engaging in "godless politics" for necessary, worldly ends.

In his *Letter of Advice* (1584) to Queen Elizabeth, Bacon at the age of twenty-three shows as much assurance in his political thinking as he does in the philosophical judgment which he delivers in his *Greatest Birth of Time* of the same year. In the *Letter of Advice* he undertakes a review of the Queen's political policies generally and more specifically of her dealing with Puritan preachers and her "strong factious subjects and foreign enemies," the Papists and the Spaniards. Bacon's concern here, as he informs the readers of his later *Observations Upon a Libel* (1593), is with "two extremities in state concerning the causes of faith and religion," the "dangerous indulgence and toleration" of permitting a number of religions and "the entering and sifting into men's consciences when no overt scandal is given." At this stage of his thinking, the author, as a Calvinist reared in a loyal household, sees no real danger to the unity of the state in the claims and contentions of the Puritans, notwithstanding the fact that they have won many sympathizers. Having made it clear to the Queen that he himself is "not given over, nor so much as addicted, to their preciseness," Bacon tells her that the Puritans are not heretical, nor do they purpose sedition, while the persecution they suffer at home creates the impression abroad of a disunity in the kingdom. Bacon also tells the experienced Queen, with a show of modesty, *"till I think that you think otherwise,* I am bold to think that the Bishops, in this dangerous time, take a very evil and unadvised course in driving them from their cures." The ecclesiastical authorities are overlooking the fact that the Puritans' "careful catechizing and diligent preaching" are producing the "fruit" of "the lessening and diminution of the Papistical number." The state might well consider the members of this sect its allies in the struggle with Rome, and extend them at least the trust which Frederick II gave the infidel Saracen soldiers whom he employed "against the Pope because he . . . knew they would not spare his sanctity." As for fears of what the Puritans might do were they to get authority in the Church, this is a remote and uncertain evil whose consideration must give way in the face of closer and more certain perils. As to meeting the danger of the present from Rome and her agent Spain, Bacon advises the cultivation of the friendship of France, the promotion of an alliance among the Dutch and northern princes, such aid to the Low Countries as may be advanced without precipitating a Spanish war, the weakening of Spain by attacks on her possessions in the Indies, and the seeking of aid from Florence, Ferrara, and Venice.

Of the Roman Catholics at home, none should be admitted to any office of government, Bacon warns, "from the highest counsellor to the lowest constable." All must be excluded from active military forces, and none is to be "trained up in the musters except his parishioners would answer for him that he orderly and duly received the Communion." No Roman Catholic is "to have in his house so much as a halbert without the same condition." Since punitive measures, even death, have proved ineffectual for the reduction of the number of Recusants—they are like the Hydra which grows several heads when one is removed—recourse should be had in the future to education as a means to bring them into a condition of loyalty.

Bacon now raises the second question, of "entering and sifting into men's consciences." In this regard, he thinks, Roman Catholic subjects have an honest cause for grievance. The Oath of Allegiance, as now framed, requires the subject to swear "that which, without the special grace of God, he cannot think." This makes him a perjurer. If for honesty's sake he refuses to take the oath, he becomes a traitor, "which, before some act done, seems somewhat hard." The proper course would be to change the oath to a form which required "that whosoever would not bear arms against all foreign princes, and, namely, the Pope, that should invade your Majesty's dominions, he should be a traitor." A subject who refused the amended oath could no longer be regarded as a martyr for his religion, but only as a deserving sufferer for his political stubbornness. The new oath would also serve to undermine the present confidence between the Pope and religious Roman Catholics disposed to loyalty towards the English throne.

After five years of further observation, reflection, and Parliamentary experience, Bacon feels called upon to prepare a second advice for the Queen, *An Advertisement, Touching the Controversies of the Church of England* (1589). In this he examines the occasions and causes of those religious controversies which are at present troubling the state. The writing is confined to the bishops of the Established Church and the Puritans—without use of the latter title and the name "Precisians," which are greatly disliked by those on whom they have been fastened by their opponents. Both parties to the controversies are brought under censure. The Puritans are now regarded by the author as "the enemy of unity, sobriety and peace" in the Church and the kingdom. Their "irreverent and violent impugning of the government of bishops" has become, in Bacon's thinking, "a suspected forerunner of a more general contempt." The Church, as an institution which has survived attacks from without by the Pope and his agents, is now faced with an internal commotion in which "truth itself" is "challenged and pretended."

The Puritans, says the author, have sought truth in "the conventicles and conciliables of heretics and sectaries, "their critics and condemners in the "external face and representation of the Church." Both parties have been seduced. There has been "forbidden" writing on the one side and "authorized" pamphlets on the other; both are deserving of suppression. If the Puritans have defamed the governors of the Church, the bishops by their attacks on Puritan preachers have disgraced religion. Through controversies kept alive by the two parties, an exaggerated report of faction and disorder in the kingdom has gone abroad, as if civil government in England "were ready to enter into some convulsion." While "sympathy" between the civil and ecclesiastical estates must be conceded, and while it is true "that . . . 'there will be kept no unity in believing, except it be entertained in worshipping,' "—as the Queen's Lord Treasurer and others contend, there is as yet in England "no such matter in the civil policy, as deserveth so dishonourable a taxation."

Unlike the disputes between the Eastern and Western churches touching images, and those in the West over the adoration of the Sacrament, current religious contentions in England are about "things indifferent," such as ceremonials and the government of the Church. "If we would but remember," reflects the author, "that the ancient and true bonds of unity are 'one faith, one baptism,' and not one ceremony, one policy; if we would observe the league amongst Christians that is penned by our Saviour, 'he that is not against us is with us'; if we could but comprehend that . . . religion hath parts which belong to eternity, and parts which pertain to time; and if we did but know the virtue of silence and slowness to speak, commended by St. James, our controversies of themselves would close up and grow together."

In the "immodest and deformed" writing of these times, the "matter of religion is handled in the stile of the stage"; a notable exception being "a challenge . . . Mr. [John] Jewel made to confute the pretended Catholics by the Fathers." "To turn religion into a comedy or satire; to search and rip up wounds with a laughing countenance, to intermix Scripture and scurrility sometimes in one sentence, is a thing far from the devout reverence of a Christian, and scant beseeming the honest regard of a sober man. . . . There is no greater confusion than the confounding of jest and earnest. The majesty of religion, and the contempt and deformity of things ridiculous, are things as distant as things may be. Two principal causes have I ever known of atheism; curious controversies, and profane scoffing: now that these two are joined in one, no doubt that sect [the Puritans] will make no small progression."

The state of mind which these violations of sobriety signalize is nothing short of a disease of which the Universities are "the seat or the continent." In these institutions, immature youths "skip from ignorance to a prejudicate opinion, and never take a sound judgment in their way." When their reasons have ripened, they are already so obsessed with prejudice that the exercise of judgment has been forever forestalled.

The occasions of present controversy are in the main four. The first is "the conversation and government of those which have chief place in the Church." The bishops, on the whole, are men of knowledge and good works. Some of their number, however, have dimmed the light of virtue and become worldly—lovers of themselves and pleasers of men. The laity in consequence have begun to doubt their leaders' succession from the Apostles, grope for religion "as in the dark," and show a readiness "to depart from the Church upon every voice." A second cause of contention is the seeker of pre-eminence. "The Church never wanteth a kind of person, which love the salutation of Rabbi, master; not in ceremony or compliment, but in an inward authority which they seek over men's minds." In the third place, the Puritan sect is obsessed with "the opinion that anything is good which differs widely from the Church of Rome, and necessarily polluted if it does not." From this conceit has stemmed the demand for the reordaining of priests and the rebaptizing of children. And fourthly, comes the "affectation and imitation of foreign churches." "God forbid," says the author, "that lawful kingdoms should be tied to innovate and make alterations." Bacon desires the removal of "some abuses" from the Established Church, but he will not countenance the ecclesiastical republicanism extolled by the Puritans. Equality of ministers and government by synods can only, he thinks, be the source of "wonderful great confusion."

The Puritans, recounts Bacon, concentrated at first on their dislike of certain abuses, such as "Romanist" ceremonies and the idleness of some among the Universities' clergy. Next, they condemned the government of the Established Church, both on "scriptural grounds," as they admitted, and also out of a desire which they did not admit, to have, even as "mercenary bands . . . the spoil of . . . endowments and livings." Next the aim of the sect became nothing less than the establishment by the magistrate of "an only and perpetual form of policy in the Church" to their liking. On this ground the majority of the Puritans now take their stand, with the consequence that there exists an open breach between their body and the Established Church. It should be said in fairness, however, that the excesses of a part, however proportionately large, must not be charged against the whole side.

The Puritans, in a misguided zeal, have gone to great extremes. They profess a reliance on Scripture, and yet ignore the precept of the apostle that the weak are not to be admitted to questions and controversies; for they entitle ignorant people to join discussions which involve abstruse questions of doctrine—a point of great peril to religion. They encourage "prophecy," not only on the part of clergy, as in the earlier practice of the Church, but by all who profess "faith," however lacking these modern "prophets" may be in Scriptual knowledge and a coherent theology. To the minimizing of worship, the sect makes preaching and the hearing of sermons essential to church services. With their "embasing" of the Church Fathers and their resort to "naked examples, conceited inferences, and forced allusions," Puritan preachers, through "an addicted respect to their own opinions," have become the entrenchers of "errors and misproceeding." The leaders of the sect are too ready to make general pronouncements on what is unlawful. They prescribe restraints and prohibitions, but fail to instruct their followers in the use of lawful liberty.

Bacon, with an emphasis on godly "works," detaches himself doctrinally from the Calvinist contention that ethical criteria have nothing to do with the wisdom or the rating of the merits of a Christian. For the strict Calvinist, a redeemed elect soul cannot himself attain or depart from a state of salvation. His condition and belief are utterly remote from humanly derived ethical principles, things which belong to the realm of "carnal" knowledge. The knowledge which saves is the "wisdom" given immediately through Divine Revelation to the redeemed soul. While Bacon agrees in the opinion that Christian conduct is not ultimately to be governed by knowledge attained through human powers, but by what is given in Revelation through faith, he rates the life of a Christian by a practical subscription in deeds and works to those moral principles which through natural human knowledge are derived from the placets given in Revelation. Bacon thinks that the views of the Calvinists in these regards are contrary to the Scriptures, which teach us "to judge and denominate men religious according to their works of the second table; because they of the first are often counterfeit, and practised in hypocrisy. So St. John saith, that 'a man doth vainly boast of loving God whom he never saw, if he love not his brother whom he hath seen.' And St. James saith, 'This is true religion, to visit the fatherless and the widow.' So as that which is with them but philosophical and moral, is, in the apostle's phrase, 'true religion and Christianity.' "

Like the Puritans, the bishops who govern the Established Church have in late times followed a dubious road. For a time they answered their critics with an admission that some of the ceremonies to which the Nonconformists objected were "indifferent" things. They acknowledged certain imperfections in the Church, which, like tares among the corn, as they said, "were not with strife to be pulled up, lest it might spoil and supplant the good corn." But of late the ecclesiastical authorities have been regarding every critic of the Established Church as an infamous outlaw. Some of their bishops have even defamed from their pulpits the Protestant churches abroad, and declared that clerics ordained by these churches are no lawful ministers.

The present bishops deserve censure for their "standing so precisely upon altering nothing," because laws, wherever found, when not refreshed with new laws wax sour. Like the good husbandman who is ever pruning his vineyard, the Church should be diligent in correcting such abuses as have issued from their proceedings; but the bishops offer no measures of reform in Parliament. "A contentious retaining of custom is a turbulent thing, as well as innovation."

The Church authorities speak and act as though their Puritan brethren were criminals, lumping the whole sect with such an infamous group as the Family of Love. They accept any accusation by persons piqued by Puritan denunciations of their sins and their vices. In their inquisitions, they make men swear to "blanks and generalities." Their requiring subscription to articles word by word have irritated sores which would otherwise have cured themselves. Such petty molestations as are rumored, such as the charging of a minister for saying in baptism, "Do you believe?" instead of "Dost thou believe?" are only to be lamented. As for the excommunication which they employ: can any man defend this, "as a base process to lackey up and down for duties and fees; it being a precursory judgment of the latter day?" While it is certainly better to live under laws than not, surely "the wrath of man worketh not the righteousness of God."

Bacon's third political writing, *Observations Upon a Libel* (1593) is a reply to a pamphlet of the Jesuit Robert Parsons, called *Responsio ad edictum reginae angliae*. In this tract Parsons assailed Elizabeth's Lord Treasurer, Burghley, and ascribed what he said were the failures and ills of England to the Queen's measures against her Roman Catholic subjects and the agents of Rome within her kingdom. Bacon's reply is enlightening for its remarks on the prosperous state of England, on Burghley's public service and character, on Elizabeth's treatment of Roman Catholics, and on the distinction which it draws between the main

body of Puritans and such minor sects as the Brownists, Barrowists, and the Family of Love. By the time the *Observations Upon a
Libel* is written, Burghley's nephew has had reasons to be angered
by the refusal of the Cecils to promote a potential rival of his
cousin Robert. The author at this juncture is relying for advancement on the patronage of Essex, the competitor of the
Cecil faction at Court. Yet Bacon makes a thoroughly objective
and just statement of his uncle's service to the Queen. "It is
rather true," he writes, "that his lordship, out of the greatness
of his experience and wisdom, and out of the coldness of his
nature, hath qualified generally all hard and extreme courses, as
far as the service of her majesty, and the safety of the state,
and the making himself compatible with those with whom he
served, would permit."

"Assuredly many princes have had many servants of trust,
name, and sufficiency: but where there have been great parts,
there hath often wanted temper of affection; where there have
been both ability and moderation, there have wanted diligence
and love of travail; where all three have been, there have sometimes wanted faith and sincerity; where some few have had all
these four, yet they have wanted time and experience: but where
there is a concurrence of all these, there is no marvel, though a
prince of judgment be constant in the employment and trust of
such a servant."

In a statesmanlike review of the affairs of the kingdom, the
author mentions several grounds for the conclusion that "if a
man weigh well all the parts of state and religion, laws, administration of justice, policy of government, manners, civility,
learning and liberal sciences, industry and manual arts, arms and
provisions of wars for sea and land, treasure, traffic, improve-
ment of the soil, population, honour and reputation, it will
appear that, taking one part with another, the state of this
nation was never so flourishing."

The greater part of Bacon's reply to Parsons concerns Elizabeth's dealings with the Roman Catholics and her protective measures against papal designs on her kingdom. Of these designs some had been covert, some overt. The Pope had excommunicated Elizabeth (1570) and absolved the faithful of obedience. Mary Stuart (1542-1587) had been made Rome's instrument, under the direction first of France and then of Spain, for the bringing of the British Isles under papal control. Reared in France as a Roman Catholic, Mary came to Scotland in 1561 with a court bent on gay pleasures, and found herself in the midst of a dour people professing a rigorous Calvinistic theology. Her hasty marriage (1567) to Bothwell, the murderer of her second husband, Lord Darnley (the father of James VI of Scotland) was too much even for her most loyal chieftains. She suffered suspension from authority "for the preservation of the Commonwealth and for that her sins appeared incurable." After her flight to England in 1568 Mary Stuart became the centre of Roman Catholic intrigue. Elizabeth was to be destroyed; English heretics were to be reconverted to the Roman faith; revolts were to be engineered; Spanish forces were to support rebellion in Ireland; and the Spanish Armada was to set sail for the subjugation of England. Jesuit agents in disguise roamed over the country and persuaded subjects, who earlier had been the religious adherents of Rome under Mary Tudor, against the acceptance of the English Prayer Book and the rule of the Established Church. Roman Catholic nobles in the north of England rose in rebellion (1569-1570). Crusaders marched under the banner of the "Five Wounds of Christ" and tore up the Bible and the English Prayer Book. The insurgents had expected help from their fellow religionists in Scotland, but those of the Scots who would have come to their aid were prevented by their government from crossing the border. The uprising was crushed and eight hundred insurgents were executed. Papal agents throughout the country were hanged. One notorious Jesuit among them, Parsons, escaped to the Continent to help

engineer the Spanish invasion. In expectation of the conquest
of England, this Jesuit had pondered the question, "What form
or manner of Inquisition to bring in, whether that of Spain
(whose rigour is misliked by some) or that which is used in
divers parts of Italy (where coldness is reprehended by more)."

When word had gone abroad that a definite plot was under
way to assassinate Elizabeth and place Mary of Scotland on the
throne, the Queen was finally prevailed upon to accept a parliamentary resolve and petition of fifteen years' standing: Mary
was beheaded (1587). The invasion of England by Spain was
repulsed by the defeat of the Great Armada in 1588. Spanish
forces aiding the Irish in revolt were repelled. England was no
longer in danger of attack by arms from without, but her
sovereign had still to contend with the undermining from within
of the unity and stability of the kingdom by determined and
resourceful papal agents.

In his *Observations Upon a Libel*, Bacon describes Elizabeth's
way of proceeding against the Roman Catholics. The Queen's
acts, he explains, have from the beginning been grounded in two
principles: that consciences are not to be forced, and that contempt and faction are to be punished even if "coloured with the
pretences of conscience and religion." Although on coming to
the throne, Elizabeth had despised the inquisitorial tyranny of
the Church of Rome, she had treated members of that body
with great lenience. While "as a prince of great wisdom . . . she
suffered but the exercise of one religion," she did not attempt
to coerce belief, but merely outlawed manifest disobedience and
treason. In the face of this toleration, the Queen was excommunicated; her subjects were rendered disobedient under threat of
damnation; and rebellion was promoted in the northern part of
her kingdom. Spain was encouraged by Rome to invade England,
and "a principal point of the plot was to prepare a party within
the realm that might adhere to the foreigner." As the "poison"
spread, most Roman Catholics "were no more papists in custom,

but papists in treasonable faction." It therefore became necessary to make laws for the punishment of renunciations of obedience, renunciations even "more insinuative into the conscience" than the papal bull which declared Elizabeth a heretic had been, since these were now joined with an absolution from mortal sin in the rite of confession. The Queen's new laws prescribed a pecuniary punishment, "not to enforce consciences" but to discover treason. Only when the secrecy of the implanted evil made it a growth extremely difficult to stamp out did the Queen stop its source and nurture. Then, "seditious priests ... were exiled; and those that were at that time within the land shipped over, and so commanded to keep hence upon pain of treason."

Among the calamities of England which Parsons instances is "the great and wonderful confusion, which he saith, is in the state of the Church." Parsons distinguishes two factions within the English Calvinists: one with professions of "purity" and the other filled with idolatry and heresies. He mentions the Brownists and their direction by "the unholy ghost." He holds it to be the Protestant belief in England—we quote Bacon—"that if the prince or magistrate do refuse or defer to reform the Church, the people may ... take the reformation into their own hands: and hitherto he addeth the fanatical pageant of Hacket."

In comment and reply, Bacon remarks that the Church in every age is beset by schisms and contentions, since there are never tares except where the wheat has been planted before. He dissociates the Brownists, the Barrowists, Hacket, the Family of Love, and other fanatics among the Puritans (in 1616 he separates specifically the Anabaptists also) from the main body of Nonconformists. The Brownists, he describes as "a very small number of very silly and base people, here and there in corners dispersed ... now, thanks be to God ... suppressed and worn out; so that there is scarce any news of them." Among their number he places Henry Barrow (d. 1593). This man Bacon describes as a "gentleman of a good house" with agreeable "table-talk" who "made a leap from a vain and libertine youth, to a preciseness in the highest degree; the strangeness of which alteration made him very much spoken of." The Family of Love, which Parsons does not explicitly mention by name, is, Bacon remarks, "banished and extinct." As for the "phrenetical and fanatical . . . Hacket": he obtained but two disciples out of the whole population of London, and his so-called uprising was "rather laughed at as a may-game."

Of the main body of Puritans or Precisians Bacon, as a loyal English Protestant replying to a traitor abroad and at the same time cautioning Nonconformists at home, speaks leniently. Some persons, he says, "with an inconsiderate detestation of all ceremonies or orders, which were in use in the time of the Roman religion, as if they were without difference superstitious or polluted, and led with an affectionate imitation of the government of some protestant churches in foreign states; have sought by books and preaching, indiscreetly, and sometimes undutifully, to bring in an alteration in the external rites and policy of the Church; but in neither have the grounds of the controversies extended unto any point of faith; neither hath the pressing and prosecution exceeded, in the generality, the nature of some inferior contempts: so as they have been far from heresy and sedition, and therefore rather offensive than dangerous to the Church or state."

Parts of *Observations Upon a Libel* amount to a panegyric on the motives and deeds of the Queen. This praise is unquestionably sincere, for in a continuing devotion to Elizabeth Bacon is to write in 1608, five years after James has ascended the throne, another panegyric equally laudatory of this beloved sovereign. The second eulogy is called *In felicem memoriam elizabethae* (*On the Fortunate Memory of Elizabeth*). In it Bacon remarks on Elizabeth's having been brought up in a hard school of fortune, her passing "from the prison to the throne" without "a mind embittered and swelling with the sense of misfortune"; her courage and constancy, strength and serenity in face of dangers from within and without her kingdom; her skill in maintaining peace at home and abroad; her controlling "at the beck of a woman" a nation "fierce and warlike"; and her sustaining the reputation of her people for military prowess.

A passage or two of this writing will serve to indicate the tone of the whole: "In a kingdom labouring with intestine faction on account of religion, and standing as a shield and stronghold of defence against the then formidable and over-bearing ambition of Spain ... it was she who by her forces and her counsels combined kept it under; as was proved by an event the most memorable in respect of felicity of all the actions of our time. For when that Spanish fleet, got up with such travail and ferment, waited upon with the terror and expectation of all Europe, inspired with such confidence of victory, came plough-ing into our channels, it never took so much as a cockboat at sea, never fired so much as a cottage on the land, never even touched the shore; but was first beaten in a battle and then dispersed and wasted in a miserable flight with many shipwrecks; while on the ground and territories of England peace remained undisturbed and unshaken."

"As for those lighter points of character,—as that she allowed herself to be wooed and courted, and even to have love made to her; and liked it; and continued it beyond the natural age for such vanities;—if any of the sadder sort of persons be disposed to make a great matter of this, it may be observed that there is something to admire in these very things, which ever way you take them. For if viewed indulgently, they are much like the accounts we find in romances, of the Queen in the blessed islands, and her court and institutions, who allows of amorous ad-miration but prohibits desire. But if you take them seriously, they challenge admiration of another kind and of a very high order; for certain it is that these dalliances detracted but little from her fame and nothing at all from her majesty, and neither weakened her power nor sensibly hindered her business:—whereas such things are not unfrequently allowed to interfere with the public fortune. But to conclude, she was no doubt a good and moral Queen; and such too she wished to appear. Vices she hated, and it was by honest arts that she desired to shine."

This sincere memorial, written as it was some years after Elizabeth's death, should in itself be sufficient to dissipate the charge commonly brought by guileless biographers that Bacon's attitude to the Queen was one of sychophantic flattery. Everyone, of course, flattered Elizabeth somehow; sometimes in plain speech and sometimes in poetry. When the man of prose flattered the Queen he felt somehow poetic in the act. No mere sprite, Elizabeth became England's "fairy-queen." She was Belphoebe, Britomartis in arms, and Gloriana, the defender of truth against religious "superstition." There had been doubt about the legitimacy of her birth. She had spent a period in the Tower (1554). For years the Papists had sought her undoing and the Spaniards had hoped for her execution. She had endured. She could act as her own prime minister and hold Parliament, and her Council too, at bay with a shake of her head. While she performed her religious exercises duly, read her books daily like a student, addressed the Universities in Greek or in Latin of her own composing, she could swear like a trooper, box Essex on the ears at a Privy Council meeting, and declare with conviction that she could fill any high or low place in the kingdom. A woman of great passion, Elizabeth never married because, while she loved men unevenly in succession, she loved England steadily always, and most of all. When the years had taken their toll and the Queen, with all her feminine finery about her, gazed sadly into her mirror and at the end was consoled with the truth of her address to the people, "I have reigned with your loves," she was then, as she always had been, the daughter of her mother, Anne Boleyn—a coquette—and the offspring of her father, Henry VIII —a Queen.

VI

BACON AND JAMES: THE EARLY PERIOD

WHEN IT BECAME EVIDENT THAT ELIZABETH'S REIGN was drawing to a close and that James of Scotland would be assuming England's throne, Bacon contemplated his future with both apprehension and hope. Of his capacity to play a part in the settlement of political questions he had not the slightest doubt. He knew that there were certain questions of magnitude which Parliament and the Privy Council had avoided in Elizabeth's lifetime, through a respect for both her person and her temperament and out of a regard for her successes without and within the kingdom. "For Queen Elizabeth," as Bacon was to write later in his *Beginning of the History of Great Britain*, "though she had the use of many both virtues and demonstrations that mought draw and knit unto her the heart of her people, yet nevertheless carrying a hand, restrained in gift and strained in points of prerogative, could not answer the votes either of servants or subjects to a full contentment; especially in her latter days, when the continuance of her reign (which extended to five and forty years) mought discover in people their natural desire and inclination towards change."

In the same writing Bacon remarked that "those that had made

their way with the King or offered their service in the time of
the former Queen, thought now the time was come for which
they had prepared: and generally all such as had any dependance
upon the late Earl of Essex ... made account their cause was
amended." Both Papists and the supporters of Presbytery felt
their brethren had fared better in Scotland under James VI than
they had in England. His mother had been a Roman Catholic.
James had accepted religious rule by Presbytery and the General
Assembly.

Bacon's immediate objective was the obtaining of a place in
political administration. He had still to bear in mind the attitude
of Robert Cecil. Yet, although the cousin had carried on the
negotiations, begun by Essex, which assured James of the
English throne, there was no certainty that he would continue
as Secretary of State under the new king. Henry Percy, Earl of
Northumberland, another promoter of James' accession, was a
strong rival for the post. Promisingly for Bacon, Northumberland had been an intimate of Anthony Bacon and shared a kinship of mind with Francis Bacon himself, for he was a scientific
inquirer, inclined to "experiments," and the patron of the mathematician Thomas Harriot. The new king would remember
Anthony Bacon as an agent of the Earl of Essex in his early
negotiations; on the other hand, he might recall with displeasure
that Anthony's brother had been a prosecutor at the trial of
Essex. James of Scotland, however, while stubborn and mindful
of past friends and foes, could nevertheless show magnanimity
in personal dealings. More important, he was proud of his learning and professed a respect for literary men. He might regard
with favor a man who showed respect for his erudition. He
might even be the sort of sovereign who, if told in apt writing
what was expected of Majesty per se, would answer by appropriate deeds.

Bacon undertook to cope with present circumstances by a
correspondence with persons who were likely to have influence

with the King. A few days before the Queen's death he had already written to Michael Hickes, Robert Cecil's confidential agent: "The apprehension of this threatened judgment of God ... if it work in other as it worketh in me, knitteth every man's heart more unto his true and approved friend.... And as I ever used your means to cherish the truth of my inclination towards Mr. Secretary, so now again I pray, as you find time, let him know that he is the personage in this State which I love most." There were grounds for the writing of this letter. Through Bacon's days in Parliament and in Elizabeth's service as Queen's Counsel Extraordinary, his cousin had treated him with great civility; he had written a friendly caution when gossip arose from Bacon's misinterpreted conversations with the Queen on behalf of Essex. Bacon for his part had grown more politically mature, and could look back with less heat on the Cecils' earlier preference of Coke and other men more experienced for senior offices in the kingdom.

Bacon also wrote to Northumberland, recalling Anthony's association with him, and likewise to the Abbot of Kinloss. To Thomas Challoner, a creditor who had been introduced by Anthony into the service of Essex, Bacon expressed the hope that in view of "the openness of the time, caused by this blessed consent and peace," the debtor's financial means could be increased, and that "our agreement, according to our time ... observed." He assumed, in a confidence, that Challoner would become an acceptable servant of the King, and requested him to "further his Majesty's good conceit and inclination" towards the debtor. Bacon even wrote to Southampton—whom James had released from the Tower immediately on his coming to the throne of England—assuring him of his goodwill and saying that, although he would gladly have waited on his Lordship in person, he chose to write him rather than risk any possible displeasure in a personal meeting over his part, as Queen's Counsel, in the Essex trial. In a letter to another conspirator with Essex,

Sir John Davies, he asked the author of the philosophical poem *Nosce Teipsum* (1599) "to be good to *concealed poets.*"

The phrase "concealed poets" has often been cited in argument for Bacon's secret authorship of poetry, more especially of the works of Shakespeare. The works of Shakespeare are not in the usual literary style of Francis Bacon, yet without touching on the Bacon-Shakespeare controversy, it may be observed that Bacon could write in many styles. When trying to bring Essex back into Elizabeth's favor, he had successfully composed a feigned correspondence in the two styles of the Earl and his brother Anthony. He had written letters to Elizabeth at the bidding of Essex in exact imitation of the Earl. His versatility in this regard is again exemplified by a communication which he now addresses to the King, where the statement moves ponderously as in James' own writings. This missive begins, for the complimenting of the learned King, with a quotation from the Vulgate and ends with another from Ovid. Part of the letter proceeds as follows:

> ... further and more nearly I was not a little encouraged, not only upon a supposal that unto your Majesty's sacred ears (open to the air of all virtues) there might perhaps have come small breath of the good memory of my father, so long a principal counsellor in this your kingdom; but also by the particular knowledge of the infinite devotion and incessant endeavours (beyond the strength of his body and the nature of the times) which appeared in my good brother towards your Majesty's service; and were, on your Majesty's part, through your singular benignity by many most gracious and lively significations and favours accepted and acknowledged, beyond the merit of anything he could effect. All which endeavours and duties for the most part were common to myself with him, though by design (as between brethren) dissembled.

> And therefore most high and mighty King, my most dear and dread sovereign lord, since now the corner-stone is laid of the mightiest monarchy in Europe; and that God above (who is noted to have a mighty hand in bridling the floods and fluctuations of

the seas and of people's hearts) hath by the miraculous and universal consent (the more strange because it proceedeth from such diversity of causes) in your coming in, given a sign and token what he intendeth in the continuance; I think there is no subject of your Majesty's who loveth this island, and is not hollow and unworthy, whose heart is not set on fire, not only to bring you peace-offerings to make you propitious, but to sacrifice himself a burnt-offering to your Majesty's service; amongst which number no man's fire shall be more pure and fervent than mine.

In this letter we have an early instance of what was to become a habit of "obsequiousness" on Bacon's part, and indeed on the part of every person at James' Court. Bacon's address here is not, of course, the spontaneous, affectionate flattery which he and others freely accorded to Elizabeth. Nor is it servile writing, nor indeed praise at all, but rather the studied abasement in address which James expected of all persons who corresponded with him. There was no more conviction behind it than there was sincerity in James' own salutation to Bacon himself, as a Lord Keeper temporarily out of favor: "Right trusty and well beloved counsellor, we greet you well." It is an example of the manner of approach required of "suppliants" by a king who regarded every subject, in or out of Court, as an inferior creature dependent on the prerogative power of an anointed, divinely endowed ruler.

Bacon had definite opinions about "praises" of sovereigns and the "pains" and "indignities" to be endured while in their service. These things he deemed necessary means to definite ends. In the case of a worthy public servant these ends included just government and the common good. "By indignities," Bacon wrote in his *Essays*, "men come to dignities"; it is "the solecism of power, to think to command the end, and yet not to endure the means. . . . Some praises come of good wishes and respects, which is a form due in civility to kings . . . when by telling men what they are, they represent to them what they should be." This last maxim Bacon was always to keep in mind when addressing

James in private letters and publicly describing his character and deeds; when confronting the King with the grievances of the Commons, when advising the Sovereign as Solicitor-General, Attorney-General, Lord Keeper, and Lord Chancellor. In reflection on the whole question as a problem confronting a philosopher, Bacon made some observations in his *Advancement of Learning* (1605). "I have no purpose," he wrote, "to give allowance to some conditions and courses base and unworthy, wherein divers professors of learning have wronged themselves and gone too far; such as were those trencher philosophers, which in the later ages of the Roman state were usually in the houses of great persons, being little better than solemn parasites." But philosophers in pursuit of becoming ends, he believed, should not be condemned for cultivating rich men in high place. Aristippus, for example, when reproved for grovelling at the feet of Dionysius, suitably answered that it was not his fault, but it was the fault of Dionysius, for he had "his ears in his feet." "The like applications and stooping to points of necessity and convenience cannot be disallowed," Bacon continued, "for though they may have some outward baseness, yet in a judgment truly made they are to be accounted submissions to the occasion and not to the person." By 1605, Bacon had prepared himself to "endure" the obsequiousness and other conditions imposed by the new sovereign of England as incidents to the pursuit of an unwavering justice, the public good, and the instauration of a new scientific learning.

Two months after James had reached Whitehall (1603), Bacon wrote optimistically of his own prospects to Tobie Matthew: "I have many comforts and assurances: but in mine own opinion the chief is, that the canvassing world is gone and the deserving world is come. And withal I find myself as one awaked out of sleep." Within three months more Bacon had been disillusioned. He had received no recognition from either the King or the Secretary of State. Even his name, to which no formal Patent had been attached in the former reign, had been omitted from the list of those reappointed as King's Counsel. Bacon wrote to Robert Cecil:

For my purpose or course, I desire to meddle as little as I can in the King's causes—his Majesty now abounding in counsel—and to follow my thrift and practice, and to marry with some convenient advancement. For as for any ambition, I do assure your Honour mine is quenched. In the Queen's my excellent Mistress's time, the *quorum* was small; her service was a kind of freehold and it was a more solemn time. All those points agreed with my nature and judgment. My ambition now I shall only put upon my pen, whereby I shall be able to maintain memory and merit of the times succeeding.

Lastly, for this divulged and almost prostituted title of knighthood, I could without charge, by your Honour's means, be content to have it, both because of this late disgrace, and because I have three new knights in my mess in Gray's Inn commons, and because I have found out an alderman's daughter, an handsome maiden, to my liking. So as, if your Honour will find the time, I will come to the Court from Gorhambury upon any warning.

Two weeks later, Bacon wrote again to his cousin:

For my knighthood, I wish the manner might be such as might grace me, since the matter will not; I mean, that I might not be merely gregarious in a troop. The coronation is at hand. It may please your Lordship to let me hear from you speedily. So I continue your Lordship's ever much bounden. . . .

A week thereafter Bacon was dubbed knight by the King, along with some three hundred others—judges, serjeants-at-law, gentlemen ushers, doctors of civil law, and other persons of diverse sorts. Soon he was made a King's Counsel with Patent, and was given an annual pension in perpetuity of £60 "in consideration of the services" of his brother Anthony. No other award came his way. Now in a condition of despair over his failure to receive an administrative post, Bacon sought the consolation of philosophy. He penned an *apologia pro vita sua*, calling it *De interpretatione naturae proœmium (Of the Inter-*

pretation of Nature: a Proem, 1603). In this writing Bacon appears as one ready to abandon politics and to devote himself entirely to the pursuit of scientific inquiry. He assumes that by the time the work is ready for publication his method of discovery—a new "formula of interpretation" which nearly twenty years before he had called "the greatest birth of Time"—will have been made ready and put to use.

Mature reflection has convinced him, Bacon now writes, that "nothing is of as much benefit to the human race as the discovery of and devotion to new truths and arts by which the life of men is cultivated. . . . And above all if a man should bring forth no particular invention . . . but were to kindle a light in nature which from its very beginning would illuminate the confines which hold within their grasp facts already discovered, and once raised aloft would straightway lay open and bring into view the most hidden things, that man seemed to me to be the propagator of man's empire over the universe, the protector of liberty, and the conqueror of necessities."

The author has reached the conclusion that, although by birth and education he had seemed committed, at an earlier stage in his life, to affairs of state, he is actually by nature more fitted to the contemplation of truth. He possesses "a mind agile enough to recognize the resemblance of things . . . and sufficiently steadfast and eager to observe the refinements of their diversity." He has desire to seek, patience to ponder, fondness to meditate, slowness to assert, readiness to reconsider, carefulness to set in order, in short, a nature with "an intimacy and kinship with truth." Until recently, he had hoped to be the better able to foster the advancement of science by obtaining place in government. He had, accordingly, learned the civil arts and sought the favor of powerful friends—yet ever mindful that "these things . . . do not penetrate beneath the circumstances and attainments of this mortal life." But his "zeal" was "taken for ambition," and his impaired health had warned him of his "tardiness." Duty now forbids further neglect of his proper task. In future he will devote himself entirely to scientific endeavors.

The science on which he is intent will be secured by "utility and works," however much the old science, with its school learning and contemplations, may suffer in consequence. Should someone demand an immediate production of works, the author will reply that he, as a man of weak health faced by "the most obscure of all subjects without guide or light," has made sufficient advance by constructing the machinery of inquiry without setting the same in motion. The restraining of all precipitous desire for "works," until some general principles of the new science are discovered, will be the wiser course for all concerned. Those who would demand specimen certainties should bear in mind that in the prevailing science men are not able even to hope for such assurances. In any event, the new science cannot be judged by recourse to precedent, "for the matter is without precedent." As for publication, those matters which "conduce to the capturing of the correspondence of men of wit and the cleansing of the threshing-floor of minds" may better be publicized by word of mouth. Scientific information should be disseminated with discretion, for both its "formula of interpretation" and discoveries are properly confined to persons of select capabilities. Finally, Bacon assures the reader that he has at heart "nothing which is dependent on externals." He is not seeking fame; he is not attempting to found a sect; nor is he moved by a desire for private gain, but only by "the consciousness of well-deserving and the effecting of things with which fortune itself cannot interfere."

Before this *Proem* can be completed, Bacon discovers that he has already made an impression on the King, an impression far from scientific in character. His written advices to James on the political union of England and Scotland and on problems of church government have been well received. His skill in mediating between the Lords and Commons and his capacity for

dominating the Lower House and putting ambitious lawyers—
the *literae vocales* of this House—in their place, has not gone
unnoticed by the new King. Bacon's prospects are greatly on
the mend. In 1607 he is made Solicitor-General. In 1608 the
Clerkship of the Star Chamber becomes vacant, and Bacon takes
over the office which he had held in reversion for nearly nineteen
years.

In 1603 Bacon had watched the new King's "progress" from
Scotland to Whitehall and, like many others, he had learned
with dismay and disquiet that during a stop at Newark, James
had ordered the hanging of a cutpurse caught in the act, without even the semblance of a trial. Clearly, the new king would
have to learn that England was not Scotland, nor Scotland
England; that the English courts were extremely jealous of their
authority; that in England even thieves were tried according to
due processes of law; that there were Englishmen who thought
even kings were subject to law; that some thought that the
Courts of the King, as they were styled, might better be called
Courts of England. James would have to learn, too, that in England Parliament was not a mere court of record, as in Scotland,
and that many among his new subjects, including Parliamentarians, placed less trust in the rule of bishops in the Church of
England than did their new monarch. By the English constitution, King James possessed an extensive Prerogative; but by
the same unwritten constitution, Parliament, courts of law,
and even the humblest subjects had their acquired privileges.
Further, there were ambitions abroad in the kingdom—ambitions held under restraint in the days of Elizabeth—of acquiring
more assured rights, independent of what any monarch might
or might not choose to grant as graces. A wise king would decrease the area of his Prerogative and gradually increase the
range of his subjects' "privileges." For some sixteen years,
Bacon would be trying to make James aware of these things;
but the King would prove neither wise nor teachable.

Bacon soon became aware that, as he told Northumberland, the King "hasteneth to a mixture of both kingdoms and nations faster perhaps than policy will conveniently bear." He addressed the new sovereign in the first year of his reign with an advice, a *Brief Discourse of the Happy Union of the Kingdoms of England and Scotland* (1603). This writing was prepared for the perusal of a king very much aware of his philosophical erudition, by a counsellor who just then was writing his *Advancement of Learning* for address to the same monarch. In the latter work Bacon was calling the metaphysics of physical nature—the only metaphysics he recognized—"magic," after the title of the wisdom of the Persian Maji. Bacon hoped that the *Brief Discourse* would serve two purposes: first, to remind the philosophically erudite James that "sudden mutations as well in state as in nature, are rarely without violence and perturbation," and, second, to prepare the mind of this learned sovereign for the reception of a work on a new sort of learning.

The *Brief Discourse* opens with the statement that the author does not find it strange that a certain book by Heraclitus, now lost, should have been regarded by some readers as a discourse on nature and by others as a treatise on politics, because "there is a great affinity and consent between the rules of nature, and the rules of policy." It was for this reason, that the education of the kings of Persia was called "magic," since this science was none other than "an application of the contemplations and observations of nature unto a sense politic; taking the fundamental laws of nature, and the branches and passages of them, as an original or first model, whence to take and describe a copy and imitation for government."

James has been in the habit of regarding his judges and other political servants after Aristotle's manner of treating the celestial spheres. It is the opinion of James, who has derived his analogy from Aristotle's theory of the heavens, that the King, as the *Primum Mobile* or "First Moved" by the First Mover or God, imparts his "motion" to his subordinates. With this view of James in mind, Bacon makes a plea for "the cherishing of inferior bodies." He tells the King that even as the planets fulfil their perpetual office of motion, constant and regular in imitation of the movement of the *Primum Mobile*, so should the activities of the officers of government proceed. He also reminds James that, while the heavens enrich themselves at the expense of the earth, "whatsoever moisture they do levy and take . . . they do spend and turn back again in showers."

Continuing the analogy of "congruity between the principles of nature and policy," Bacon in Peripatetic vein distinguishes *compositio* from *mistio* (putting together from mingling), "the one being a conjunction of bodies in place, the other in quality and consent." The former is exemplified in the mixing of water and oil, where fusion is never successful, and the latter in the union of earth, water, and oil in vegetable growths, where the "mingling" is so complete that the contributing "simple" bodies cannot be separated. In a *compositio* there is a lack of a new integrating form; in a *mistio* this factor proves a *commune vinculum*. Without this, the old forms of bodies conjoined remain in strife and discord. Natural philosophers say for good reasons that "composition" is the work of man and "mingling" the work of nature and of time, which "perfect fermentation and incorporation."

Having cautioned the King against a hasty uniting of his two kingdoms, Bacon specifies five of the components of a united nation: sovereignty, name, language, laws, and employments. Sovereignty and language, allowing for local dialects in both England and Scotland, are already one in the Island of Britain. Employments are "indifferent" things. "Name, though it seem but a superficial and outward matter, yet it carrieth much impression and enchantment: the general and common name . . . always apt to unite." Within laws, "the principal sinews of government," Bacon includes *jura*, or "abilities and freedoms";

leges, or laws proper; and *mores,* or customs. Of abilities he
instances "kinds, or rather degrees" which are recognized by the
Roman jurists: naturalization, voice in Parliament, place in
council or office. As for specific laws, those of England and
Scotland are so many, various, and disparate, that there is no
possibility of bringing them together in one system. All that can
be hoped for in the beginning is some uniformity in the principal
and fundamental laws, both ecclesiastical and civil. When the
time comes for a consideration of such of these laws as pertain
to the Church, it will be well to call to mind that Christ's coat,
while without seam, was of many shades and colors. As "for
manners: a consent in them is to be sought industriously, but not
to be enforced: for nothing amongst people breedeth more
pertinency in holding their customs, as sudden and violent offer
to remove them."

The *Brief Discourse* made an impression on the King. The
Commons elected Bacon to a committee designed to make
James' two kingdoms one. He prepared another writing for the
King's guidance, *Certain Articles or Considerations Touching
the Union of the Kingdoms of England and Scotland* (1604).
This dealt with the union under many headings: sovereignty,
subjection, territory, statutes, naturalization of Scottish subjects,
customs, the Churches and their disciplines and doctrines, commissions, councils of state, Parliaments, offices of the Crown,
nobilities, courts, trials and processes, finances, garrisons and
navies, freedoms and liberties, merchandisings, taxes, and fitting
title for the Sovereign. The author reminds the King that "for
the sovereignty, the union is absolute in your majesty and
generation." In his discussion of naturalizaton Bacon set down
for James' consideration the principle "that all Scotsmen from
the very instant your majesty's reign begun are become denizens,"
but not as yet "subjects." The *post-nati,* however, like the inhabitants of Ireland, are "for the time forwards" natural subjects
of the Crown of England, "not by any statute or act of parlia-

ment, but merely by the common law, and the reason thereof."

Bacon suggested and James took "the stile and title of King of Great Britany." The Crowns of England and Scotland were now united, but their Parliaments and Churches were to remain separate. The coalescence of the former was not to take place for a century; the union of the latter was to be indefinitely deferred. James decisively refused to accept Bacon's opinion that Scottish "denizens" required naturalization, after Bacon had all but succeeded in bringing into agreement the commissioners appointed to deal with the union. A majority of the members of the Commons showed a readiness to entertain the naturalization of every subject of James VI of Scotland, who was now James I of England, when the King indicated that he was not of a mind to have his people in Scotland created subjects either by act of the elected representatives of other subjects or through the operation of English law. He himself would be the *Primum Mobile*, God's first agent in the creation of subjects. His Prerogative alone would be the source of their being. Members of Parliament then began to exercise unrestrainedly the right of free speech. James' Scots were called, in turn, a horde of savages intent on a foray into a civilized land, beggars eager to feast at the well-laden English board, impoverished cattle from the north about to be turned loose on the rich pastures of the south. Some members of the Commons opposed the union, in a more reasonable manner, on the ground of competition in business and trade. Bacon, who had composed a *Preparation toward the Union of the Laws of England and Scotland* for the King and, in expectation of a successful outcome of negotiations, had made ready for presentation to Parliament a *Certificate or Return of the Commissioners of England and Scotland* (1604), raised his voice in the Commons. There has been, he admitted, "some inequality in the fortunes of these two nations, England and Scotland, by the commixture whereof there may ensue advantage to them and loss to us," but these differences have consisted only in "the external goods of fortune." As for the goods

of mind and body, the Scots are *"alteri nos,"* other ourselves."
They are ingenious, valiant, industrious, strong and active in
body, and so much like us generally that "we are participant
both of their virtues and vices." If they seem less than tractable
in government, we ourselves are not free of this fault, it "being
a thing indeed incident to all martial people." "I hope, Mr.
Speaker," said Bacon, "I may speak it without offence, that if we
did hold ourselves worthy, whensoever just cause should be
given, either to recover our ancient rights, or to revenge our late
wrongs, or to attain the honour of our ancestors, or to enlarge
the patrimony of our posterity, we would never in this manner
forget considerations of amplitude and greatness, and fall at
variance about profit and reckonings; fitter a great deal for
private persons than for parliaments and kingdoms."

While engaged with the problem of political union, Bacon
was also concerned with other constitutional questions. Sir
Francis Goodwin's election in 1604 to Parliament had been
declared illegal, but the House of Commons had ordered him to
take his seat, and asserted the principle that it alone had the right
to pronounce upon the legality of its membership. King James,
however, insisted that the question be settled in Chancery.
Bacon was called upon to mediate the case, which involved
Parliament, courts of law, and the sovereign. He managed to
find a solution whereby a writ would be issued for a new election
in the present instance, and the King and other disputants in the
case would undertake to see that hereafter the Commons would
possess the right it now vocally asserted. Goodwin's case was
probably the one which provided James with the occasion, as
James Spedding surmises, for uttering the opinion in a case on
the use of the Royal Prerogative—as Bacon was to report in his
De augmentis (1623)—"That kings ruled by the laws of their
kingdoms, as God did by the laws of Nature, and ought as rarely
to put in use their supreme prerogative, as God does his Power
of working miracles."

In the same year the question of the King's Purveyance was

brought before the Commons. Bacon, being one of those members who held the opinion that Purveyance was now being carried on illegally, was nominated by the Lower House to present a case to the King. He prepared an address in the form of a *Petition Touching Purveyors* and delivered this to James in "the withdrawing-chamber" at Whitehall. In it he wrote: "In the course of remedy which we desire, we pretend not, nor intend not, in any sort, to derogate from your majesty's prerogative. . . . For we seek nothing but the reformation of abuses, and the execution of former laws whereunto we are born." The present grievance is this: the King's purveyors are taking what they ought not to take, and may appropriately be called taxers. They demand the poor man's hay, wood, or poultry, which he has reserved as provision for his family; and then tax him on the money he is given in return. The purveyors put their axes to trees, "which are the beauty, countenance, and shelter of men's houses; that men have long spared from their own purse and profit." If the possessor is too difficult to deal with while he is at home, purveyors strike while he is away. When the representatives of the Crown are asked to reimburse for goods illegally taken, a fee of twelve pence per pound is exacted. Incredibly, such poundage is sometimes taken twice over on the same transaction.

To compound their wrong the purveyors take much more than ever comes to the King's use. For every pound's worth of goods that the King receives, it is affirmed on good authority that three pounds of damage is inflicted on the populace. Purveyors conceal their thievery by failing to register their exactions as the law provides. Illegally they set their own prices. They cheat in appraising goods. By law they are required to procure only in the daytime, but now they are abroad in twilight and at night. By law they are required to show their commission, but this they refuse. "A number of other particulars there are," Bacon adds, "whereof as I have given your majesty a taste, so the chief of them upon deliberate advice are set down in writing by the labour of some committees, and approbation of the whole house, more particularly and lively than I can express them, myself having them at the second hand by reason of my abode."

About this time the courts, the Privy Council, and the King were deliberating the constitutional question, whether the Council of the Marches lay beyond the jurisdiction of the ordinary courts of law. The Council of the Marches had been set up in an effort to reduce the power of the nobles in outlying districts, notably the frontier areas of Wales and Yorkshire. Because of the manner in which the King had empowered local magistrates, these areas had become veritable crown colonies as far as the dispensing of justice was concerned. The motives behind the present agitation for a change were not unmixed. There were representations against the efficiency of magistrates by noblemen who deemed the inhabitants of these regions their special "care." There was a preference on the part of inhabitants for trial by jury, because jurors could be brought under local influence. There were arguments by lawyers greedy for costs. And there was another opportunity for Edward Coke—who never missed one—to make a case against the King's holding within his power any court which could establish new law by precedent. The question was brought before a series of tribunals and then sent back to the King. The matter was settled, for the time being, by James with the declaration, in keeping with his own political doctrine and according to Bacon's constitutional advice, that the empowering and the continuance of the Court of the Marches lay within the Prerogative of the King.

It was the opinion of Bacon that in this instance, at least, the poor could obtain better justice at less expense from the King's courts than from "lawyers' courts," that the "power of the gentry is the chief fear and danger of the good subject." Bacon also thought that an unconstitutional assault on the sovereign's

Prerogative in any instance could be more dangerous in the long run to subjects' liberties than the retaining within the Prerogative of what was assumed by certain judges and lawyers bent on constitutional changes to lie within subjects' so-called "rights." A debate in the Commons on the question of the Marches called forth one of Bacon's most notable constitutional utterances. In this he affirmed by legal argument, with citation of precedents established in the days of King Alfred, William the Conqueror, Henry III, Edward III, Edward IV, and Henry VIII, that the King acting on his Prerogative could establish courts by a power of initiative divinely bestowed upon rulers *qua* rulers. Bacon's speech on that occasion would not be forgotten by some of those who were to try him before the High Court of Parliament in 1621.

The King, argued Bacon, "holdeth not his Prerogatives of this kind mediately from the Law, but immediately from God, as he holdeth his Crown; and though other Prerogatives by which he claimeth any matter of revenue or other right pleadable in his ordinary courts of justice, may be there disputed, yet his Sovereign Power, which no Judge can censure, is not that of nature; and therefore whatever pertaineth or dependeth thereon, being matter of government, and not of law, must be left to his managing by his Council of State. And that this is necessary to the end of all government, which is preservation of the public, may in this particular appear. For no doubt but these grave and worthy ministers of justice have in all this proceeding no respect but their oaths and the duties of their places, as they have often and deeply protested; and in truth it belongeth not to them to look any higher, because they have charge but of particular rights. But the State, whose proper duty and eye is to the general good, and in that regard to the balancing of all degrees . . . will happily consider this point above Law, that monarchies, in name, do often degenerate into Aristocracies, or rather Oligarchies, in nature, by two insensible degrees." These degrees are the making of the Sovereign's Prerogative subject to the constructions of law and the affixing of law to some office, where it can be over-ruled or inspired by a judge, to the enablement of magistracy to stand independent by itself. "God forbid," said Bacon, "that we should be governed by men's discretions and not by the Law; 'for certainly a King that governs not thereby,' as his Majesty has written, 'can neither be comptable to God for his administration, nor have a happy and established reign.' But God forbid also, upon pretence of liberties or Laws, Government should have any head but the King. . . .

"We say that in the King's Prerogative, there is a double power: one which is delegate to his ordinary judges in Chancery or Common Law; another which is inherent in his own person, whereby he is the supreme judge both in Parliament and all other Courts; and hath power to stay suits at the Common Law." Acts of Parliament may be suspended by the King's sole authority. The inherent power of the Sovereign is exempt from control by any court of law.

James, while making his initial "progress" from Edinburgh to London (1603), had been presented with a petition from the Nonconformist clergy. This document came to be known as "the Millenary Petition" because of its supposed one thousand signatures—it actually contained some eight hundred. The petitioners described themselves as not "factious" men nor "schismatics," but as faithful ministers of Christ, who humbly desired redress of certain abuses. As one who had surveyed the Established Church of England from a distance, James had thought of this as a communion which could countenance a sufficient variety of doctrines and modes of worship to satisfy all reasonable men. He was inclined to listen, however, to the complaints of any worthy Nonconformists who, because of troubled "consciences," were finding it difficult to conform to the letter of some of the ecclesiastical laws. On meeting with his first Parliament, the King and Head of the Church stressed his reluctance to persecute or threaten his subjects "in matters of conscience," referred to Puritans as persons "impatient of any superiority," and reminded his hearers that he had been born a Roman Catholic. He affirmed that he had ever been considerate of persons of that faith, but added in warning that priests who contended that the Bishop of Rome could exercise political power over the subjects of other lawful sovereigns, or held that excommunicated kings could be lawfully assassinated, would not be permitted to enter or remain within his kingdom. There would be no condoning, moreover, of attempts on the part of Roman Catholic laymen to convert other subjects either by argument or coercion.

James advised the Universities that he intended to make provision for preaching ministers who would travel from one vacant parish to another, as need required, by such impropriate tithes as he was able to set aside for this purpose. This project, however, was abandoned when Whitgift remonstrated that it would amount to a capitulation to Puritans bent on the undermining of the rule of bishops by spreading through the agency of itinerant "prophesying" clergy the doctrine of rule by Presbytery. It soon became apparent to Bacon that the King, while aware of the threat of the Recusants to the unity and independence of his kingdom, was not fully informed of the demands and the connivings of the Puritans, the extent of their following throughout England, and the influence of the sect within Parliament.

His advice on the union of England and Scotland had been well received; the King might entertain *Certain Considerations touching the better Pacification and the Edification of the Church of England* (1603). In this latter advice Bacon introduces the subject with this statement: "The unity of your Church, excellent Sovereign, is a thing no less precious than the union of your kingdoms; being both works wherein your happiness may contend with your worthiness. Having therefore presumed, not without your majesty's gracious acceptation, to say somewhat on the one, I am the more encouraged not to be silent in the other: the rather, because it is an argument I have travelled in heretofore." Bacon then sets down three premises: first, that "all actual and full obedience is to be given to ecclesiastical jurisdiction as it now standeth"; second, that "mutation" in church affairs, for the "taking away abuses," will not necessarily "undermine the stability . . . of that which is sound and good"; and third, that there is not "one form of discipline in all churches, and that imposed by necessity of a commandment and prescript out of the word of God." He tells James that he can find nothing in Scripture contrary to the view that "God had left the like liberty to the Church government, as he had done to the civil government," so that the forms of the former can befit the time, as Divine Providence may order and dispose. It is his opinion, nevertheless, that government by bishops, which is warranted by the practice of the ancient Church, is "much more convenient for kingdoms, than parity of ministers and government by synods." The "sympathy" between the state ecclesiastical and the state civil is of such a nature that it is not possible to alter the government of the one without endangering the stability of the other.

There are, however, two features of the present administration by bishops in the Established Church which might well be changed; the first is their "sole exercise" of rule, and the second their deputation of certain parts of their authority to chancellors, commissaries, and other officers. As for the first: there were in the original government of the Church Presbyters and Consistories who, with the bishops, had to do not only with endowments and revenues but also with general ecclesiastical jurisdiction. It would seem fitting, therefore, that in ordaining, suspending, or depriving ministers, and in judging cases of blasphemy and the like, bishops should not proceed "sole and unassisted." This is a point in which present-day bishops might concede without perturbation to the Church and to their own strengthening and better proceeding in causes. Yet, while this is so, the bishop as bishop cannot properly put his authority from him by means of deputation, as a civil sovereign may. The imitation of kings by bishops, through their having chancellors and judges, is not contained in their "original grant." The bishop's "trust and confidence . . . is personal and inherent: and cannot, nor ought not to be transposed."

Turning to the liturgy and the ceremonies of the Church, Bacon finds the emphasis on preaching so extreme that reverence in worship is declining and "superstition" is in prospect. "As the extolling of the sacrament bred the superstition of the mass; the extolling of the liturgy and prayers bred the superstition of the monastical orders and oraisons: and so no doubt preaching likewise may be magnified and extolled superstitiously, as if all the whole body of God's worship should be turned into an ear." The Puritans "inveigh against a dumb ministry," but make too "promiscuous an allowance" for those of their number whom they account prophets. Many of their preachers have no acquaintance with learning or regard for the arts and sciences which are the handmaidens of theology, nor indeed respect for the true gift of preaching, which in many cases among them is no gift at all. While it must be acknowledged that there is a great variety in auditories and congregations, there is surely some level below which preaching ought not to descend. As for prophesying, an exercise which because of abuses has been put down by an order of the Church, the question might profitably be considered whether this should be revived by having the clergy within a precinct meet upon a weekday, with an "ancient grave minister" presiding, for the exposition by those who attend of a selected and previously announced text of Scripture. Such an exercise, an earlier custom of the Church, would prove an excellent means for the training of preachers in the proper handling of the Word of God.

In the remainder of *Certain Considerations* Bacon grants several concessions to the Puritans. He advises that bishops act in council with Presbyters and Consistories. "The word, priest," he says, "should not be continued, especially with offence, the word, minister, being already made familiar." When dealing with the cap and surplice, Bacon asks whether the Church should insist more on what belongs to the unity of the Christian faith in articles of doctrine, and less on a common conformity with outward rites and ceremonies. Cap and surplice, in Bacon's opinion, are among things "in their nature indifferent." In the conflict between those who do and those who do not wear them, Bacon would have the Church obey "the apostle's rule, which is: 'that the stronger do descend and yield to the weaker.' " This would make for toleration, bring about liberty within the law, and discourage that connivance which encourages disobedience. As part of church worship there should be "singing of psalms and spiritual songs," but no employment of "figures of music" which "have no affinity with the reasonable service of God, but were added in the more pompous times." The ceremony of the ring should be dropped from the marriage service; even vulgar persons think it not "grave" or an "essential part."

Having, next, considered the rites of confirmation and of absolution, the latter of which he thinks was "first allowed in a kind of spiritual discretion," Bacon turns to "the abuse" of excommunication. This, in his opinion, is a punishment too indiscriminately prescribed by bishops for persons who fail to conform with "indifferent" practices. "Excommunication," he writes, "is the greatest judgment upon earth; being that which is ratified in heaven; and being a precursory or prelusory judgment of the great judgment of Christ in the end of the world. And therefore for this to be made an ordinary process . . . how can it be without derogation to God's honour, and making the power of the keys contemptible?"

After touching on the questions of nonresident clergy and the placing of several parishes under one minister, Bacon makes a brief reference to penal measures against Roman Catholics. "I am persuaded," he writes, "that the papists themselves should not need so much the severity of penal laws, if the sword of the Spirit were better edged, by strengthening the authority, and suppressing the abuses in the Church."

Certain Considerations was written to prepare the mind of the King for a conference in prospect between the ecclesiastical authorities and representative Puritans. Whether James gave any thought to Bacon's advice, in whole or in part, it is impossible to say. Certainly, any effect it might have had on his thinking was soon dissipated by the behaviour of both Puritans and bishops at this meeting. The conference was convened at Hampton Court in 1604: nine bishops and nine other dignitaries represented the Church; there were four Puritans present. The Puritans moved to have the doctrine of the Church of England made so extremely Genevan in character that John Whitgift, who was sufficiently Calvinist in theology to believe that "it is not placed in the will and power of every man to be saved," could not even consider their proposals. It occurred to the bishops that the Puritans hoped that by their first precipitating an involved and lengthy doctrinal debate, in which they would undoubtedly make a good showing, their later propositions of reform in church government might be the more readily entertained, as having to do with "less essential" matters. The Puritans requested that a pastor be provided for every parish and that pluralities be abolished. This proposal was, in the surmise of the bishops, shrewdly motivated by a twofold desire, to bring to an end the silencing of Puritan preachers by ecclesiastical courts and to have vacancies in parishes about the country filled with untrained pastors of a "prophesying" sort. Archbishop Whitgift thought the motives of the Puritans in every discussion serpentine. In a letter to Robert Cecil he called the "contentious brethren" so many "vipers" who "have made petitions and motions correspondent to their natures." Bishop Bancroft countered a Puritan proposal for democratic church government with an assertion of the doctrine of the divine right of the King and Head of the Church. He called for a more rigid statement of Articles. When the question of rituals was raised the Puritans repeated their familiar charge that all the "forms" of the Established Church, from the surplice to the Sign of the Cross in baptism, were "relics of Popery, and had been abused to idolatry, and therefore ought to be abolished." Their leader, John Reynolds, taking hold of the Archbishop's sleeve, told him mockingly that he was clad in the "rags of Popery." In a brief on discipline the Puritans asked that in the case of grave decisions the bishops be required to consult with Presbyters. James, on hearing this request and remembering what he had suffered at the hands of the Presbyterians in Scotland, flew into a rage and exclaimed that its proposers were aiming at a Scotch Presbytery which, he said, "agreeth as well with a monarchy as God with the devil. Then Jack and Tom, and Will and Dick shall meet and at their pleasure censure me and my council and all our proceedings." The King told the Conference plainly: "I will have one doctrine, one discipline, one religion, in substance and ceremony." To the Puritans he addressed the threat: "If this be all your party have to say I will make them conform, or I will harry them out of this land, or else worse."

The Conference produced nothing of consequence for theology or ritual except a few minor changes in the catechism and the service of worship. It had, however, one issue of great consequence, the authorized translation of the Bible—what was to be the King James Version—long to continue as a standard work. This translation would be read or heard by Protestants everywhere, and was to do more for the furtherance of principles on which the Puritans stood than any concession which could conceivably have been obtained through debate or by any other strategy from any bishops at any conference in the seventeenth century.

As a result of the Hampton Court Conference, "many cripples in conformity were cured of their former halting therein; and . . . for the future quietly digested the Ceremonies of the Church." More robust persons among the Puritans, however, were to become stronger in conviction and bolder in speech. In the thinking of many of these, repugnance against the severe rule of bishops was to be associated with aversion for the exercise of the Royal Prerogative in secular acts by the King. The disappointment, and fear too, of the Recusants, who had been awaiting the results of the Conference, and then learned of the King's announcement respecting "one doctrine, one discipline," was great.

The strong sense of frustration in some of their number showed itself vehemently the following year in the unsuccessful Gunpowder Plot (1605). The design of this "Powder Treason" was to kill the King, members of the Privy Council, the Lords, and Commons all at one blow. The conspiracy made a great impression on the mind of Bacon. He was to recall it in his writings time after time. Two years after the "Powder Treason" was hatched, Bacon in a letter to his friend Tobie Matthew, who earlier had become a Roman Catholic, described the conspiracy as "the extreme effects of Superstition . . . fit to be tabled and pictured in the chambers of meditation, as another hell above the ground; and well justifying the censure of the heathen that superstition is far worse than atheism."

VII

BACON AS SOLICITOR-GENERAL

Bacon ASSUMED HIS FIRST ADMINISTRATIVE POST in government, that of Solicitor-General, in 1607. So many and exacting were the duties attached to this office, that he came to regard it as one of the "painfullest places in the Kingdom." Bacon was now required to consult with the King, the Privy Council, the judges, the Lords, and the Commons. He prepared proclamations for the Star Chamber, cases for the courts, and measures for presentation to Parliament. Because, as Henry Howard, Earl of Northampton (d. 1614), Lord Privy Seal, said, the present Solicitor was "a person very apt . . . to apprehend," Bacon was assigned duties which ordinarily would have been performed by the Attorney-General. Bacon gave advice on the continuing case of Court of the Marches, the pacification of unquiet Ireland, the amelioration of laws which were harsh and the repeal of those which were obsolete, the abuses of those who made it their business to be "informers" against others, the duties and dignities of the juror's office, and the practice of duelling. In addition, he undertook heavy tasks in the Commons, wrote twelve philosophical pieces, and became a judge and the President of the new Court of the Verge. The high regard in which James held Bacon's services became very evident when, in 1611, on establishing by Patent the Court of the

Verge, he decided to appoint the Solicitor to its Presidency. The King's intention was that the new tribunal, which he was establishing on his own warrant, should supersede the old Court of the Marshalsea. The range of the latter had been too narrow and uncertain. The new court's jurisdiction would extend to all offences, except breach of private contract, committed by any subject within the Verge of the King's House, an area with a radius of twelve miles. James still retained vivid memories of the Gunpowder Plot. He was apprehensive of the Recusants, who were ever plotting, and of conniving Puritans, who were becoming increasingly bolder in their demands. He had been reflecting of late, too, on the assassination of Henry IV of France (1610). He had also been taking advice from his Solicitor-General.

In his address on the occasion of the opening of the new court, his first speech as a judge, Bacon describes the Verge as a "carpet spread about the king's chair of estate," and declares that "where the king cometh, there should come peace and order, and an awe and reverence in men's hearts." The newly appointed judge does not overlook a reminder to the court of the privileges of the King's subjects. "It is," he says, "the happy estate and condition of the subject of this realm of England, that he is not to be impeached in his life, lands, or goods, by flying rumours, or wandering fames and reports, or secret and privy inquisitions; but by the oath and presentment of men of honest condition, in the face of justice." Sections of his address present evidence of a change in Bacon's attitude towards the Roman Catholics after the Gunpowder Plot, and towards the Puritans after the Hampton Court Conference. The toleration manifest in his *Letter of Advice* (1584) to Elizabeth and in his more recent *Certain Considerations* (1603) is now modified. He bluntly asserts that there are to be no "contempts" of "the service of Almighty God," and illustrates what he means by his words: "For contempts of our church and service," he says, "they are comprehended in that known name ... recusancy; which offence hath many branches and dependencies; the wife-recusant, she tempts; the church papist, he feeds and relieves; the corrupt schoolmaster, he soweth tares; the dissembler, he conformeth and doth not communicate." In a second reference, this to the Puritans, Bacon reminds the jurors that "because the vulgar people are sometimes led with vain and fond prophecies; if any such shall be published, to the end to move stirs or tumults, this is ... punished by a year's imprisonment and loss of goods; and of this also shall you inquire." The judge further instructs the jury on a question which concerns both Puritans and Roman Catholics: "If any minister refuse to use the book of Common-prayer, or wilfully swerveth in divine service from that book; or if any person whatsoever do scandalize that book, and speak openly and maliciously in derogation of it; such men do but make a rent in the garment, and such are by you to be inquired of."

Bacon's speech on this occasion contains some of his early reflections on the subject of duelling. He observes that, with the increase in this practice, life has grown so cheap that it is "set at the price of words, and every petty scorn and disgrace can have no other reparation." Through duelling "the very life of the law is almost taken away." English law makes many distinctions in the question of the taking of life, "but yet no such difference as the wanton humours and braveries of men have under a reverend name of honour and reputation invented." In a later speech when, as Attorney-General, he argues a case of duelling before the Star Chamber, Bacon finds occasion to remark that if this practice continues and prevails, English legal yearbooks and statute books must give way to French and Italian pamphlets. Already it is being said, sometimes in scorn, that the law of England makes "no difference between foul murder and the killing of a man upon fair terms as they now call it." The seed of the mischief is being nourished by "vain discourses, and green and unripe conceits." As by a kind of be-witching or sorcery, which enchants immature minds, the evil has so grown that "the stream of vulgar opinion" makes it necessary to attempt the life of another, "or else there is no living or looking upon men's faces." The growth of duelling is a consequence of a misunderstanding and wrong conception of fortitude and valor. "For fortitude distinguisheth of the grounds of quarrels whether they be just; and not only so, but whether they be worthy; and setteth a better price upon men's lives than to bestow them idly; nay it is weakness and dis-esteem of a man's self, to put a man's life upon such liedger performances: a man's life is not to be trifled away; it is to be offered up and sacrificed to honourable services, public merits, good causes, and noble adventures." The notion underlying what are deemed affairs of honor is a "fond and false disguise or puppetry of honour" which is set up in defiance of the "honour of religion, law, and the king." In English tradition "the fountain of honour is the king and his aspect." From these flow justice to the courts of law. When revenge for wrong is taken out of the magistrates' hands, contrary to God's ordi-nance, "and every man shall bear the sword, not to defend, but to assail; and private men begin once to presume to give law to themselves, and to right their own wrongs . . . the state by this means shall be like to a distempered and imperfect body, con-tinually subject to inflammations and convulsions."

During the years of his Solicitorship other matters besides those of Recusants, Puritans, and duellists were disturbing Bacon's mind. There was no support in sight for his projected instauration of the sciences. The *Advancement of Learning* had failed to make an impact on the King, to whom it was addressed, or on members of the Court, who ignored it. Political pro-motion had been slow; Bacon, already in his late forties, was still only Solicitor-General, a subsidiary officer at the beck and call of every official in authority. Hobart, the present Attorney-

General, was, in Bacon's opinion, seriously lacking in the capacities required for this office. Robert Cecil, Lord Salisbury, the Secretary of State was transacting the nation's business by covert negotiations at home and abroad. He was playing England's enemies, the French and the Spaniards, one against the other, while secretly collecting pensions from both parties. His allowances from the state and the perquisites which he was collecting from office holders and agents, who sought his goodwill and support, were making the Secretary financially rich, but by his deplorable trading, this cousin was gradually bringing the King to poverty and the constitutional affairs of the kingdom to an impasse.

For the impasse in prospect, not only Cecil but the King, certain judges, and the Commons also were partly to blame. James could better have refrained from interfering continuously with the operation of the established institutions of state and have left the Council, the courts, and the Commons to work out their own problems. His incessant assertion of the Sovereign's Prerogative, sometimes for the maintaining of his own dignity but mainly in justification of questionable Impositions, burdensome Monopolies, improper Purveyance, and outmoded Tenures and Wardships, was bringing that Prerogative under regrettable discussion, even indeed into disrepute.

There was no doubt in Bacon's mind about the historical and continuing priority of the Sovereign's Prerogative in the unwritten constitution of England. The Prerogative, as Bacon often affirmed, was as old as the law itself. Such curbs as had been put upon it had been slowly accumulated by the establishment of precedents from reign to reign, as in the case of the privileges of the Houses of Parliament and the assured jurisdictions of the courts of law. Yet the sovereign himself, in Bacon's opinion, had never been brought under the rule of Parliament or the law. The courts, despite what some lawyers might think and some judges might say, were still King's Courts.

The source of political initiative and of justice as well, no matter how fervently some members of the Commons might contend to the contrary, was still the Throne.

In English history, the initiator and dispenser of law was the King. From early times the King had had his *curia*, or court, and his councillors, but he himself had always remained the source of legislative and judicial power. The King in Council—privy to himself—was in early days a judiciary and parliament combined. Gradually, definite modes of procedure and precedents in judging took shape to form the basis of a law applicable to like cases, common to the whole of England. In the sorting of precedents judges and lawyers, as counsel, had played a part. Parliament, or "parley," had its beginnings in a feudal assembly of knights, summoned for consultation with the King and his Council on such questions as territory, taxes, internal and external policies, and arrangement of governmental offices. While the early "parley," whose members often responded but grudgingly to the King's call, discussed these matters, it never, as a Parliament, assumed the power or right of final judgment or settlement. This lay with the King in Council. Under the Edwards, Parliament was enlarged to include representatives of King and Church, barons, knights, and burgesses. Edward I (1272-1307) invited the enactment of statute after statute by this body. In consequence, the offices of Parliament and King's Council became more or less distinct. Petitions addressed directly to the King were sometimes presented to Parliament for discussion. Gradually it became an assumption that Parliament's consent was proper for the passing of certain statutes, as distinct from judicial precedents, Council's proclamations, and levies of extraordinary taxes. Gradually two Houses of Parliament emerged, one of Commons and another of Lords. Each body became increasingly jealous of its own privileges. Yet, before the days of the present King, it had never been seriously assumed that either House derived its power of "initiative" from any source but the King.

Each court had been established permissively by the King in Council for purposes. The presumption continued that the sovereign remained the final source of right, of law, of justice. The courts remained King's Courts, their advocates King's Counsel. When, in the present reign, Edward Coke called himself "Lord Chief Justice of England" and not "Lord Chief Justice of the King's Bench," he had already made himself a party to far-reaching constitutional change. Probably this fact was not fully comprehended by this judge, who never showed much discernment of constitutional matters. His failure in comprehension was to make him an unwitting precursor of political revolution.

The Court of Common Pleas was a bench of judges, sanctioned by the King and set up at Westminster in King John's reign (1199-1216) for the convenience of subjects who would find it difficult or impossible to follow about the country a king who might be given to journeying. The Court of Chancery was designed by the King in Council as a means to redress miscarriages of justice in courts where the common law, based on precedents, largely prevailed. And so it was in the case of the origins of other courts. Yet early in James' reign the two Houses of Parliament and a variety of courts were advancing definite claims for their respective jurisdictions without any reference, in some instances, to the King's power of initiative.

Constitutional advancement from privilege to privilege, from precedent to precedent, was, in Bacon's opinion, sound and desirable, provided there was no attempt on the part of Parliament, courts of law, or any commission to destroy continuity in constitutional development or to dissipate unity in constitutional administration. A comprehending king would take care to grant more and more political authority to subjects and developing courts of law and to the Commons—which contained the elected representatives of loyal and desiring subjects. Wise kings in the past had done so. If the present occupant of the throne would not so concede, then, in Bacon's mind, two things had firmly to be kept in mind: first, there was to be no giving way on the concessions already won by courts and by Parliament. Second, the continuity of the constitution, according to which the Throne retained powers never conceded to any other institution, was to be guarded against inroads by judges or by members of Parliament who might attempt to set up, as Coke and some lawyers undoubtedly would, *imperium in imperio*.

Time after time in the reign of the present sovereign the Commons had already undertaken to debate what it constitutionally could not question, namely, the King's power within his Prerogative to impose Impositions, grant Monopolies, to establish and continue the Court of the Marches. The chief promoters of unconstitutional debates in the Commons had been the lawyers. The judges of the common law courts had gone so far in their boldness as to warn the Council of the Marches, which had been set up by the King, that if it went beyond certain jurisdictional limits, a Prohibition would be issued to restrain it. They had declared that cases arising in four specified English counties were not to be kept within these limits. The judges, too, had been interfering in increasing degree with the proceedings of the Commissions of the Privy Council and ecclesiastical courts, by issuing Prohibitions for their inhibition until they proved their own right to proceed in cases. When Archbishop Bancroft claimed that the King had "power to take what causes he pleased out of the Judge's hands and to determine them himself," Coke, now Chief Justice of the King's Bench, issued a flat denial. "Then," exclaimed James, "I shall be under the Law, which is treason to affirm." Coke, in comment, quoting Henry de Bracton, replied that "the King ought not to be under any man but under God and the Law."

While pondering these several problems in 1608, Bacon set down in a private notebook called *Commentarius solutus* (*Casual Commentary*) some reflections on current perils to the state, on the King's conduct, the Royal Prerogative, the Secretary of State, the Attorney-General, recent foreign policy, law and judges, lawyers in Parliament. The diarist also made notes on ways and means to promote his scientific projects, and on his private and personal difficulties, such as monetary affairs and certain aspects of his temperament which might be preventing his political promotion. Some of Bacon's "ethical" biographers have raised a great to-do over certain of the personal items in his *Casual Commentary*. Their revulsion, in a display of "moral sensibility," has ranged from indignation to horror. Yet when approached simply, as they should be, those jottings in a diary appear as artless memoranda, largely in self-criticism. As directions for future conduct, they portend nothing sinister; they are but self-helps to a man seeking promotion in public office when he is not of a "politic" nature, as such a nature is regarded in his time. Bacon from his youth had shown shyness, formality in speech, and alternating timorousness and self-assurance, qualities commonly found together in a reserved person of capacity. He had in his make-up some of the stiffness of manner and the censoriousness of speech which belonged to persons reared under Calvinist influence. To his complaining uncle, Lord Burghley, he had found it necessary to explain, in his youth, some of these qualities as the characteristics of a student who lived *in umbra*. Bacon from the beginning had been certain of his gifts of reflection, tongue, and pen. His assurance in these regards had enabled him to give political advice of consequence to sovereigns and the members of the three estates, Lords Spiritual, Lords Temporal, and Commons. It had carried him from success to success in Parliament. Yet even after these achievements and his demonstration of administrative efficiency in the Solicitor-General's office, he was still being looked upon and treated as a person theoretically remote, a man not quite fitted to high public office. On such facts as these Bacon had been ruminating before he jotted down the items of his diary. It had dawned upon his thought that if his political and scientific ends were to be achieved some incidental difficulties would have to be overcome.

In the *Casual Commentary* the diarist reckons that his current income is £4,975, his present debts in sum £4,481, and the monetary worth of his property and offices £24,155. Turning from personal finance to public matters, he notes, among present perils to the state, the King's "poverty and empty coffers," an irresolute Privy Council, daring judges, a hostile Commons, religious unrest, a devious Secretary of State, possible invasion from Scotland, foreign wars, and James' interference with institutions of government. Through the diarist's mind there pass, during the few days in which the *Casual Commentary* is written, some thoughts on ways to obviate these perils: the fixing of the respective jurisdictions of the political and the legal offices in the kingdom; the restoring of the Church to its true limits of authority; the putting into office of "persons *act(ive)* and in their nature *stir(ring)*"; the making use of the Presbytery and nobility of Scotland; the practice by the King of what is majestic and not of a meddling and bargaining sort; "new laws to be compounded and collected"; persuasion of the King to be "lawgiver perpetuus princeps" after a compilation of laws has been made by his present Solicitor-General; "confederacy and more straight amity with the Low Countries"; means for providing the King with funds.

In a note Bacon reveals his own immediate political ambition. He will "succ(eed) Salisbury and amuse the K(ing) and P(rince) [Henry] with pastime and glory." The cousin is, in Bacon's opinion, not fitted in capacity or by motive to be the King's first minister, and James, Bacon thinks, could do much to further the affairs of the kingdom by giving more time to his esteemed amusements and less to attempts to bring under his personal direction settled offices of government. (Bacon's opinion in this regard was to be one of the causes for his optimism when the King's second "favorite," George Villiers, began to undertake the King's tasks in the administration of state.) Three months before the *Casual Commentary* is written, Salisbury has assumed the office of Lord Treasurer; and Bacon includes a reference to means employed by his cousin for replenishing the King's Treasury without recourse to Parliament: "My L(ord) of Salisbury is to be remembered of the great expectation wherewith he enters that he will *moderate new Impositions.*"

On the capacity and performance of Hobart, the Attorney-General, Bacon sets down the jotting, "Solemn goose . . . they have made him believe he is wondrous wy (wise). He never beats down unfit suits with law. In persons as in people, some shew more wise than they are." "He will alter a thing, but not mend." "Nibbling solemnly, he distinguisheth, but not apprehendeth." On the subject of judges, lawyers, Prohibitions, and the Royal Prerogative the Solicitor-General records the following reflections:

"The K(ing) assembled his Judges—not all, but certain of them—before their Circuits, and found fault with multitudes of Prohibitions. . . . The K(ing) was vehement, and said that more had been granted in four years of his Reign than in forty of former time; and that no kingdom had more honourable Courts of Justice; but, again, none was more cursed with confusion and contention of Prohibitions. Seemed to apprehend the distribution of justice after the French manner was better for the people and fitter for his greatness, saying that this course, to draw all things to Westminster was to make him K(ing) as it were of the Isle of France. . . . Warned a surceance of granting Prohibitions for the vacation following."

"Judges to consult with King as well as the King with Judges. . . . Query, of making use of my Lord of Canterbury his opposition to the la(wyers), in point of reforming the laws and disprizing mere lawyers."

"To prepare either collect(ions), or at least advice, touching the equalling of laws."

"Rem(inder); to advise the K(ing) . . . to keep the lawyers in awe."

"Summary justice belongeth to the King's prerogative. The fountain must run, where the conduits are stopped."

"Being prepared in the matter of Prohibitions. Putting in a claim for the K(ing). The 4 necessities, (1) time, as of war; (2) place, as frontiers remote; (3) person, as [for example] poor [persons] that have no means to sue those that come in by safe-conduct; (4) matter, mixed with State."

As helps to his demeanor, Bacon mentions in advice to himself "struggling against shyness, hurry in speech, brusqueness or formality," and the suppression of "panting and labour of breath and voice" when speaking. Hereafter he will try "not to fall upon the main too sudden; but to induce and intermingle speech of good fashion," and also to "free myself at once from payment of formality and compliment, though with some shew of careless-ness, pride, and rudeness." He intends also, "To set foot and maintain access with his Majesty. . . . To attend some time his repasts and to fall into a course of familiar discourses. To find means to win a conc(eit), not open but private, of being af-fectionate and assured to the Sco(tch) and fit to succeed Sa(lis-bury). . . . To have ever in readiness matter to minister talk with every of the great counsellors *respective*, both to induce familiarity and for countenance in public place. . . . Insinuate myself to become privy to my L(ord) of Salisb(ury's) estate. . . . To correspond [i.e., conform] with Salisbury in a habit of natural but no way's perilous boldness, and in vivacity, invention, care to cast and enterprise, but with due caution . . . to listen how the King is affected in respect of the Prince, and to make use of my industry in it towards the Pr(ince). . . . To make them [the Lord Chancellor and Lord Treasurer] think they shall find an alteration to their contentment over that [Attorney] which now is. . . . To furnish my Lord of Suffolk with ornaments for public speeches; to make him think how he should be reverenced by a L(ord) Chancellor, if I were:—princelike. . . . To take notes, in tables, when I attend the Council; and sometimes to move out of a memorial, shewed and seen. To have particular occasions, fit and grateful and continual, to maintain private speech with every the great persons, and sometimes drawing more than one of them together, *ex imitatione* Att(orney). This especially in public places and without care or affectation."

In the optimistic mood of a dreamer Bacon sets down some thoughts about his instauration of the sciences. He thinks of "a place to command wits and pens, Westminster, Eton, Winchester, specially Trinity College in Cambridge, St. John's in Cambridge, Magdalene College in Oxford, and bespeaking this betimes with the King, my Lord Archbishop, my Lord Treasurer." It occurs to him that either Salisbury or Bancroft, the respective chancellors of Cambridge and Oxford, may be induced to influence one or the other of the Universities towards the granting of a college for the promotion of a new knowledge. He entertains the hope that the junior scholars of the Universities will prove receptive of a new kind of fruitful inquiry in replacement of frustrating Peripatetic argumentation. Possible backers of his plan would include his friend Bishop Andrewes, "single, rich, sickly, a professor to some experiments," and the Earl of Northumberland—who was his late brother's friend and is now the patron of Thomas Harriot, the mathematician—and perhaps Harriot himself. He also thinks of the imaginative Sir Walter Raleigh "in the tower," the court physicians Leonard Poe and John Hammond, and one of the Scottish Murrays who is treasurer to Prince Henry. If an already established college could be put to new use, or a new foundation obtained, it will be provided with "laborities and engines, vaults and furnaces, terraces for insulation," and the like, for the carrying on of experiments and observations and the compiling of histories of operations in nature and the mechanical arts. Investigations in all sorts of phenomena, including those of motion, will be pursued. There will be scientific correspondence with members of foreign societies. The diarist thinks of "giving pensions to four, for search to compile the two histories"; of marvels and the mechanical arts; of providing facilities for inventors; of having "two galleries with statuas for Inventors past, and spaces, or bases, for Inventors to come. And a library and an Inginary." These practices will, in his opinion, further a scientific advance, since "marvels" or monsters, the manual arts, and "works" in practical operation—which inventions are—have no sanctioned place, strictly speaking, in traditional histories of natural science.

The *Casual Commentary* continues with more notes on the institute of science: "Query, of the order and discipline, to be mixed with some points popular to invite many to contribute and join. Query, of the rules and prescripts of their studies and inquiries. Allowance for travelling. Allowance for experiments. Intelligence and correspondence with the Universities abroad. Query, of the manner and prescripts touching secrecy, tradition, and publication. Query, of removes and expulsions in case, within a time, some invention worthy be not produced. And likewise query of the honours and rewards for inventions."

As for the diarist's own philosophical writings: the *Advancement of Learning* will be translated into Latin; a new piece, *Cogitata et visa (Thoughts and Impressions)*, will be circulated privately; the Aphorisms on scientific method will be added to; and the Tables of Heat, Cold, and Sound, on which some work has been done, will be completed. In pieces to be prepared the author will "discuss scornfully of the Grecians, with some better respect to . . . the utmost antiquities and the mysteries of the poets," and perhaps make an "oration '*ad filios*' " to prospective disciples. The issue of the last of these musings are *Redargutio philosophiarum (Refutation of Philosophies*, 1608) and *Sapientia veterum (Wisdom of the Ancients*, 1609).

In 1610, two years after he made a note in his *Casual Commentary* on Salisbury's management of the King's Treasury, Bacon was to see the Sovereign of the Realm turned into a

bargainer without kingly majesty—as Bacon later told James—
under the leading of this Lord Treasurer. When Salisbury took
over the office of Lord Treasurer, in 1608, he found a disparity
of £83,000 a year between the King's ordinary revenue and his
ordinary expenditure. There was, besides, an accumulated debt
of £1,000,000, half as much as Elizabeth had been voted in
supply during her whole reign. (Elizabeth had left James with
debts.) To relieve the situation, Salisbury had been relying on
the King's Prerogative for the levying of Impositions on exports
and imports, and by these unpopular means had acquired an
additional annual revenue of £60,000. He had also collected
£10,000 by a tax on alehouses. Early in 1610 the Lord Treasurer
presented the House of Commons with a detailed statement of
the King's revenues and his necessary expenditures. He then
made an intimation of a "retribution" in prospect from James,
as a response to a desired "contribution" from the Commons.
The "retribution," Salisbury indicated, would be conditional
upon the receipt of a requested "contribution." In plain words,
the Lord Treasurer, who was also the Secretary of State, was
undertaking to arrange with the Commons a straight business
deal, in which a portion of the King's Prerogative—the histori-
cally originating source of justice and rights—would be negoti-
ated away at a price.

On announcing his plan, Salisbury found the mood of the
Lower House far less pliant and conciliatory than he had hoped
for. Members of the Commons were conscious of too many
accumulated grievances. In 1604, the first year of his first English
Parliament, James, whose Parliament in Scotland had been but
a court of record, had provoked the Lower House into making
the Remonstrance that "The privilege of our House, and therein
the liberties and stability of the whole Kingdom, hath been
more universally and dangerously impugned than ever, as we
suppose, since the beginning of Parliaments." The Commons
was now of the opinion that in the mind of the King its "privi-

leges" did not exist. Ever since the Remonstrance had been presented, James had been acting as if this petition of grievance had never been. His Lord Treasurer had been using dubious means to obtain what it was the Common's office to supply. After petition by the Lower House only the lesser of many offensive Monopolies, granted by the King, had been suppressed. The rest had been left intact, to the continued constraint of manufacture and trade, and to the increasing of the wealth of the rich and the decreasing of the means of the poor. There was still the continuance of the abuse of power by ecclesiastical commissions, and of legislative arbitrariness on the part of the King's Privy Council in dealings with Wardships, Feudal Tenure, and the Council of the Marches. These three outmoded institutions, despite complaints and entreaties in and by Parliament, were still being retained, as institutions within the King's Prerogative. The evils of Purveyance still flourished after a petition, on proven legal grounds, had been presented to the Sovereign. Clergy who could not meet the requirements of the ruling bishops were still undergoing persecution for opinions on which God alone, and no prelate, could pass judgment. The silencing, depriving, and excommunicating of Puritan clergy for relatively minor offences was increasing the number of parishes without resident ministers.

In the opinion of many members of the Commons the inhabitants of the Marches were subjects who deserved availability to courts similar to those within cities, where ordinary judges made their circuits and employed the common law. As for Wardship and Tenure: there had been a time when minors were conveniently made wards of the Crown and parts of the revenues from their estates sequestered because they could not be enrolled in the King's forces; when knights who held their lands in tenure were fittingly required to render an equivalence if they themselves could not do battle for their sovereign. But this time was long past. The occasions of present exactions from wards and knights had little relation to original military reasons and circumstances.

The Commons had already advanced a proposition of grievances over Tenure and Wardships. The King, through Salisbury,
had indicated a "gracious construction of their proposition," but
had added the observation that it was their duty to "attend his
Majesty's times at his good pleasure." On that occasion Bacon
had been chosen as the representative of the Commons "to treat
of compounding for tenures" with the King. On commission
from the Commons he had addressed the Lords, "moving and
persuading" them to join with the members of the Lower House
in petition to the King, "to obtain liberty to treat of a composition with his Majesty for Wards and Tenures." In his speech
he had said: "We have grave professors of the common law,
who will define unto us that those are parts of sovereignty, and
of the regal prerogative, which cannot be communicated with
subjects: but for tenures in substance, there is none of your
lordships but have them, and few of us but have them . . . . the
subject is capable of tenures; which shews that they are not
regal, nor any point of sovereignty. . . . So have we many deputy
lieutenants to your lordships, and many commissioners that have
been for musters and levies, that can tell us, that the service and
defence of the realm hath in these days little dependence upon
tenures. So then we perceive that it is no bond or ligament of
government; no spur of honour, no bridle of obedience. Time
was when it had other uses, and the name of knight's service
imports it: but *vocabula manent, res fugiunt*."

Despite such representations and earlier petitions on other
grievances, the King's Lord Treasurer was offering no more
than a "retribution" for a monetary "contribution." Once more
the House of Commons was being treated as if it were a mere
source of financial supply, devoid of political power and even
of political sense. What was more, the Lord Treasurer was confronting the House, not with a proper supplication for supply,
or even with a request, but simply with a business offer, a mere
"contract," with "consideration"—which is the essence of contract—attached. Some two weeks after Salisbury had announced

what came to be known as the "Great Contract," he began his bargaining in earnest. His first request was for a payment to the King of £600,000 down and £200,000 annually. The Commons, after four weeks' consideration of this, offered the King £100,000 annually on condition that he make the services of knights, as King's tenants, a matter of tenure of land with fixed and determinate, and not arbitrary, equivalence. A month later the Commons repeated their counteroffer. But the day before they did this, the King had obtained a loan of £100,000 from the City of London. Immediately his Treasurer became a more difficult party to negotiation.

Salisbury now raised the price of a royal concession. The King, he said, while not intending to diminish his Prerogative, would meet the known wishes of the Commons on the question of Wardships, provided that they paid him £200,000 annually and made a grant of £600,000 immediately, and in addition reimbursed him with a sum equivalent to the worth of the Wardships. The Commons replied by withdrawing their counteroffer. Salisbury, now resorting to intimidation, warned the Lower House that to engage in any discusssion of the King's right to levy any Impositions his Majesty thought fit "were to bark against the moon." The Privy Council also sent an order to the Speaker of the House to make a statement, "as from the King," warning its members that any question "as to his right to impose duties upon merchandise exported and imported had been settled judicially, and was not to be disputed in the House." The Commons took note that this message was not from the King himself, but from the Council, and then declared "that the same message, coming not immediately from his Majesty, should not be received as a message; and that in all messages from his Majesty, the Speaker, before he delivered them, should first ask leave of the House, according as had anciently been accustomed."

Bacon, who regarded this declaration as a constitutional

affront to the King—which it was intended to be—took the opportunity to remind both parties to the controversy of their places in the government of the kingdom. "The King's sovereignty," he said, "and the liberty of parliament, are as the two elements and principles of this estate; which, though the one be more active, the other more passive, yet they do not cross or destroy the one the other; but they strengthen and maintain the one the other. Take away liberty of parliament, the griefs of the subject will bleed inwards: sharp and eager humours will not evaporate; and then they must exulcerate; and so may endanger the sovereignty itself. On the other side, if the king's sovereignty receive diminution, or any degree of contempt with us that are born under an hereditary monarchy, so as the motions of our estate cannot work in any other frame or engine, it must follow, that we shall be a meteor, or *corpus imperfecte mistum*; which kind of bodies come speedily to confusion and dissolution."

Soon the King appeared in person to address the two Houses of Parliament. He declared that he had the right to levy any Impositions he thought proper, implying that he had the right not only to make levies on exports and imports but to impose taxes on merchandise and all other properties. The next morning the Commons, thus affronted with what they regarded as a threat to "liberties" and "privileges," appointed a committee "to devise upon some course to be taken to inform his Majesty how much the liberties of the subject and the privileges of the Parliament were impeached by this inhibition to debate his Prerogative."

Bacon advised the House not to press for, or even to assume, the right to question the King's Prerogative, but to proceed by petition, since the matter had been so determined within the Commons itself in the reign of Elizabeth—on Bacon's own advice. The Commons, this caution notwithstanding, sent a message to the King with a Petition of Right to discuss Impositions. James

informed them that the House had misinterpreted the Council's
intention. Bacon again advised the Commons, on constitutional
grounds, not to press explicitly for a right. Accordingly a
petition was framed "by way of grievance, implying the right,
though not in express terms." In response to this, some Impositions were removed, and the King, in a great concession, declared his willingness to assent to an Act whereby his power
would be suspended to levy further Impositions upon merchandise without consent of Parliament. Three days after James had
granted these concessions, the Commons decided to supply him
with £180,000 a year. Salisbury, however, now quoting a letter
from the King, said his bargaining price was £200,000, and
added the warning that if this offer was not accepted, it would
never again be repeated and Parliament would be immediately
dissolved. The Commons agreed to pay the Lord Treasurer his
price, but only on condition that some eight specified concessions
would be granted by the King in return. Parliament was then
prorogued for three months.

The Privy Council, meanwhile, became apprehensive of the
temper of the Commons and began to question whether their
forbidding of certain actions, under penalties, by Proclamation
was not presumptive of a power to legislate which they did not
possess. The Lord Chancellor, Egerton, expressed the opinion
that this power lay within their disposing, as a power of the
King, and that, if there was no precedent in law to justify the
exercise of the power, then the courts should establish one which
would. When the Chief Justice of the Common Pleas, Edward
Coke, was invited to state his view on this question, he asked for
time to consult with the other judges. Bacon, aware that Coke
would be put into a state of confusion when confronted with this
constitutional problem, reminded him of the fact that he had
already sanctioned the King's power to legislate, when as a
judge in the Court of Common Pleas he had in "divers cases"
given sentence in keeping with a Proclamation against building

in or about London. Coke, who did not want the King's power mentioned in any discussion of the law courts, replied that "it was better to go back than to go on in the wrong way." After consultation, the judges reported their opinion that "the King by his Proclamation cannot create any offence which was not an offence before." With this James intimated his agreement.

James, after Parliament was again convened, asked the Commons for a "resolute and speedy answer whether they would proceed with the Contract, yea, or no." The Lower House, suspicious that Salisbury was up to some new mischief, demanded the inclusion of certain provisory clauses within what the King now called "the Contract." The Commons asked for the guarantee, first, that hereafter Parliament would be regularly summoned; secondly, that the £200,000 granted annually would go into the kingdom's Treasury and not be alienated to other purposes—such as gifts to the King's favorites—and, thirdly, "that this £200,000 be not doubled or trebled by enhancing of the coin by the King." When faced with these stipulations, the King became enraged and, perhaps with the intention of bringing a shameless negotiation to an end, countered the demands of the Commons by mentioning an exorbitant sum in price. James in the end had probably recoiled from his Treasurer's putting his regal Majesty up for sale. The King dissolved Parliament on February 29th, 1611. Three months before, November 25th, 1610, Salisbury had received a letter filled with rage and fury from James. In this the King reminded his Treasurer that the Privy Council had "parted irresolute" after a meeting, and, as for Parliament, he had suffered with forbearance "this assembly these seven years, and from them received more disgraces, censures, and ignominies than ever Prince did endure." The Council had advised patience on his part, and this he had already exercised; but he could not "have asinine patience."

The Lord Treasurer was now reaping the fruits of a policy

begun and continued without regard to political principle. He had been squeezed by King and Commons in a deal which had turned a sovereign ruler of a kingdom into a huckster. The Sovereign was showing something more than annoyance. Salisbury became ill. Failure in dealing with Parliament and resultant cares, including a failing confidence on the part of the King, were increasing his infirmities.

Bacon had long been aware that Salisbury had kept him out of political office, yet he had always been on civil terms with his cousin. Bacon had not forgotten their family kinship. He had been meticulous in his service to Robert Cecil; had gone to him after he had been bullied as a counsel in court by Coke; had appealed to him on occasions for help when hard presssed by debtors, and had received aid. Salisbury had arranged for the dedication of the *Advancement of Learning* to the King, after getting its author a knighthood. Before that, he had warned him about rumors arising from his discussing with the Queen the conduct of Essex. Bacon had dedicated *De sapientia veterum* to his cousin. After Salisbury had been ailing for several months, Bacon wrote his cousin a New Year's letter, in January, 1612:

It may please your good Lordship,

I would entreat the new year to answer for the old, in my humble thanks to your Lordship . . . for many your favours . . . *though I find age and decay grow upon me*—yet I may have a flash or two of spirit left to do you service. And I do protest before God, without compliment or any light vein of mind, that if I knew in what course of life to do you best service, I could take it, and make my thoughts, which now fly to many pieces, be reduced to that centre. But all this is no more than I am, which is not much, but yet the entire of him that is.

Salisbury died on May 24th, 1612. The King was now without an experienced Secretary of State. His Privy Council was ineffectual. There was no Parliament in fact or in prospect. The Treasury was empty. Accumulated debts could be paid only by what might be raised through Impositions, Monopolies,

Feudal Tenure, Wardships, and other means within the Prerogative. Until 1621 there would be no Parliament in England, except one of two months' duration, which Bacon would arrange. This would be summoned on April 5th and dissolved on June 7th, 1614. The destiny of the kingdom for a period of nine years was to be in the hands of the King, his Council, his judges, two of James' rascally favorites, Robert Carr (created Earl of Somerset in 1613) and George Villiers (created Duke of Buckingham in 1617)—and Francis Bacon. During these years, rule in England, so far as James was concerned, might have reverted to a primitive form, but for certain institutions which the King could neither decimate nor reduce: the courts with their rights, the law with its statutes and precedents, and the hard-won "privileges" of subjects. Parliament was in abeyance because the Commons would neither surrender their privileges, nor allow the King to take them captive through threat or specious promises. Throughout the kingdom there was dissatisfaction with the exercise of the Royal Prerogative and disquiet over the operations of the commissions and courts of the Privy Council. The times, in Bacon's opinion, were dangerous in the extreme for the unwritten constitution of England. Even the common law judges, under the leadership of Coke, were far from certain of what was and what was not proper constitutional procedure. The courts and the constitution were to be preserved in a continuity through great trials and hazards by one man and one man alone, Francis Bacon. In this regard he became for a period the axial officer of the kingdom. He managed, without ill-deserving, to keep the constitution intact and in operation, to maintain the law and liberty of subjects, and to preserve "the King's honour," through wise, skilful, and just resorts.

VIII

BACON AS ATTORNEY-GENERAL

Bᴀᴄᴏɴ's ʜᴜᴍᴀɴᴇ ʀᴇɢᴀʀᴅ ᴏꜰ ʜɪs ᴄᴏᴜsɪɴ notwithstanding, it was definitely his opinion that the King should not appoint another of Robert Cecil's sort to the office of Secretary of State. The Solicitor-General made no attempt to conceal from James this opinion or his desire to obtain the place for himself. Long denied promotion by Salisbury, Bacon believed, for good reasons, that he was the one subject of the King who could prove successful in mitigating James' financial, Parliamentary, and general constitutional circumstances. Bacon had been dismayed by the manner of Cecil's bringing of the Throne into disrepute with members of the Commons and their constituencies. He was distressed at the lack of a Commons, the proper, constitutional source of the King's supply. He deplored the prospect of seeing the coffers of the King filled through means which depended solely on the use of the Prerogative. He began a draft of a frank, unfinished letter to James with these words:

If I shall seem in these few lines to write *majora quam pro fortuna*, it may please your Majesty to take it to be an effect not of presumption but of affection. For of the one I was never noted; and for the other I could never shew it hitherto to the full; having been as a hawk tied to another's fist [Salisbury's], that mought sometimes bate [i.e., flutter] and proffer, but could never fly.

148

In a completed letter (May 31st, 1612), Bacon wrote the King:

Your Majesty hath lost a great subject and a great servant. But if I should praise him in propriety, I should say that he was a fit man to keep things from growing worse, but no very fit man to reduce things to be much better. For he loved to have the eyes of all Israel a little too much upon himself, and to have all business still under the hammer, and like clay in the hands of the potter, to mould it as he thought good; so that he was more *in operatione* than *in opere*. And though he had fine passages of action, yet the real conclusions came slowly on. So that although your Majesty hath grave counsellors and worthy persons left, yet you do as it were turn a leaf, wherein if your Majesty shall give a frame and constitution to matters, before you place the persons, in my simple opinion it were not amiss. But the great matter and most instant for the present, is the consideration of a Parliament, for two effects: the one for the supply of your estate, the other for the better knitting of the hearts of your subjects unto your Majesty . . . for both which, Parliaments have been and are the antient and honourable remedy.

Now because I take myself to have a little skill in that region . . . though no man can say but I was a perfect and peremptory royalist, yet every man makes me believe that I was never one hour out of credit with the lower house; my desire is to know, whether your Majesty will give me leave to meditate and propound unto you some preparative remembrances touching the future Parliament.

In another letter Bacon entreated the King to employ his services. He wrote:

My principal end being to do your Majesty service, I crave leave to make at this time to your Majesty this most humble oblation of myself. . . . Your Majesty may have heard somewhat that my father was an honest man, and somewhat you may have seen of myself, though not to make any true judgment by, because I have hitherto had only *potestatem verborum*, nor that neither. I was three of my young years bred with an ambassador in France; and since, I have been an old truant in the school-house of your council-chamber, though on the second form; yet longer than any that now sitteth hath been upon the head form. If your Majesty find any aptness in me, or if you find any scarcity in others, whereby you may think it fit for your service to remove me to business of State; although I have a fair way before me for profit (and by your Majesty's grace and favour for honour and advancement), and in a course less exposed to the blasts of fortune, yet ... I will be ready as a chessman to be wherever your Majesty's royal hand shall set me.

In the last of the sentences quoted from this letter Bacon employs an analogy from the game of chess. The same analogy, whose meaning would be immediately clear to James, is to be found in Bacon's statement of the relationship between the placets of Revelation and ethical modes of conduct, which are derived, as "inferences," from these. Chessmen are moved on a chequered board according to prescribed rules. Similarly, specific modes of ethical action are governed by rules, or placets, which are declared and given in Divine Revelation, and not made by those who perform or contrive these actions. In the present use of the analogy, Bacon is regarding kingship as a Divine bestowal of sovereignty and political initiative. The sovereign by virtue of this bestowal is the source of political justice. Legal precedents, statutes, and judicial "mercies" are but derivations from the King's sovereign justice. The makers and administrators of these derivations are to be "moved" in accordance with the Sovereign's supreme justice, which is not originated by persons subject to it or engaged in dispensing it, whether they be members of the Privy Council, judges, Attorneys, Solicitors, Parliamentarians, or ordinary voters. Political legislation and legal dispensing are, so far as initiating sovereignty is concerned, always permissions on the part of the King.

Bacon, despite his entreaties to the King, was given neither the Secretaryship of State, which he greatly desired, nor the Mastership of the Wards, which he also sought—although he felt so sure of obtaining the latter that, as William Rawley later reported, he "put most of his men into new cloaks" for the occasion of its assumption. For almost two years, James refused to entrust any person with the Secretaryship. Finally, in 1614, he gave the office to Sir Ralph Winwood, a diplomat in the foreign service, a man without Parliamentary experience and —what was more to the point in James' thinking—with no Parliamentary ties.

However, in 1613 Bacon was granted the office on which he had set his heart twenty years before, the Attorney-Generalship. To make this accommodation, the occupant, Sir Henry Hobart, was moved into the Court of Common Pleas and Sir Edward Coke, one of the judges in this court, was promoted to the office of Chief Justice of the King's Bench. On his being thus promoted, Coke was made a member of the Privy Council. Three years later, Bacon, too, became a member of the Council. In 1617 Bacon was promoted to Lord Keeper; one year thereafter he was made Lord Chancellor and Baron Verulam, and in 1621 Viscount St. Albans.

Chief among the causes for Bacon's failure to obtain the Secretaryship in 1612 was the belief, shared by the King and the Council, that the Solicitor-General, despite his defences of the Royal Prerogative against assaults by Commons and common law judges, was a Parliamentary man. Risking and suffering Elizabeth's displeasure, Bacon had supported the claims of the Lower House. More than once he had been chosen by the Commons as their delegate in dealings with the Lords, the Council, and the King. Bacon was undoubtedly bent on allowing only so much to remain within the Prerogative as could not be taken away by appeal to precedent. On more than one occasion his arguments, filled with historical erudition and framed with great resource, had been employed to this end. His speeches were full of deferences to the King, but his deeds, when he acted as the spokesman of the Commons, spoke louder than his words. Those who held this opinion of the Solicitor-General were to have their belief confirmed by the Commons' treatment of the Parliamentarian they still trusted in the short-lived Parliament of 1614. Then, with a new sense of authority, members of the Lower House were to question the propriety of an Attorney-General's occupying a seat in the Commons. Yet they would make an exception in Bacon's case. After enacting the rule that no Attorney-General should frequent the Lower House, the Commons would indeed make Bacon their spokesman in a proposed dealing with the House of Lords.

Although denied the office of Secretary of State, Bacon was immediately called upon for advice by the frustrated, suspicious, and somewhat fearful James. While still Solicitor, Bacon found himself confronted with great problems. There was the question of the King's debts, of the emptiness of the Treasury, of James' conflicts with Parliament, and his proneness to interfere in the administration of the offices of government. The courts of law required attention. The law itself required study, especially because Coke had been making digests of cases according to his own formulas and under the assumption that the common law contained all that was essential in legal justice. Not to be overlooked were the problems occasioned by the agents of Rome and by the Puritans, both parties bent on overthrowing the presumably settled principles and practices of the Established Church. In dealing with each of these difficult matters, in whatever capacity, Bacon would feel required to see that the Sovereign's honor was kept intact while the liberty and rights of his subjects were sustained. There was one complicated puzzle which could not be evaded, or seemingly solved: this concerned the King's Scottish "favorite," Robert Carr, a physically vigorous, morose, and sly individual, who once had served as James' personal page, and was now, as Viscount Rochester (1611), distributing public offices according to the amounts of the perquisites he could exact, and advising the King on questions of domestic and foreign policies in the secrecy of his closet.

Bacon made a successful attempt to lessen the influence of

the King and his favorite on the ordinary administration of state by suggesting the restriction of the sovereign's own signature to documents of unusual importance and requesting permission from James to have the Council certify the others. At the King's behest the Solicitor examined such means as might serve for the replenishment of the Treasury: revenues from crown lands, customs, taxes, Monopolies, and industries which, in an opinion of James, could be aided through loans from a bank established to this end. Bacon successfully advised against the establishment of the bank in question and reported on inefficiency and fraud in the administration of customs and taxes. The Solicitor, who held that Parliament was the rightful source of the King's main revenue, warned James against expecting too much from the sources he had examined. He wrote James in caution, employing references which might make an impression on the learned recipient: "Generally upon this subject of the repair of your Majesty's means, I beseech your Majesty to give me leave to make this judgment: that your Majesty's recovery must be by the medicine of the Galenists and Arabians, and not of the Chemists and Paracelsians. For it will not be wrought by any one fine extract or strong water, but by a skilful compound of a number of ingredients, and those by just weight and proportion. . . . And secondly, that as your Majesty's growing behindhand hath been the work of time, so must likewise your Majesty's coming forth and making even." Bacon then added the pointed warning: "I forsee that if your Majesty shall propound to yourself to do it *per saltum*, it can hardly be without accidents of prejudice to your honour, safety, or profit."

Bacon gave the King some comfort in his present misery by observing that financial debts do not necessarily bring diminution to the greatness of persons; and that the Divine Majesty sometimes prefers uncertainties to certainties for those dependent on Him, because the former teach "a more immediate dependence on his providence." The Solicitor also made the entreaty "that your Majesty, in respect of the hasty freeing of your State, would not descend to any means, or degree of means, which carrieth not a symmetry with your majesty and greatness. . . . To have your wants and necessities, in particular, as it were hanged up in two tablets before the eyes of your Lords and Commons, to be talked of for four months together. . . . To have such worms of Aldermen to lend for ten in the hundred upon good assurance. . . . To pretend even carriage between your Majesty's rights and the ease of the people and to satisfy neither—these courses and the like I hope are gone with the deviser of them: which have turned your Majesty to inestimable prejudice."

It was Bacon's hope that the King, in order to speed both his financial and his political recovery, could be persuaded to summon a Parliament, "the ancient and royal way of providing the King with treasure." He expressed the desire that "this Parliament may be a little reduced to the more ancient form . . . which was to voice the Parliament to be for some other business of state, and not merely for money." Bacon was aware that any subsidy voted by any conceivable Parliament would be far from enough to supply the Treasury; there would still have to be taxes and duties. It had long been so with the exchequers of sovereigns. The twelve subsidies granted to Elizabeth by Parliament during her whole reign had not amounted to more than £2,000,000. In consequence, she had been hard-pressed to pay her ministers abroad and officers at home. To make ends meet, her household staff had been driven to exacting bribes and her political officers to collecting perquisites. The Queen had been thought parsimonious when she was in fact poor. Elizabeth, however, had enjoyed certain advantages over James: she was beset by threatening enemies, and Parliament would never seriously question any subsidy required for the protection of their Queen and her kingdom against the designs of Spain and France.

Moreover, as a queen, Elizabeth was regarded with awe, as a person partaking in the divinity which in Tudor times had still been accorded without question to sovereigns. But in this later reign, the Commons was refusing to support a king who had thought it wise to buttress popular belief with reasoned argument. The doctrine of the divine right of rulers had been expounded by James in theologico-philosophical treatises, and yet his very Prerogative was being questioned—in confirmation of Bacon's opinion that there are abstruse questions whose solutions should not be submitted to the general public for a verdict.

The Privy Council, when confronted with the fact that the King could not meet his pressing debts or pay his officers, bestirred themselves. They appointed a committee to consider ways and means to curtail expenditures and to tap such legal sources of supply as might be available. This committee's proposals, however, promised but little increase in revenue. Bacon, now Attorney-General, strenuously advised that a Parliament be called, pointing out that "few actions of Estate that are harsh, have been in agitation or rumour of late; and the old grievances, having been long broached, wax dead and flat." He argued that "if any man dissuade a Parliament, he is exposed to the imputation of creating or nourishing diffidence between the King and his people; he draweth upon himself the charge of the consequences of the King's wants; and he is subject to interpretation that he doth it for private doubts and ends." Bacon also uttered another caution, saying, "I conceive the sequel of good or evil not so much to depend upon Parliament, or not Parliament, as upon the course which the King shall hold with his Parliament." The Council decided, in February, 1614, that a Parliament should be summoned. In preparation for its meeting, Bacon compiled various notes and prepared a letter of advice for the King. He asked James to "put off the person of a merchant and a contractor," and said in warning: "Until your Majesty have tuned your instrument you will have no harmony. I for my part think it a thing inestimable to your Majesty's safety and service that you for once part with Parliament with love and reverence." He advised that Impositions by the Council be *"buried and silenced,"* and asked for a consideration of "gracious and plausible laws" designed for the "comfort and contentment" of the people. He mentioned, as one of many matters of serious concern, "the winning or bridling of the Lawyers (which are the *literae vocales* of the House) that they may further the King's causes or at least fear to oppose them."

Lawyers had become prominent in the Commons after the relaxing of a rule which required that a member reside in the constituency which he represented. The solicitors of London and other large centres offered themselves as candidates, and were elected in considerable proportion to the Commons. Many of them, skilled in speech, were prone, for obvious reasons, to accommodate their rhetoric to the opinions of an ever-increasing body of elected Nonconformists from the shires. "Law and pulpit," to use a phrase of John Chamberlain, became a combined means for giving a bad "colour" to the reputation of the King, his Council, and the Council's courts and ecclesiastical commissions. Not a few of the lawyers, under the influence of Coke, became promoters of a legal *imperium in imperio.*

Parliament was summoned and met on the fifth of April, 1614. It was to be known as the Addled Parliament. The King addressed the two Houses and professed his affection for both, and for all his subjects as well. Some members of the Commons immediately charged that the Lower House had been "packed" by "small undertakers," persons pledged by varied means as individuals, and not as proper representatives of constituencies, to support the King's cause. The House demanded their expulsion. Bacon, who was fearful lest Parliament again "be dissolved, as gamesters use to call for new cards when they distrust a pack," argued against any attempt at an impossible sifting of rumors to discover "deputies" suspected of betraying "the people" to the defeat of the "public good." As one long associated with courts of law, he knew "how far men will ingenuously confess, how far they will politically deny, and what we can make and gather upon their confession, and how we shall prove against their denial; it is an endless piece of work." "For protestations, and professions, and apologies," he told the House, "I never found them very fortunate; they rather increase suspicion than clear it." Keeping in mind the Lords, the Council, and the King—whom he had warned against using "undertakers"—Bacon exclaimed: "That private men should undertake for the Commons of England! Why, a man mought as well undertake for the four elements. It is a thing so giddy, and so vast, as cannot enter into the brain of a sober man."

Winwood, the inexperienced Secretary of State, tried at the beginning—contrary to established Parliamentary procedure—to have a measure for supply considered immediately. The Commons began to debate whether hereafter an Attorney-General, as the King's officer, should be admitted to the House, and determined in the negative. Bacon they would, however, allow to remain for the present sitting. A member offered a bill against Impositions, and another a bill against ecclesiastical courts. The House asked for a meeting with the Lords on the question of Impositions, and appointed Bacon their spokesman. The discovery had been made that since the meeting of the last Parliament, whose protest had led to the removal of many Impositions, there had come into operation three or four hundred more, some of which were of greater profit to the King. Worse still, certain of these Impositions were for the benefit not only of the present sovereign, but of his "generation" as well, his heirs in perpetuity. Bacon, who on more than one occasion had told the Commons that the power to institute Impositions lay within the Royal Prerogative, was now, as he always had been, jealous of maintaining whatever had by precedent restricted the employment of this Prerogative. The present case was one in which the Royal Prerogative was not running in what Bacon regarded as "the ancient channels and banks." An ominous feature of the King's grant of the Monopolies now under discussion was the undermining for all time of a privilege of the House of Commons, the constitutionally sanctioned providing of the sovereign with supply. Impositions had been recognized as necessities of the time, but their present granting was being associated, on an assumed principle, with sovereignty forever. The profits were being assigned not to the King in present circumstances, but to his "generation," the royal line, in perpetuity. For the conference in prospect Bacon prepared a pointed introduction to the "business" to be discussed between the two Houses. It ran as follows:

An Introduction, briefly declaring the matter in fact and state of the question. Direction to him in three things, wherein we conceive the King, to have, by misinformation, done other than any of his ancestors.

1. *The time:* for now by letters patent, and in print, these Impositions set for him and his heirs for ever: which never done before; which strange; because no proclamation bindeth longer than the King's life; so could not impose but during his own life.

2. *Multitude of Impositions:* Queen Mary—gascoigne wines and clothes, Queen Eliz. added only one, of sweet wines. From Ed. III to Queen M. none. In Ed. III, Ed. II, Ed. I, but five in all. —That upon a petition last Parliament divers hundredths of these taken away; so now not remaining above 300 or 400; yet that those remaining far more worth than those abolished.

3. *The Claim:* for none of his ancestors ever did so, but pretended [i.e., alleged] wars, needs, &c.: prayed continuance, but for a time.

The proposed conference with the Lower House was debated, and then rejected, by the Lords. One of the members, Richard Neile, a bishop, insulted the Commons by declaring that their present proposal was both seditious and mutinous. Neile's remarks were resented especially by many members of the Commons because the Cecils, father and son, had been his patrons, and he had served as chaplain to Burghley and Salisbury in turn. An outraged Lower House demanded satisfaction. The King interposed and told the Commons to proceed with their business, which was the problem of supply. Thereupon the Lower House resolved that no business would be done until such time as explanation and satisfaction from the Lords were forthcoming. Nor were they pacified when the offending bishop undertook to have them believe, "with many tears" and "sorrow" on his part, that his words had been misconstrued. There had been no indication that his peers intended to censure the culprit. It was the belief of many angry members of the Lower House that what the bishop had uttered in contempt of the Commons was the settled opinion of more than a few of the Lords. James became impatient with these goings-on, and by Friday, the third of June, threatened the Commons with dissolution on Thursday the ninth if they refused to vote on his Secretary's motion of supply. The Commons called for a committee of the House to compose an answer to the King. Thereupon James dissolved Parliament, two days before the date named in his threat. Bacon's efforts to have the Commons function again had come to naught.

After James' dissolving, for a second time, of Parliament, the Council was again faced with the acute problem of providing the King with funds. Now at their wits' end, its members decided to ask for a "benevolence," from corporations, counties, noblemen, bishops, and individuals of all ranks. Circulars were sent out, recommending bountiful giving and intimating that contributions could not "without discredit and note fall too low." Soon there was widespread complaining that the Benevolence was an illegal tax. The contributions received were not great, only some £66,000 over a two-year period. Bacon at the outset had advised the Council against the use of the term "benevolence." In the reign of Richard III a law had been

passed to the effect "that the subjects and commons of this realm
from henceforth should in no wise be charged *by any charge or
imposition called a Benevolence, or any such like charge, and
that such exactions called a Benevolence* shall be damned or
annulled forever."

A "principal person" of Marlborough, Mr. Oliver St. John,
when asked to support an appeal for the Benevolence, made the
charge that in calling for this exaction the King had performed
an illegal act, had violated the Magna Charta, and was indeed
"a Prince perjured in the great and solemn oath of his coronation." St. John also claimed that Parliament was being cur-
rently slandered by a rumor to the effect that the Commons
had refused to supply the King with necessary funds. St. John
was summoned before the Star Chamber, the Council's court.
In the absence of the Lord Chancellor, Bacon was assigned the
prosecution. The Attorney-General took this opportunity to
call the court's attention to what he considered a too hasty dissolution of the late Parliament. He told members of the Council
plainly that he "never could perceive but that there was in that
house a general disposition to give, and to give largely. The
clocks in the house perchance might differ; some went too fast,
some went too slow; but the disposition to give was general."
(The Secretary of State, Winwood, had introduced his measure
of supply too soon, at the beginning of the proceedings, contrary to recognized procedure; and the business of the House
had been slowed and, finally, stopped through altercation with
the Lords.) For the benefit of Anti-Parliamentarians among his
hearers Bacon described Parliament as "the great intercourse
and main current of graces and donatives from the king to the
people, from the people to the king." For the informing of the
King's subjects generally, he pointed out that the call for a free
benevolence was made after the summoning and the dissolving
of a Parliament which "made profession to give, and was interrupted." The Benevolence, then, could be considered an "after-

child" of this Parliament. In justice to the King in Council, Bacon explained that the present Benevolence was not to be confused with that earlier sort of Benevolence which had been made illegal by statute, because there is "a great difference between a Benevolence and an exaction called a Benevolence." The present Benevolence was of the former kind. In its case every man could exercise "a prince's Prerogative, a negative voice." It was not compulsory, and no rate of giving had been set down. There was no certifying by name of any who refused. The accused, therefore, was not being tried for his declining to give, but for his assault upon the King. If St. John had been satisfied with refusing a donation, no case would or could have been made against him.

Before the accused was sentenced to a short imprisonment and a heavy fine—this was remitted on the prisoner's making an abject apology—Bacon took occasion to say some things about the office of the sovereign within the constitution of England. In his address to the court, Bacon had already, by implication, criticized James for his having gotten rid of the late Parliament; now he praised him, not to declare what the King did in practice, but rather to make clear to the King and his Council what the duty of the sovereign *qua* sovereign was. "Is it so," Bacon asked, "that king James shall be said to be a violator of the liberties, laws, and customs of his kingdoms? Or is he not rather a noble and constant protector and conservator of them all? I conceive this consisteth in maintaining religion and the true Church; in maintaining the laws of the kingdom, which is the subject's birth-right: in temperate use of the prerogative; in due and free administration of justice, and conservation of the peace of the land.

"For the maintaining of the laws, which is the hedge and fence about the liberty of the subject, I may truly affirm it was never in better repair. . . . Neither doth the universality of his own knowledge carry him to neglect or pass over the very forms of the laws of the land. Neither was there ever king, as I am persuaded, that did consult so oft with his judges, as my lords that sit here know well. . . .

"As for the use of the prerogative, it runs within the ancient channels and banks: some things that were conceived to be in some proclamations, commissions, and patents, as overflows, have been by his wisdom and care reduced; whereby, no doubt, the main channel of his prerogative is so much the stronger. For evermore overflows do hurt the channel."

As the Attorney- or Procurator-General of the Crown, Bacon at this period was continuously in the courts, where he took the more difficult cases, especially those with constitutional involvements. In two notable instances the accused persons were Roman Catholics, and in a third, a Puritan minister. William Talbot, an Irish member of Parliament, had asserted the opinion—which he credited to the Jesuit philosopher Francisco Suarez (1548-1617)—that tyrannicide was legally justified in the case of heretics, including the Protestant sovereigns of England. When brought before the Court of Star Chamber, Talbot claimed that for him the doctrine of Suarez concerned a matter of "faith," and that on all questions respecting faith he submitted his opinion to the judgment of the Roman Catholic Church. In his plea he said, "*And for matter concerning my loyalty, I do acknowledge my Sovereign Liege Lord King James, to be lawful and undoubted King of all the kingdoms of England, Scotland, and Ireland; and I will bear true faith and allegiance to his Highness during my life.*" The Attorney-General regarded this submission as the going "backward and forward," the "repenting and relapsing" of a coward. Bacon was less concerned with the prosecution of the offender than with the branding of the crime, which in his view had arisen out of "the swelling pride and usurpation of the see of Rome *in temporalibus*, tending altogether to anarchy and confusion." Talbot was fined as a formality and then discharged from custody, his four months' earlier incarceration in the Tower having been deemed a sufficient punishment.

Bacon's address to the court on this occasion is informative of his political thought, for in it he expressly puts political sovereignty within the "prerogatives of God." "The Pope of Rome," argues Bacon, has pretended "by cartels to make sovereign princes as the banditti, and to proscribe their lives, and to expose their kingdoms to prey. . . . Surely I had thought they had been the prerogatives of God alone, and of his secret judgments: '*Solvam cingula regum*, I will loosen the girdles of Kings'; or again, 'He poureth contempt upon princes'; or, 'I will give a king in my wrath, and take him away again in my displeasure'; and the like: but if these be the claims of a mortal man, certainly they are but the mysteries of that person which 'exalts himself above all that is called God, *supra omne quod dicitur Deus.*' Note it well, not above God, though that in a sense be true, but above all that is called God; that is, lawful kings and magistrates."

A second case concerned John Owen. The accused was a Roman Catholic who had spent some time in Spain. On his return to England, Owen made "divers most vile and traitorous speeches confessed and subscribed with his own hand; as, among others, that it was as lawful for any man to kill a king excommunicated, as for the hangman to execute a condemned person." He was not an Irishman with the usual grievances, like William Talbot, nor had he been convinced of a doctrine, as Talbot had been, through theological speculation. Owen, in Bacon's opinion, had simply imbibed the political "poison" which had long been spread about the southern part of Europe in talk about the rulers of England. Owen was brought before the Court of Star Chamber and charged with treason. The Attorney-General informed the court that the accused was not being indicted according to any statute against the Pope's supremacy or with any religious implication, but on a law made when the Pope was "received" in England, to the effect that the "compassing and imagining" of the King's death is treason. Owen's defence was that, while he meant kings generally in his utterances, he did not intend specifically the King of England. Bacon, who understandably could not accept this distinction, charged Owen with maintaining that "it is lawful to kill the king, but conditionally; that if the king be excommunicated, it is lawful to kill him: which maketh little difference either in law or peril."

In his address to the court Bacon argued that were the Bishop of Rome able to absolve a subject from allegiance to his king, any English bishop could free any person from his duty, say, a son from his duty to his father. An opinion which allowed the killing of a sovereign excommunicated by a high Romanist official would also permit the slaughtering of any individual on his excommunication by a bishop. Surely this is putting the bishops, whether in Rome or in any other see, above the commandments of God Himself. The words of Owen remind one, Bacon continued, of the teaching of the Anabaptists, for they too advocate the "pulling down of magistrates: and they can chaunt the psalm, 'To bind their kings in chains, and their nobles in fetters of iron.' " Taking unto themselves "the glory of the saints," these sectaries maintain that their teaching is of a "spiritual" order and for the salvation of souls, even when they make God Himself "in the likeness of the prince of darkness." "What is there" of evil, asked Bacon, "that may not be made spiritual by consequence: especially when he that giveth the sentence may make the case?" Owen was found guilty of treason and sentenced to death. After three years' imprisonment he was permitted to leave the country.

A third case concerned Edmond Peacham, a Puritan minister in Somersetshire. Peacham, on becoming disgruntled over some acts of his bishop, made accusations against his ecclesiastical superiors. For these he was brought before the Court of High Commission. When the house of the accused was being searched for evidence, among his papers was found a sermon, not yet publicly preached, in which the King and his family were threatened with the fates of Ananias and Nabal, and reference was made to the assassination of the King's heir at such time as he should come to the throne. The King and members of the Council suspected that behind this particular sermon lay something more universal within a not untypical shire. In their opinion the unpublished statements of an individual Puritan portended a general disloyalty to the Sovereign and clandestine agitation in contempt of the acts of ecclesiastical commissions and the use of the Royal Prerogative. James himself had been made so nervously apprehensive by the attitude of Parliament, the scheming of the Puritans, and the intrigues of the Recusants that he could sleep at night only when his bed was surrounded by a barricade of other beds.

Peacham was summoned before the court of the Privy Council. The warrant for his trial, which was formally addressed to the Secretary of State and *ex officio* to the Attorney-General and the Solicitor-General, carried the signatures of the Archbishop of Canterbury, the Lord Treasurer, the Lord Steward, the Secretary of State, the Chancellor of the Exchequer, the Master of the Rolls, and a representative of the Lords. Because the offence in question was regarded as treasonable, the accused, when he failed to explain the reasons for his statements, was put on the rack and "stretched" for discovery of the circumstances of the writing of his sermon, including probable instigators, but not for evidence against himself—for, "by the law of England"—as Bacon had written—"no man is bound to accuse himself." Bacon was not, of course, responsible for Peacham's torture, although as Procurator-General he was required to sign, with others, the official report. The accused confessed and denied his guilt by turns. Sometimes he refused to recognize his own handwriting. No evidence of specific consequence could be got from his utterances.

Lest the public should think the indicting of Peacham before

the Council was designed to make an example for the terroriz-
ing into submission of Puritans and other malcontents, his case
was submitted to the judgment of the Court of the King's
Bench. Edward Coke, the Chief Justice, refused to consider a
charge of treason against the accused on other grounds than his
having impugned the King's title. Scandal, defamation, and
even contention that the King was an unworthy sovereign did
not, in the opinion of the present Chief Justice, constitute
treason. The several judges of the King's Bench were unable to
agree in a judgment on the case. Peacham was then tried in
Somersetshire before a jury composed of seven knights, "taken
from the bench," and found guilty of high treason. The prisoner
was left to languish in the Taunton jail for the remainder of his
life. When he died he left behind "a most wicked and desperate
writing, worse than that he was convicted for."

IX

BACON, COKE, AND THE LAW

It had long been the ambition of Edward Coke to bring the Sovereign of England "under the law." That fact had become very evident in the protracted negotiation over the Council of the Marches and was seen more recently in the case of Peacham. In the former instance, a conflict arose when Coke required a resort to a conference of the judges before answering the King's questions concerning this council's jurisdiction. Some members of the Commons had been given to understand that, on that occasion, the opinion of the company of judges under Coke, which was delivered in writing and not published, was opposed to that of the Crown. Soon thereafter, Coke and the other judges in the court which he controlled began to issue a series of Prohibitions designed to obstruct and inhibit the proceedings of the Court of the King's Council. When the case of Peacham was referred to the Court of the King's Bench, James proposed that the judges should be asked to state their opinions severally "to put Coke in doubt that he shall be left alone." To this Coke, as Chief Justice, objected on the ground, as Bacon found necessary to report to the King, that "particular and . . . auricular taking of opinions was not according to the custom of this realm." A contest between the Chief Justice and the King in Council now began to take definite shape. In this conflict Bacon was to be on the side of the Sovereign because of a constitutional principle. For other reasons the contest was to his liking.

A rivalry between Bacon and Coke had begun when the latter was preferred before Bacon for the office of Attorney-General. Following this defeat, Bacon lost out to his rival for the hand of Lady Hatton, a wife who subsequently did not make Coke's life "comfortable," and who refused to use his name. Bacon, while recognizing Coke's very considerable acquaintance with the law, came to have sufficient reasons for regarding him as an indifferent scholar, who invented law when his memory or information failed him; a poor legal thinker, who thought of law as a body of "almost infinite particulars"; and a crude performer at trials. When the two rivals were required to act together in the prosecution of Essex, Coke had allowed the introduction of irrelevant matters and brought confusion into the case. Then Bacon was made to appear as a punitive agent against a former benefactor because he had stressed apt points and made sharp distinctions in fact and in law. When Coke became a judge, a lack of capacity to clarify causes left him open to impression by doubtful evidence. In his behavior in court while Attorney-General, Coke showed the disposition of a bully. When presiding as a judge he intimidated accused persons, browbeat witnesses, and insulted counsel. At the trial of Sir Walter Raleigh, he behaved like an executioner before the fact. Bacon during his early days in the courts had found it necessary to send a report on Coke's conduct to the Secretary of State, Robert Cecil. In one incident this Attorney-General, as Bacon complained, had introduced into court proceedings the personal matter of Bacon's having been charged for indebtedness and had made derogatory remarks about his acting as Counsel without Patent, when the Queen herself had not deemed the usual warrant necessary.

Bacon, in due time, found an opportunity to take a verbal revenge on Coke, but not in court. When Judge Coke had been elevated, to his disliking, from the Common Pleas to the King's Bench, he told the new Attorney-General, "This is all your doing." Then Bacon made the retort: "Ah, my lord, your lordship has all this time grown in breadth; you must needs now grow in height, else you will become a monster."

One of Coke's major shortcomings, in Bacon's view, was his failure to recognize the commanding place of the King's Prerogative in the constitution of England. This failure was manifest in his subscribing himself Chief Justice of England and not of the King's Bench, his habitual dissatisfaction with proceedings in all courts where the common law did not suffice, his misconstruction of cases in his *Reports* for the confirmation of his own prejudices, his proneness to make justice the business of lawyers, his encouragement of lawyers to inveigh against ecclesiastical courts and thereby to bring comfort to Nonconformist members of Parliament, and his presumption that in the common law, as interpreted by a judge with little capacity to discern principle within particulars and the spirit beneath the letter, was to be found the beginning and the end of justice.

Coke had great influence over lawyers and judges. His admirers within the Commons were many. He continued in unabated judicial power after he had inhibited the Council's commissions and courts and presumed that the Court of Chancery could not review judgments pronounced in lower courts. Coke was beginning to regard himself as the ruler of a kingdom of justice within the Kingdom of England. Indeed, he had begun to subdivide the latter kingdom in a judicial way when he and the judges under his sway told the Council which shires should and which should not be placed under the jurisdiction of the Court of the Marches. When Coke refused consultation by the judges with the King, he had in effect told James that the Throne was no longer—if, in his opinion, it ever had been—the source of justice. James had met these affronts to his person and Council with unusual forbearance. The time was at hand, however, when Coke was to go too far in a pursuit of legal victories.

The events which led to Coke's downfall involved three cases. In one of these the Chief Justice achieved a partial triumph, and in the others ignominious defeat. The first of the three was occasioned by the King's granting Mr. John Murray of his Majesty's Bedchamber a Patent for making writs in the Court of Common Pleas. A prothonotary whose profits were threatened with decrease by this appointment brought an action, probably at Coke's prompting, for the denial of the legality of the Patent. The Patent was annulled in Coke's court. Thereupon Bacon and other Crown Counsel made a strong protest, and a compromise was arranged whereby the King's present appointee should take office, but no successor should similarly be issued a Patent. Encouraged by this partial success, and at the same time suffering pique at being forced to retrace a step, Coke was to overplay his hand. He was to demonstrate what Bacon called his "over-ruling nature." Two fraudulent debtors had been granted judgments in their favor by the King's Bench, and these findings had then been reversed in the Court of Chancery. Coke thereupon persuaded the culprits to ask for indictments of *praemunire* in his own court against the several persons involved in the proceedings in Chancery, against the plaintiffs, the counsel, the Solicitor, even the Master of Chancery himself. So determined was the Chief Justice of the King's Bench to make a case that the action which he had promoted, over a matter of debt, was grounded on a statute of Edward III which had been designed to deal with persons given to appealing to Rome in ecclesiastical cases adjudged in England! A grand jury threw out the bill, despite remonstrances and threats by Coke and the other judges of the King's Bench.

Bacon told the King that something should be done "for the settling of your authority and strengthening of your Prerogative according to the true rules of Monarchy." Bacon thought this " a just and fit occasion to *make some example against the*

*presumption of a Judge in causes that concern your Majesty,
whereby the whole body of those magistrates may be contained
in better awe*; and it may be this will light upon no unfit subject
of a person that is rude and that no man cares for"—meaning, of
course, Judge Coke. Bacon advised also that each of the several
courts be required to keep within its own limits and precedents,
and that in "these high causes that touch upon State and Monarchy, your Majesty give [the judges] strait charge that upon
any occasions intervenient hereafter they do not make the
vulgar party to their contestations by public handling them before they have consulted your Majesty, to whom the reglement
of those things only appertaineth."

Meanwhile, another significant case was taking shape.
Richard Neile, Bishop of Lincoln—the bishop who had pre-
cipitated a tumult in the late short-lived Parliament by insulting
the Commons—had been granted a benefice temporarily *in com-
mendam* by the King. A claimant who thought he should have
the place brought action against the bishop of the diocese concerned. The bishop was asked by the King to provide a full
report of the circumstances. James, on receiving this, instructed
Bacon, as Crown-Attorney, to inform Coke and the other
judges that they should not proceed with the case until they
had consulted with the King, who would know the conditions
surrounding the appointment. This command the judges refused to obey. They went on with the action, and sent a letter
to the King stating that they were bound by oath "in case any
letters come unto us contrary to law that we go forth to do the
law." James called a meeting of the Privy Council and summoned the judges of the King's Bench—twelve in number—to
attend. He informed the assembled gathering of a letter he had
already written the judges to the following effect:

"You might very well have spared your labour in informing
us of the nature of your oath; for although we never studied
the Common Law of England, yet are we not ignorant of any

points which belong to a king to know: we are therefore to inform you hereby, that we are far from crossing or delaying any thing which may belong to the interest of any private party in this case; but we cannot be contented to suffer the prerogative royal of our crown to be wounded through the sides of a private person: we have no care at all which of the parties shall win this process in this case, so that right prevail, and that justice be truly administered. But on the other side, we have reason to foresee that nothing be done in this case which may wound our prerogative in general; and therefore so that we may be sure that nothing shall be debated amongst you which may concern our general power of giving Commendams, we desire not the parties to have one hour's delay of justice: but that our prerogative should not be wounded in that regard for all times hereafter, upon pretext of private persons' interest, we sent you that direction; which we account as well to be wounded if it be publicly disputed upon, as if any sentence were given against it: we are therefore to admonish you, that since the prerogative of our crown hath been more boldly dealt withal in Westminster-Hall, during the time of our reign, than ever it was before in the reigns of divers princes immediately preceding us, that we will no longer endure that popular and unlawful liberty; and therefore we were justly moved to send you that direction to forbear to meddle in a cause of so tender a nature, till we had farther thought upon it."

After this statement had been read, the King went on to speak of what he deemed the errors of the judges in their dealings with this and other cases. He said that "it was a fault in the judges, that when they heard a counsellor at the bar presume to argue against his majesty's prerogative, which in this case was in effect his supremacy, they did not interrupt and reprove sharply that base and bold course of defaming or impeaching things of so high a nature by discourse; especially since his majesty hath observed, that ever since his coming to the crown, the popular sort of lawyers have been the men that most affrontedly in all parliaments have trodden upon his prerogative: which being most contrary to their vocation of any men, since the law or lawyers can never be respected, if the king be not reverenced; it doth therefore best become the judges of any, to check and bridle such impudent lawyers, and in their several benches to disgrace them that bear so little respect to their king's authority and prerogative: that his majesty had a double prerogative, whereof the one was ordinary and had relation to his private interest, which might be, and was every day, disputed in Westminster-Hall; the other was of an higher nature, referring to his supreme and imperial power and sovereignty, which ought not to be disputed or handled in vulgar argument: the courts of the common law are grown so vast and transcendent, as they did both meddle with the king's prerogative, and had incroached upon all other courts of justice; as the high commission, the councils established in Wales and at York, the court of requests."

The sovereign in this instance had desired "to know of the judges how his calling them to consult was contrary to law, which they could never answer unto," for it was "no bare supposition or surmise, that this cause concerned the king's prerogative," and that a delay of the consultation requested by the King was not for an "infinite nor long time, but grounded upon his majesty's weighty occasions, which were notorious . . . and that there was a certain expectation of his majesty's return at Whitsuntide: and likewise that the cause . . . would not receive judgment by Easter term next, as the judges themselves afterwards confessed."

The King further told his Council and the judges of his Bench that "it was a new thing, and very indecent and unfit for subjects to disobey the kings commandment, but most of all to proceed in the mean time, and to return him a bare certificate; whereas they ought to have concluded with the laying down and representing of their reasons modestly to his majesty, why they should proceed; and so to have submitted the same to his princely judgment, expecting to hear from him whether they had given him satisfaction."

Thereupon Coke and the other judges fell on their knees, and acknowledged "their error for matter and form, craving his majesty's gracious favour and pardon for the same." Coke, however, put in the remark that the King's request through the Attorney for a delay in the recent action "mentioned no day certain, and that an adjournment must always be to a day certain." James replied that this "conceit ... was mere sophistry, for that they might in their discretions have prefixed a convenient day."

The King now asked the Lord Chancellor for his opinion on the question whether he had acted illegally in making his request for a delay to the judges. The Chancellor suggested that James invite the opinion of his "Learned Counsel." Bacon, as Crown-Attorney, then said that "the putting off of the day in manner as was required by his majesty, to his understanding was without all scruple no delay of justice, nor danger of the judges' oath." To this he added the remark that the judges should "consider seriously with themselves, whether they were not in greater danger of breach of their oaths ... to counsel his majesty when they are called." Coke immediately took exception to this statement, saying it was the duty of the King's Counsel to "plead before judges, and not to dispute with them." To this opinion Bacon replied that he found the "exception strange," because the King's Counsel, by oath, office, and the King's express command, were "without fear of any man's face, to proceed or declare against any the greatest peer or subject of the kingdom; and not only any subject in particular, but any body of subjects or persons, were they judges, or were they of an upper or lower house of parliament, in case they exceed the limits of their authority, or took any thing from his majesty's royal power or prerogative."

The Lord Chancellor then declared himself in agreement with the Attorney's opinion, and requested that the oath pertaining to judges be read out of the statute. This was done by the Solicitor. At this point James and the Lords thought it proper to ask the judges severally their opinion on the question now at issue, whether they would or would not stay particular court proceedings at the request of the King. In reply, all the judges present, with the exception of Coke, said that they would, and acknowledged it their duty to do so. The Chief Justice of the King's Bench made, for his answer, the statement that "when the case should be, he would do that which should be fit for a judge to do."

The King had been annoyed at Coke's behavior over a period of several years. When Chief Justice Coke had enunciated the thesis that there can be "no appeal from the King's Bench to any court except the High Court of Parliament," the outraged James had called this statement "treason" and "blasphemy." The King on one occasion had become so enraged with Coke's criticism of proceedings within the ecclesiastical courts that he "clenched his fists as if to strike the Chief Justice." When the Chief Justice of the King's Bench had called himself Lord Chief Justice of England, he had been guilty of sufficient misdemeanor in the eyes of James to warrant his dismissal from office. James' view of the Sovereign's relation to law and judicature was definite and positive. He had written shortly after his accession to the throne of England, in his *True Law of Free Monarchies*, "Although a good King will frame all his actions to be according to the law, yet he is not bound thereto, but of his own will and for example-giving to his subjects." The King had repeated the same theme in a speech in the Star Chamber after becoming angered at what Archbishop Bancroft called Coke's "contempt of the command of the King." James had then told his listeners: "Kings are properly Judges, and judgment properly belongs to them from God, and thence all judgment is derived. It is atheism and blasphemy to dispute what God can do; so it is presumption and high contempt in a subject to dispute what a King can do, or say that a King cannot do this or that."

Bacon, the King's chief advisor during his late dealings with Coke, had previously written in his *View of the Differences in Question betwixt the King's Bench and the Council of the Marches* (1606): "We say that in the King's Prerogative there is a double power: one, which is delegate to his ordinary judges in Chancery or Common Law; another, which is inherent in his own person, whereby he is the supreme judge both in Parliament and all other Courts; and hath power to stay suits at the Common Law; yea, *pro bono publico,* to temper, change, and control the same; as Edward III did, when, for increase of traffic, he granted juries to strangers *de medietate linguae,* against the Common Law. Nay, our Acts of Parliament by his sole authority may be mitigated or suspended upon causes to him known. And this inherent power of his, and what participateth thereof, is therefore exempt from controlment by any Court of Law."

Bacon had ever been of the opinion that the source of justice was the Throne itself; that the sure friend of the wronged subject seeking justice, of the penitent criminal begging mercy, of the litigant under the pressure of book-lawyers and even common law judges, was the King himself. As for the conferring of judges with kings, now in sharp dispute: this practice had been sanctioned by time immemorial. Bacon's opinion on this matter was to be succinctly stated in his essay "Of Judicature": "Judges ought, above all, to remember the conclusions of the Roman Twelve Tables; *Salus populi suprema lex*; and to know that laws, except they be in order to that end, are but things captious, and oracles not well inspired. Therefore it is an happy thing in a state when kings and states do often consult with judges; and again when judges do often consult with the king and state: the one, when there is matter of law, intervenient in business of state; the other, when there is some consideration of state intervenient in matter of law. For many times the things deduced to judgment may be *meum* and *tuum*, when the reason and consequence thereof may trench to point of estate: I call matter of estate, not only the parts of sovereignty, but whatsoever introduceth any great alterations or dangerous precedent; or concerneth manifestly any great portion of people. And let no man weakly conceive that just laws and true policy have any antipathy; for they are like the spirits and sinews, that one moves with the other. Let judges also remember, that Salomon's throne was supported by lions on both sides: let them be lions, but yet lions under the throne; being circumspect that they do not check or oppose any points of sovereignty." Then Bacon was to add, characteristically: "Let not judges also be so ignorant of their own right, as to think there is not left to them, as a principal part of their office, a wise use and application of laws."

Three weeks after the meeting with the judges and the Privy Council, the King directed the latter to inform Coke that he was not for the present to sit either at the Council Table or on the Bench. Instead, he was to employ his leisure time in correcting his *Reports* and the "many exorbitant and extravagant opinions set down and published for positive and good law ... and having corrected what in his discretion he found meet in these Reports, his Majesty's pleasure was that he should bring the same privately to himself that he might consider thereof, as in his princely judgment should be found expedient." After a period of three months Coke reported that he had gone over eleven volumes of some six hundred reported cases and had found only five examples of questionable statements on his part, and these of no consequence. When told that certain of his interpretations, now cited by Bacon and Sir Henry Yelverton, the Solicitor-General, cast doubt on the Royal Prerogative, Coke stubbornly affirmed that this was not so.

James finally decided that Coke must be removed from office. Bacon, as both Attorney-General and a member of the Privy Council—a combination with rare precedent in English history—

was invited to prepare an advice on what the King should declare in explanation of the dismissal of his Chief Justice. In this document Bacon mentioned Coke's "perpetual turbulent carriage" towards the liberties of the Church and its ecclesiastical commissions; towards the "prerogative royal, and the branches thereof; and likewise towards all the settled jurisdictions of all his other courts . . . in all which he had raised troubles and new questions." The Attorney reminded the King in a reference to the trial of Peacham, that there had been "turbulent carriage" also in what might concern the safety of the Sovereign, namely, the interpretation of the law in cases of high treason. James was invited to recall that Coke in his dealings had been "neither civil, nor affable, nor magnificent," that he "made himself popular by design only, in pulling down government . . . that whereas his majesty might have expected a change in him, when he made him his own, by taking him to be of his council, it made no change at all, but to the worse, he holding on all his former channel, and running separate courses from the rest of his council; and rather busying himself in casting fears before his council, concerning what they could not do, than joining his advice what they should do." The Attorney requested the King to keep in mind how he had given Coke a vacation "to reform his 'Reports' wherein there be many dangerous conceits of his own uttered for law, to the prejudice of his crown, parliament, and subjects; and to see, whether by this he would in any part redeem his fault," but that "after three months time and consideration, he had offered his majesty only five animadversions, being rather a scorn, than a satisfaction to his majesty."

Shortly after preparing this advice, Bacon found great satisfaction in being able to send the King a letter which read:

May it please your excellent Majesty,
I send your majesty a form of discharge for my lord Coke from his place of chief justice of your bench.
I send also a warrant to the lord chancellor, for making forth

a writ for a new chief justice, leaving a blank for the name to be
supplied by your majesty's presence.

Bacon's motives in his dealings with Coke were not, of course,
merely personal. As one learned in the law, Bacon had not been
greatly impressed by Coke's *Reports*. He was aware that his
rival in the law had distorted records of cases through his own
legal propensities; that his digests were neither accurate in
citation nor properly informative by induction of rules; that
Coke had been given to exalting the common law beyond what
it could bear; that he had undertaken the impossible task "to
reduce the common laws of England to a text-book as the statutes
are." Bacon himself had two legal Propositions in an early stage
of preparation for the King's consideration, one the making of
a "Digest . . . of the Laws of England," and the other "the Compiling and Amendment of the Laws of England." The first
Proposition Bacon was calling, in the very words he had employed when he described his instauration of the sciences,
"means to perpetuate . . . memory and merits." The second
Proposition had been in its author's mind for years. As early as
1592, in a digression within a Parliamentary speech—an aside
which made an impression on Elizabeth—Bacon had intimated
the need for a compilation and a reform of the laws. Ever since
then he had maintained a scholarly interest in the development
of English law, which he found "as mixt as our language, compounded of British, Saxon, Danish, Norman customs." Bacon
believed that even as the language of England was richer for an
intermingling of native and foreign roots and idioms, so were
her laws the more complete because of their past drawing on the
resources of many peoples.

In the first Proposition, Bacon, in words which contain a
moral for sovereigns, tells the King: "Certain it is, that good
laws are some bridle to bad princes, and as a very wall about
government. And if tyrants sometimes make a breach into them,
yet they mollify even tyranny itself, as Solon's laws did the

tyranny of Pisistratus: and then commonly they get up again, upon the first advantage of better time." Bacon instances among "the better works of perpetuity in princes" colleges, learned lectures, the education of the young, the founding of noble orders, and the like. Such things are, however, "but like plantations of orchards and gardens, in plots and spots of ground here and there; they do not till over the whole kingdom, and make it fruitful, as doth the establishing of good laws and ordinances; which makes a whole nation to be as a well-ordered college or foundation." Here Bacon has in mind a projected *New Atlantis*, a writing in which he hopes to delineate the practices and regulations of an ideal kingdom with informed learning and ideal laws. In a mildly veiled reference to the constitutional struggles of the present and the part he himself could play as an English Justinian, the author makes the observation that in former times, after the days of Augustus and the rest, "there was such a race of wit and authority, between the commentaries and decisions of the lawyers, and the edicts of the emperors, as both law and lawyers were out of breath." It was Justinian who in the end compiled a system of laws, an "edifice or structure of a sacred temple of justice, built indeed out of the former ruins of books, as materials, and some novel constitutions of his own."

Bacon introduces his second Proposition, which concerns the "compiling and amendment" of laws, by saying that he will be a "workman" under his "master," the King. He tells James: "Your majesty hath set me in an eminent place, whereby in a work, which must be the work of many, I may the better have coadjutors." Here, one is immediately reminded of the author's plea to the King, on several occasions, for helpers to collect a natural history for the instauration of a new learning and science.

Bacon informs James that it is not his intention to bring charges against the law of England generally; he is bent only on perfecting English laws that already exist, giving them "rather light than any new nature." In the beginning he will mention, and meet, some objections which may be raised against this undertaking. It will be said that English law, as it stands, "is in good estate comparable to any foreign law"; whereas in fact, the laws of England and their administration are subject to delays, evasions, and great uncertainties which include fluctuating opinions. There is multiplicity of suits and endless litigation. "The contentious person is armed, and the honest subject wearied and oppressed." The judge becomes the more absolute, since in doubtful cases he has the "greater stroke and liberty." Chancery is filled to overflowing because the law is often obscure. Lawyers cover their ignorance by arguing what is doubtful. Many legal transactions hang on hollow questions.

It will be objected by some, again, that in purging the common laws and statutes much that is sound may be taken away. To this, Bacon replies that "in all purging, some good humours may pass away; but that is largely recompensed by lightening the body of much bad." In face of any remonstrance to the effect that the labor required for the undertaking in prospect could be better employed in "bringing the common laws of England to a text law, as the statutes are," the common law, as it stands, deserves a defence. Certainly in legal practice more doubts arise over statutes, which are text law, than over the common law, which is not.

Turning from objections to the particulars of his Proposition, Bacon recommends a proper "digest or recompiling," first of the common laws, and, then, of the statutes. In the case of the common laws, three things, he says, are required:

1. The compiling of a book *De antiquitatibus juris*. This will involve a sifting of ancient legal records and a selecting of the most informing of these for summary and chronological arrangement. Cases thus compiled will serve "for reverend precedents, but not for binding authorities."

2. The reducing and "perfecting" of the course or, if you will, the body of common law. This may be done by compiling year-

books from the time of Edward I to the present. Here five
directions will help. First, cases "which are at this day clearly
no law, but constantly ruled to the contrary," are to be omitted,
while cases whose legal points are not now questioned may be
entered as judgments simply, without arguments "which are
now become but frivolous." Second, repetitious cases are to be
purged away. Third, cases which show contradictions among
judgments rendered should be noted in a special manner, so that
the doubts to which they give rise may be settled either by
Parliament or by assembly of judges. Fourth, idle queries should
be omitted; and fifth, cases reported with too great prolixity are
to be shortened in statement by the omission of "tautologies and
impertinences."

3. The preparation of certain auxiliary books which can both
further the study and develop the science of law. These books
will be of three sorts, in keeping with three subjects: legal institutions, the rules of law, and legal terms. A work on legal institutions generally will serve as a general preparative to the reading
of a course of law. This book should be perspicuous, clear in
method, and comprehensive, like "a model towards a great
building." A work which dealt properly with the second subject,
the rules of law, would be "of all other things the most important
to the health . . . and good institutions of any laws . . . like the
ballast of a ship, to keep all upright and stable; but I have," says
Bacon, "seen little in this kind, either in our law or other laws,
that satisfieth me. The naked rule or maxim doth not the effect:
It must be made useful by good differences, ampliations, and
limitations, warranted by good authorities; and this not by
raising up of quotations and references, but by discourse and
deducement in a just tractate. In this I have travelled myself, at
the first more cursorily, since with more diligence, and will go
on with it, if God and your majesty will give me leave. And I
do assure your majesty, I am in good hope, that when Sir Edward Coke's Reports, and my rules and decisions shall come to

posterity, there will be, whatsoever is now thought, question, who was the greater lawyer?" Yet "to give every man his due . . . Sir Edward Coke's Reports . . . though they may have errors, and some peremptory and extrajudicial resolutions more than are warranted," do nevertheless contain "good decisions and rulings of cases." They, too, may be compared to the "ballast" of which we speak.

In the case of statute law, recompiling and reforming will require four undertakings: 1. The clearing of statute books of obsolete laws and of enactments long since expired and clearly repealed. Where the repeal of any of these is in doubt recourse should be had to Parliament. 2. The repeal of all statutes which "are sleeping and not of use, but yet snaring and in force: in some of those it will perhaps be requisite to substitute some more reasonable law, instead of them, agreeable to the time; in others a simple repeal may suffice." 3. The mitigation of harsh penalties attached to many statutes. 4. The reducing of concurrent statutes, heaped one upon another, to one clear and uniform law. "Towards this," Bacon writes, there "hath been already, upon my motion, and your majesty's direction, a great deal of good pains taken by Lord Hobart, myself," and others. The work is already considerably advanced.

Finally, Bacon tells the King, in a reminder both of the legislative capacity of the Houses of Parliament and of his own work on the Commission for the Union of the Kingdoms of England and Scotland, that "because this part of the work, which concerneth the statute laws, must of necessity come to parliament, and the houses will best like that which themselves guide, and the persons that themselves employ," the best procedure will be to follow Parliamentary precedents, such, for example, as the arranging of the union of England and Scotland, when the commissioners were named by both Houses.

Needless to say, had James placed at his Attorney-General's disposal time and means for the effecting of his Propositions,

English law would have been freed of much obscurity and conflict, for Bacon had a skill which amounted to genius in the
mastering of legal details and in the induction and enunciation
of principle. Undoubtedly, he would have ordered and brought
consistency into the main body of English law without destroy-
ing its structure and function, its principles and capacity for
growth.

X

BACON AND JAMES' FAVORITES

WE HAVE HAD OCCASION TO MENTION JAMES' "FAVORITES." There were two of these, Robert Carr and George Villiers. Bacon had been given the Attorney-Generalship by the King himself, yet, as he said, one of the favorites sought to "thrust himself into the business for a fee." This was Carr, Viscount Rochester. Bacon became a member of the Privy Council (1616) partly through the goodwill of the succeeding favorite, Villiers, and from him received the promise of the Lord Chancellorship. There was accuracy in the statement made in 1613 concerning Carr: "The Viscount Rochester sheweth much temper and modesty without seeming to press or sway anything; but afterwards the King resolveth all business with him alone." Three years later it was said in equal truth of Villiers: "This is now the man by whom all things do and must pass."

Among the causes for the King's cultivation of favorites were a complete lack of sympathy between him and his Parliament and the opposition which he encountered from judges, lawyers, Puritan gentry, Roman Catholic Recusants, and subjects commonly opposed to his Impositions and Monopolies. The King sought in the company of favorites escape from difficulties of state, which were compounded by conflicts within his Privy Council and between Commons and Lords, Sovereign and Parliament, Crown and courts of law, and upholders of the common law and members of the Privy Council. There could be no composure or unity of purpose in a Council which included the anti-Romanist, Calvinist George Abbot, Archbishop of Canterbury; Lancelot Andrewes, a bishop who detested Calvinism; Sir John Digby, the favorer of Spain; Sir Ralph Winwood, the Puritan Secretary of State and desirer of a Spanish war; Sir Thomas Edmondes, who sought an alliance with France; the Earl of Suffolk, the chief promoter of the large Howard interests; and the Earl of Arundel, the heir of the Roman Catholic Norfolks.

The first of the two favorites, Robert Carr, was a physically robust Scot who had been a personal page to the King in Scotland. When James came to England, Carr had been left behind. But in three years he appeared at the English Court; and while taking part in a contest on the tilting field, in James' presence, broke a leg. The sympathetic King, impressed by Carr's continuing physical exuberance and his present misfortune, again took him under his personal care. Soon the former page was knighted (1611). He had previously been provided, too, with an estate (1609), after Salisbury found a flaw in the deed of Sherborne Manor and dispossessed Sir Walter Raleigh's wife and children. Soon Carr, who was far from stupid, became the King's personal political minister. He was permitted to dispose of public offices, both high and low, for perquisites in return. When Bacon sought the Mastership of the Wards, he found it necessary, as much as he deplored the agency, to negotiate his request through the favorite. So successful was Carr in the business of selling offices, that he was eventually able to accumulate, for his personal spending, as much as £90,000 a year.

In 1613, Carr, who two years before had become Viscount Rochester, was created Earl of Somerset. The new honor was bestowed in order to provide him with a fitting title to offer in

marriage to Frances Howard, after this lady had obtained a
"disgraceful" divorce from the third Earl of Essex, the son of
the Essex who had been Queen Elizabeth's favorite. Sir Thomas
Overbury, an intimate friend of Somerset, became displeased
with the divorce proceedings, and gave Somerset some plain
advice against his forthcoming marriage. Before long, Frances
Howard, now Lady Somerset, and Carr too, partly because he
had previously communicated secrets of state—secrets which,
as Bacon said, had never been brought to the Council Table—
to Overbury, was anxious to have him put out of the way. The
Somersets plotted his arrest on a technical charge. Overbury was
put into the Tower (1613). The Countess then arranged a plan
whereby her agents were made his keepers. After experiments
had been made on animals with noxious drugs, Overbury was
poisoned, and the rumor was circulated that he had died of a
loathsome disease. When charged with the murder (1615), the
Countess confessed her guilt. Somerset, who was later (in 1616)
found guilty of a part in the crime, maintained his innocence.
Actually, his guilt was never finally established in the court
where he was tried. Coke determined the case on doubtful
evidence. The chief agent in the murder, Weston, was hanged,
but the lives of the Somersets were spared. Soon the Countess
was pardoned (1616), as one who was not "a principal, but an
accessory before the fact." Carr was confined to the Tower.
Bacon, whatever he thought of the legal proceedings, was "far
from the opinion that the re-integration or resuscitation of
Somerset's fortune can ever stand with his Majesty's honour or
safety." The succeeding favorite of James, Villiers, kept Carr
incarcerated for six years, trying unsuccessfully all the while
to exact from the prisoner, as the price of his freedom, the "gift"
of Sherborne Manor. James, shortly before his death, issued a
pardon for Somerset.

George Villiers had come to James' notice in 1614. A year
thereafter he was knighted and, to Carr's great annoyance, made

a Gentleman of the Bedchamber. An opportunity now presented itself to those about the Court to displace the morose, cunning, feared, and despised Carr. Villiers had been trained in France as a courtier under the guidance of no less a person than Sir John Eliot. He was intelligent, approachable, affable, diplomatic, literary, and appreciative of things of the mind. Archbishop Abbot and lay members of the Privy Council, including Bacon, the Attorney-General, commended Villiers to James. Bacon in a letter to the King in 1616 described Villiers as a man of "a safe nature, a capable mind, an honest will, generous and noble affections, and a courage well lodged; and one that I know loveth your Majesty unfeignedly, and admireth you as much as it is in a man to admire his Sovereign upon earth."

Villiers' advancement at Court was exceedingly rapid. Knighted in 1615, he was made a Viscount, Master of the Horse, and a Knight of the Garter in 1616. In 1617 he was given the rank of Earl and in 1618 that of Marquis. In 1621 he assumed the office of Lord High Admiral. In 1623 he was created Duke of Buckingham. Within a very short period this perceptive and resourceful courtier took over the political will of an arbitrary king. James was happy in the fact; his dealings with the Council, Parliament, judges, and Secretaries of State had been very troublesome. So complete was James' attachment to Villiers by 1617 that the King put himself on record with this statement: "I James am neither a god nor an angel, but a man like any other. . . . I wish to speak in my own behalf and not to have it thought to be a defect; for Jesus Christ did the same, and therefore I cannot be blamed. Christ *had his John and I have my George.*"

After Villiers had read the letter in which Bacon commended him to the King—James had showed it to him—the new favorite displayed an affectionate regard for the writer, like the esteem of a devoted son for a benignant and discerning parent. Villiers sought the older and politically experienced man's advice, and

Bacon in return assumed a paternal role. When, as Attorney-General, he sent Villiers his Patent of creation as Viscount, he enclosed with the document a letter of personal advice. Remembering what had happened in Carr's case, Bacon gave a frank warning to the new favorite against some of the besetting temptations of his position. He wrote to Villiers:

> After that the King shall have watered your new dignities with his bounty of the lands which he intends you, and that some other things concerning your means which are now in intention shall be settled upon you, I do not see but you may think your private fortunes established; and therefore it is now time that you should refer your actions chiefly to the good of your Sovereign and your country. It is the life of an ox or beast always to eat, and never to exercise; but men are born (and especially Christian men) not to cram in their fortunes but to exercise their virtues; and yet the other hath been the unworthy and (thanks be to God) sometimes the unlucky humour of great persons in our times. Neither will your further fortune be the further off; for assure yourself that fortune is of a woman's nature, that will sooner follow you by slighting than by too much wooing.

Having offered this admonition, Bacon made the request to the new favorite that he do something "which was never done since I was born, and which, not done, hath bred almost a wilderness and solitude in the King's service." He asked that men of capacity and merit be placed in offices. The filling of places, said Bacon, still depends too much on "money and turn-serving and cunning canvasses and importunity." Far from being piqued by this frank counsel, Villiers expressed a desire for more. Bacon thereupon prepared a comprehensive *Advice*. Two drafts or versions of this have survived. One of these, the longer, may have been put in shape at a later period, perhaps in 1619, to serve as a record of what Bacon regarded as proper opinions on certain questions of state and offices of government. There is no discrepancy between the two documents, and it is not improbable that the parts of the second which are omitted from the first draft were orally, and in a more casual way, communicated to Villiers.

In the shorter and first version of the *Advice* (1616), which Bacon sent in written form to Villiers, the Attorney-General first admonishes the new favorite on his relations with the King: "Remember well," says Bacon, "the great trust you have undertaken; you are as a continual sentinel, always to stand upon your watch to give him true intelligence. If you flatter him, you betray him; if you conceal the truth of those things from him which concern his justice or his honour, although not the safety of his person, you are as dangerous a traitor to his state, as he that riseth in arms against him. . . . Kings must be answerable to God Almighty, to whom they are but vassals, for their actions, and for their negligent omissions: but the ministers to kings, whose eyes, ears, and hands they are, must be answerable to God and man for the breach of their duties, in violation of their trusts, whereby they betray them."

Turning to matters of religion and the Established Church, Bacon tells the favorite: "If any question be moved concerning the doctrine of the Church of England expressed in the thirty-nine articles, give not the least ear to the movers thereof: that is soundly and so orthodoxly settled, as cannot be questioned without extreme danger to the honour and stability of our religion; which hath been sealed with the blood of so many martyrs and confessors, as are famous throughout the Christian world. The enemies and underminers thereof are the Romish Catholic, so stiling themselves, on the one hand, whose tenets are inconsistent with the truth of religion professed and protested by the Church of England, whence we are called protestants; and the anabaptists, and separatists, and sectaries on the other hand, whose tenets are full of schism, and inconsistent with monarchy: for the regulating of either, there needs no other coercion than the due execution of the laws already established by parliament.

"If any attempt be made to alter the discipline of our Church, although it be not an essential part of our religion, yet it is so necessary not to be rashly altered, as the very substance of religion will be interested in it . . . it is dangerous to give the least ear to . . . innovators; but it is desperate to be misled by them."

"If any transplant themselves into plantations abroad, who are known schismatics . . . they [should] be sent for back upon the first notice; such persons are not fit to lay the foundation of a new colony."

Bacon's present disposition of mind towards Roman Catholics and Nonconformists shows the effect on his thinking of not only the Hampton Court Conference and the Gunpowder Plot, but the regicidal theories of some Papists, the attitude of the Puritan gentry towards the King's ecclesiastical courts and the use of his Prerogative, the aims of the Presbyterians, who seem determined on setting up a Genevan church government, and the contempt for law and magistrates by the Brownists, Anabaptists, and other fanatical sects. Thirteen years before, Bacon, as one who "lived more than two centuries ahead of his time," had advised the King to grant a greater religious toleration to his subjects than would be found in England for more than two hundred and fifty years. But events of the last dozen years have convinced him that such a toleration is not yet feasible. He no longer speaks as a theoretical Calvinist, still under the spell of his "fanatical" mother (d. 1610), but as a statesman taking a considerable part and about to take a greater part in the government of a kingdom. He thinks that the unity of the Established Church must be maintained, if grave political conflicts are to be averted. In the next reign these conflicts would come, as Bacon now knows they could; and after the downfall of King Charles I—the present Prince—Genevan ecclesiastical rule would be established in the Church of England. In succession to that, in the days of the Protector, Oliver Cromwell, there would be ecclesiastical chaos throughout the kingdom under the dispensation of disagreeing sects and a variety of self-designated

"Saints." Bacon's present task was the averting of such happenings.

The remainder of the first draft of the *Advice* contains admonitions respecting plantations or colonies. These remind one of the contents of the humanitarian letter of advice on Ireland which Bacon had sent, years before, to Robert Cecil. Bacon still wants "no extirpation of the natives under pretence of planting religion." The inhabitants of colonies are to "be governed according to the laws of this realm." Care is to be taken that "some few merchants and tradesmen, under colour of furnishing the colony with necessaries, may not grind them, so as shall always keep them in poverty." There are to be "such governors as may be qualified in such manner as may . . . lay the foundation of a new kingdom."

The second and longer draft of the *Advice* shows the range and variety of matters under the control of Villiers, who, Bacon says, is not merely a King's courtier, but a person "in his bosom also . . . for kings and great princes, even the wisest of them, have had their friends, their favourites, their privadoes in all ages." In this version Bacon brings under review the many institutions and offices of state, from the sovereign to embassies abroad. He lists the subjects on which Villiers will be receiving "petitions" and "petitioners" under eight headings:

I. Matters that concern religion, and the Church and churchmen.
II. Matters concerning justice, and the laws, and the professors thereof.
III. Councillors, and the council table, and the great offices and officers of the kingdom.
IV. Foreign negociations and embassies.
V. Peace and war, both foreign and civil, and in that the navy and forts, and what belongs to them.
VI. Trade at home and abroad.
VII. Colonies, or foreign plantations.
VIII. The court and curiality.

This second version of the *Advice* is a lengthy document.

Mention of some of its salient points will serve our present purpose. We shall continue to quote Bacon's own writing as definite evidence against misrepresentation, in "probabilities," of his understanding of the place and function of certain offices of government. At the beginning, Bacon tells Villiers, some of whose family connections have Roman Catholic inclinations, to be "rightly persuaded and settled in the true Protestant religion, professed by the Church of England, which doubtless is as sound and orthodox in the doctrine thereof, as any Christian church in the world." Of this church's discipline, "I will not positively say, as some do, that it is *jure divino*; but this I say and think *ex animo*, that it is the nearest to apostolical truth; and confidently I shall say, it is the fittest for monarchy of all others."

After warning the favourite against his being made "an instrument of Rome," Bacon tells him that "besides the Romish catholics, there is a generation of sectaries . . . they have been several times very busy in this kingdom, under the colour of zeal for reformation of religion: the king your master knows their disposition very well; a small touch will put him in mind of them; he had experience of them in Scotland, I hope he will beware of them in England; a little countenance or connivency sets them on fire . . . the true Protestant religion is seated in the golden mean; the enemies unto her are the extremes on either hand."

Bacon proceeds next to make clear his views respecting the place of laws, courts, and Parliament in the kingdom. "Let the rule of justice," he writes, "be the laws of the land, an impartial arbiter between the king and his people, and between one subject and another: I shall not speak superlatively of them, lest I be suspected of partiality, in regard of my own profession; but this I may truly say, they are second to none in the Christian world. . . ."

"And as far as it may lie in you, let no arbitrary power be

intruded: the people of this kingdom love the laws thereof, and nothing will oblige them more, than a confidence of the free enjoying of them."

"The execution of justice is committed to [the King's] judges, which seemeth to be the severer part; but the milder part, which is mercy, is wholly left in the king's immediate hand: and justice and mercy are the true supporters of his royal throne."

"By no means be you persuaded," Bacon warns the favorite, "to interpose yourself, either by word or letter, in any cause depending, or like to be depending in any court of justice, nor suffer any other great man to do it where you can hinder it, and by all means dissuade the king himself from it, upon the importunity of any for themselves or their friends."

Since the administration of justice has, in the Attorney's view, suffered from the interference of one court with the jurisdiction of another, he writes in admonition, "There are many courts . . . some superior, some provincial, and some of a lower orb: it were to be wished, and is fit to be so ordered, that every of them keep themselves within their proper spheres. The harmony of justice is then the sweetest."

Treating next of the two Houses of "the high court of parliament in England, which is superlative," Bacon affirms that "no new laws can be made, nor old laws abrogated or altered, but by common consent in parliament . . . but nothing is concluded but by the king's royal assent; they are but embryos, it is he giveth life unto them."

"But the house of commons have only power to censure the members of their own house, in point of election, or misdemeanours in or towards that house; and have not, nor ever had, power so much as to administer an oath to prepare a judgment."

"Yet the house of peers hath a power of judicature in some cases: properly to examine, and then to affirm; or, if there be cause, to reverse the judgments which have been given in the court of king's bench, which is the court of highest jurisdiction in the kingdom for ordinary judicature." However, when the House of Lords acts as a court of justice its office is not to make new laws but to determine causes "according to the known laws of the land."

Bacon would have occasion to recall these statements about the Houses of Parliament when, a few years hence, the Commons would be sending his own case on to the Lords. Now almost prophetically—when one thinks of the treatment of holders of Monopolies with Patents by the Commons in 1621 and of ensuing events in the reign of Charles I and during the Commonwealth—Bacon remarks that the "true use of parliaments in this kingdom is very excellent . . . but if they should be unjustly enlarged beyond their true bounds, they might lessen the just power of the Crown, it borders so near upon popularity."

There can be no doubt that the elder statesman's advice exercised for a number of years a restraining influence on Villiers. The favorite, however, was not to live up for long to the monitor's early hopes in several regards. The temptations which surrounded his place and his power were to prove too great for his nature. As Villiers' political experience and authority increased, he yielded to an ever-increasing desire to accumulate wealth. To this end he sold political offices, reputations—indeed, everything that could be rendered a subject of bargaining. In his financial negotiations, Villiers did not hesitate to use his mother, his brother, any relative. He even bought Coke's daughter for his worthless brother John at a large monetary price. Villiers would probably have sold justice itself, the law, and the constitution, had Bacon, as a mentor and a holder of high office, not stood in his way. Yet when Bacon had undergone an undeserved political trial before the court of the Lords and had been found guilty on a technical count, Villiers alone, of all his peers, refused to give his word of assent, and uttered Nay.

In 1616, the year in which Bacon presented the first draft of his *Advice* to Villiers, he became a Privy Councillor. The year after he was made Lord Keeper. So great a conception did Bacon have of the Lord Keeper's office, he even supposed that he should convey to the King's favorite the thought that its present incumbent could take over the government of the king-dom—under the advice of the Monarchy, of course, through correspondence by letter—while the King was absent in Scot-land. Bacon wrote to Villiers: "I had a conference with some Judges (not all, but such as I did choose), touching the High Commission and the extending of the same in some points; which I see I shall be able to despatch by consent, without his Majesty's further trouble. . . . And I see now that his Majesty is as well able by his letters to govern England from Scotland, as he was to govern Scotland from England." Bacon also told the judges, who were proceeding to their summer circuits, that "at this present [they] ought to make the people know and consider the King's blessed care and providence in governing this realm in his absence; so that sitting at the helm of another kingdom, not without great affairs and business; yet he governs all things here by his letters and directions, as punctually and perfectly as if he were present."

A month before writing this letter to Villiers, the Lord Keeper had assumed that he, as the Sovereign's deputy, could exercise his discretion by withholding a King's Proclamation to the Privy Council which commanded the nobles to absent them-selves from London during his Majesty's "progress" in Scot-land. (Bacon had either known or assumed that most of the nobility had already left the city.) James, on learning of the disregard of his order, made his displeasure known and re-minded the members of his Council that "obedience is better than sacrifice, and that he knoweth he is King of England."

Having made it evident to Villiers and the judges that he regarded himself as the Sovereign's deputy, both in form and in fact, and having disobeyed an order of the King, the Lord Keeper overstepped discretion a third time while both James and Villiers were in the north. At this period, Edward Coke was engaged in improving his political lot, to "make a faction," as Bacon thought, by ingratiating himself with Villiers. Some time before, the favorite's brother, Sir John Villiers, had begun to look with favor on Coke's daughter, whose father and mother both had considerable means. After the favorite began a negotiation for a marriage between the two, and then demanded a large dowry, the transaction was suspended. The favorite had asked for an immediate payment by Coke of £10,000 with an annual gratuity of £1,000, but Coke had offered only £6,666 all told. The girl's father, after being dismissed from office and "disgraced," renewed the bargaining. He finally settled for £30,000. Coke's wife, Lady Hatton, a woman of character and spirit, had been far from pleased from the first with the negotiation between her husband and Villiers. She claimed that her daughter was not of a mind to marry Sir John, having another admirer—real or fictitious—in view and desire. Lady Hatton removed her daughter, without the father's knowledge, to a place near Oatlands, and afterwards hid her in a house of the Lord of Argyle near Hampton Court. Coke, who discovered the place of the daughter's seclusion, asked Villiers' mother to obtain a warrant from the Lord Keeper for her recovery. When this was refused by Bacon, another writ was sought and obtained from Winwood, the Secretary of State. Then with a troop of retainers, including a pugilist, Coke went to the house where the daughter was secreted, "but indeed went farther than his warrant, and brake open divers doors before he got her." Bacon meanwhile—still remembering, no doubt, that he once had wooed Lady Hatton and lost her to his rival in both love and the law—helped the mother to obtain a warrant

for the custody of her child, who by this writ was now brought
within the care of the Privy Council. Lady Hatton had received
promise of his aid in this regard after she had affrighted Bacon
by entering his private quarters and bouncing against the door
of his bedroom during one of his periodic illnesses. She had
acted, as she admitted when begging the Lord Keeper's pardon,
with the fury of "a cow that had lost its calf." Coke, for his
violent rescue of the daughter, was summoned before the Privy
Council where an order was made to charge him in the Court
of Star Chamber with "force and riot." Winwood, however,
when requested to explain to the Privy Councillors his part in
the proceedings, as one threatened with a *praemunire* by the
Lord Keeper, produced a letter from James which approved
of the Attorney-General's action. Thereupon the Council made
a retraction and sent information to this effect to the King.

Bacon had meddled earlier in the nuptial business by sending
Villiers a letter which reflected on the favorite's judgment, his
friends, and his place in the King's service. Bacon had also
written the King, mentioning the "humbled Sir Edward Coke"
and warning James that if Coke were restored to the Council—
an eventuality which Bacon surmised might be the result of the
present business—division in that body would inevitably follow.
To Villiers he had written respecting the match in prospect as
follows:

I hold it very inconvenient both for your brother and yourself.
First, he shall marry into a disgraced house. . . . Next, he shall
marry into a troubled house of man and wife, which in Christian
discretion is disliked. . . . Thirdly, your lordship will go near
to lose all such your friends as are adverse to Sir Edward
Coke. . . . Lastly, it will greatly weaken and distract the King's
service. . . . Therefore my advice is . . . your lordship will signify unto my lady, your mother, that your desire is the marriage
be not pressed or proceeded in without the consent of both
parents . . . the rather for that it hath been carried so harshly and
inconsiderately by Secretary Winwood; as, for doubt that the

father should take away the maiden by force, the mother, to get the start, hath conveyed her away secretly. . . . Hoping your lordship will not only accept well, but believe my faithful advice, who, by my great experience of the world, must needs see further than your lordship can.

When Bacon came to realize that he had gone much too far in pursuing something which was in truth not his legitimate concern, he wrote the King a letter by which, he knew, he could provide only an extremely lame excuse. This letter was, in fact, one of the few halting, disjointed, and irrelative statements Bacon ever carefully penned. Even the scriptural references, put in for James' appeasing, carried no point. In the missive Bacon admitted that in his recent advice to Villiers he had been "a little too parent-like, this being no other term, than his lordship hath heretofore vouchsafed to my counsels. . . . But yet I was afraid, that the height of his fortune might make him too secure; and as the proverb is, a looker-on sometimes seeth more than a gamester." Bacon acknowledged, too, that at the Council Table he had sometimes been "sharp, it may be too much," in statements where Sir Edward Coke was concerned. This admission was followed, however, by a reference to Coke's "riot or violence." Bacon brought his "explanation" to an end with an unfortunate reference to Solomon, to whom he had often before compared the King, saying, "Solomon were no true man, if in matter of malice the woman should not be superior."

Sir Henry Yelverton, Bacon's successor in both the Solicitor-Generalship and the Attorney-Generalship, who also had incurred the King's displeasure for his opposition to the Villiers-Coke negotiations, found it politic to make a journey to Coventry to meet James in an attempt to bring himself and the Lord Keeper into the King's good graces. He was accompanied on his journey by none other than Coke. Yelverton reported to Bacon by letter that "Sir Edward Coke hath not forborne by

any engine to heave both at your Honour and at myself." The
Attorney said that he had "seen the face of . . . the King . . .
more clouded towards me than I looked for," and, when he had
been given the royal hand to kiss, he had been told by James
that he "deserved not that favour, if three or four things
were true." In his letter Yelverton advised Bacon to present
himself to the King "bravely and confidently, wherein you
can excel all subjects." The Attorney also thought it well
to incite the Lord Keeper to heroic action on the present
occasion by intimating some things touching the latter's reputation. He mentioned his belief that "it is too common in every
man's mouth in court, that your greatness shall be abated; and
as your tongue hath been as a razor to some, so shall theirs be
to you." He also warned the Lord Keeper that "there are laid
up for you, to make your burden the more grievous, many
petitions to his majesty against you."

The King, before he reached London, during his progress
homeward, put Bacon in his place by a letter which contained
"some observations" on the Lord Keeper's conduct in the
present affair. James had suffered on more than one occasion
from Bacon's barbed comments on his handling of the nation's
business. Even Bacon's high praises had been lessons in regal
conduct. Now an opportunity had come to return this treatment. The King censured his Lord Keeper for his official legal
proceeding—a very touchy point. James wrote:

And was not the thefteous stealing away of the daughter from
her own father the first ground whereupon all this great noise hath
since proceeded? For the ground of her getting again came upon
a lawful and ordinary warrant, subscribed by one of our council,
for redress of the former violence: and except the father of a
child might be proved to be either lunatic, or idiot, we never read
in any law, that either it could be lawful for any creature to steal
his child from him; or that it was a matter of noise and streperous
carriage for him to hunt for the recovery of his child again. . . .
[In] your opposition to this business . . . you either do, or at

least would seem to, mistake us a little. For first, whereas you excuse yourself of the oppositions you made against Sir Edward Coke at the council-table, both for that, and other causes; we never took upon us such a patrociny of Sir Edward Coke, as if he were a man not to be meddled withal in any case.

James also reproached Bacon for the unfriendliness and bad manners he had displayed throughout his recent treatment of Villiers, and continued:

We will not speak of obligation; for surely we think, even in good manners, you had reason not to have crossed any thing, wherein you had heard his name used, till you had heard from him. For if you had willingly given your consent and hand to the recovery of the young gentlewoman; and then written both to us and to him what inconvenience appeared to you to be in such a match; that had been the part indeed of a true servant to us, and a true friend to him. But first to make an opposition; and then to give advice by way of friendship, is to make the plow go before the horse.

The King charged Bacon with suspicion and jealousy and wrote:

You say, that you were afraid that the height of his fortune might make him too secure; and so, as a looker-on, you might sometime see more than a gamester. Now we know not how to interpret this in plain English otherwise, than that you were afraid, that the height of his fortune might make him misknow himself. And surely, if that be your 'parent-like affection' toward him, he hath no obligation to you for it. And, for our part, besides our own proof, that we find him farthest from that vice of any courtier, than ever we had so near about us: so do we fear, that you shall prove the only phenix in that jealousy of all the kingdom.

In an attempt to retreat from the perilous position in which his persistent dislike for Coke had landed him, Bacon made an oral "submission" to Villiers, who turned this into a plea for forgiveness to the King. Villiers wrote a reply in pencil:

I do freely confess that *your offer of submission unto me, and in writing (if so I would have it)*, battered so the unkindness that

I had conceived in my heart for your behaviour towards me in my absence, as out of the sparks of my old affection toward you I went to sound his Majesty's intention how he means to behave himself toward you, specially in any public meeting; where I found on the one part his Majesty so little satisfied with your late answer unto him, which he counted (for I protest I use his own terms) *confused and childish,* and his vigorous resolution on the other part so fixed, that he would put some public exemplary mark upon you, as I protest the sight of his deep-conceived indignation quenched my passion, making me upon the instant change from the person of a party into a peacemaker; so I was forced upon my knees to beg of his Majesty that he would put no public act of disgrace upon you, and, as I dare say, no other person would have been patiently heard in this suit by his Majesty but myself, so did I (though not without difficulty) obtain thus much: —that he would not so far disable you from the merit of your future service, as to put any particular mark of disgrace upon your person.

Villiers added, as a solicitous observer writing in portent:

I protest all this time past it was no small grief unto me to hear the mouth of so many upon this occasion open to load you with innumerable malicious and detracting speeches, as if no music were more pleasing to my ears than to rail of you: which made me rather regret the ill-nature of mankind, that like dogs love to set upon him that they see once snatched at.

A relieved Bacon wrote in reply:

My ever best Lord, now better than yourself, your Lordship's pen, or rather pencil, hath portrayed towards me such magnanimity and nobleness and true kindness, as methinketh I see the image of some ancient virtue and not anything of these times. It is the line of my life and not the lines of my letter that must express my thankfulness; wherein, if I fail, then God fail me, and make me as miserable as I think myself at this time happy by this reviver through his Majesty's clemency and your incomparable love and favour.

The now chastened Lord Keeper, who had been soaring too high, knew that he was never again to presume that he might be the deputed ruler of England; that his jurisdiction was to be confined to the courts of law; that in his dealings with the favorite, whose will was one with that of James, he could no longer play the part of one *in loco parentis.* Lady Hatton's daughter became Lady Villiers. Coke paid his £30,000 and again became a member of the Council. The Villiers family took another step forward on the road to riches. The Lord Keeper of the Great Seal, having been reminded of his place, and having acknowledged this, was restored to royal favor. The next year (1618) he was made Lord Chancellor and Baron Verulam of Verulam.

Villiers was fast becoming a very wealthy man, the wealthiest, it was said, of all save one in England. With the accumulating of a monetary fortune he was not, however, satisfied. The favorite would also establish in perpetuity the Villiers family as the foremost in the land. To the disposition of the Scottish King, this ambition was quite agreeable. "Of myself," said James, "I have no doubt, for I live to that end; and I hope that my posterity will so far regard their father's commandments and instructions so as to advance that house above all others whatever." In order to effect the desire for such eminence on the part of the Villiers family, one other clan would have to be reduced, namely, the powerful Howards. Its members and dependents were in occupancy of most of the commanding places in government: the offices of Lord Treasurer, Lord High Admiral, Master of the Wards, Secretary of State, and Attorney-General. The holders of the first and second of these offices were Howards, of the third the son-in-law of a Howard, of the fourth and fifth dependents of the Howard family. It occurred to the favorite that if it became necessary to pay present holders for the relinquishment of one or two of these offices, the filling of enforced vacancies in the others would provide more than compensating perquisites. In any event, no matter what the immediate profit or loss might be, the occupants of all five places must be ousted by whatever means.

Villiers himself was already Master of the Horse (1616); he

would assume the office of Lord High Admiral as well (1621).
Charles Howard, Earl of Nottingham, the present occupant,
was old and incompetent. As luck would have it, he had resisted
an inquiry by a Naval commission, whose report had in the end
showed many abuses in administration. The suggestion was
conveyed to Nottingham that he should give up the office. To
this he agreed as a return for a pension from the King and other
compensation from the favorite. The Master of the Wards,
Viscount Wallingford, the son-in-law of Thomas Howard,
Earl of Suffolk, surrendered easily after an offer of compensation had been made, and after he had been told, among
other things, of the King's displeasure at his wife's lampooning
the Villiers faction.

In the reduction of other members of the Howard connection, Bacon's duties as judge rendered him an agent in
furthering Villiers' family designs, because these holders of
office had either left or would leave themselves open to attack
through legal causes. The Secretary of State, Sir Thomas Lake,
despite his offering the favorite a bribe of £15,000—which
probably found its way into the purse of Villiers' mother—was
charged with malfeasance, found guilty, sentenced to fine and
imprisonment, and put out of office. The Lord Treasurer,
Thomas Howard, Earl of Suffolk, was put out of his place for
malpractice, and brought to trial along with his wife for em-
bezzlement. The sentence imposed on the guilty parties was a
fine of £30,000. Coke had wanted to make the penalty £100,000.
Bacon was to have occasion to remember this sentence, when
Suffolk was his accuser and a party to his sentencing in the
court of the House of Lords.

The Attorney-General, Yelverton, came to grief through his
self-assurance, a quality which characterized members of the
Howard family and faction, even the most irresolute among
them. This characteristic was displayed when Yelverton failed
to obey an order of the King in cases involving a Monopoly,

and when afterwards he amended on his own authority the clauses of a Royal Charter. The Monopoly concerned had been granted to a company in which Sir Edward Villiers, the favorite's brother, had invested £4,000. The reason advanced by the patentees to the certifying judges for its granting was the furtherance of national prosperity by keeping the goldsmiths from melting down the gold coin of the realm. Under the Monopoly only imported gold was to be used in the manufacture of thread and laces, two articles in wide demand for uniforms and elegant clothes. The goldsmiths put up a strong resistance and, as opponents of a Monopoly, received large support from London manufacturers generally.

Violators of the Patent were charged, but cases brought against them in the Court of Exchequer were abandoned. The King then wrote to Yelverton as Attorney-General, telling him to have offenders detained. Yelverton failed to act, presuming, as he explained, that the King, who had been in the north, was not aware of the extent of the current opposition to the Monopoly and to the arrest of its violators. Bacon, as Lord Chancellor, and as one of those responsible for passing on the Patent, argued that by an Act of Henry VII goldsmiths had been forbidden to melt gold and silver except for the making of certain objects; the Monopoly was, therefore, good in precedent. As violations of the Patent increased, a commission was appointed to undertake the discovery of offenders; this included a kinsman of Buckingham, Sir Giles Mompesson, who himself held the Patent for Inns. The commissioners were instructed to bring persons charged before the Star Chamber, but the cases they brought there were abandoned one after another. The patentees then appealed to the Attorney-General to maintain the Monopoly as a grant good in law. Yelverton, for answer, resorted to the questionable device of simply putting offenders into prison and then throwing the onus of their continued confinement, or disposal otherwise, upon the Lord Chancellor.

When the Attorney-General refused to keep arrested persons under further restraint, the Lord Chancellor promptly had them recommitted. An uproar arose in the City, where bail in the amount of £100,000 was raised. A deputation was sent to the King and the prisoners were released. The outlawed goldsmiths were now the victors in what was a skirmish against the Royal Prerogative, within which the Monopoly had been granted. This skirmish was to prove but an incident in a constitutional battle which was now taking shape. A breach, however small, had been made in a constitution sustained by the Prerogative. Coke and his judges had made earlier breaches. These had been repaired, but only temporarily. There would come a time, even in the next reign, when the traditional line of constitution would be broken and its holding forces put to rout.

Yelverton now began to feel a little too sure of himself after his success in refusing an order of the King and then throwing a legal onus, which he himself should have dealt with, on the shoulders of the Lord Chancellor. He was even growing "pert" with the Chancellor, as Bacon had occasion to note. When, as Attorney-General, Yelverton was called upon to draw up the Charter recently granted to the City of London, he proceeded to insert nonauthorized clauses of his own, clauses "not agreeable to his Majesty's warrant, and derogatory to his honour." For this act he was brought before the Star Chamber. On the accused's making a submission, denying "corruption" and acknowledging only "error" in "mistaking" the King's directive, a majority of the councillors voted to stay proceedings until James had been informed of the submission. The reason for this course of action was doubtless the fact that Yelverton had paid James £4,000 for his office! (The King had used the money to buy needed dishes for the Palace.) Bacon wrote to Villiers: "I do not like of this course, in respect that it puts the King in a strait; for either the note of severity must rest upon his Majesty if he go on; or the thanks of clemency is in some part taken away, if his Majesty do not go on." James did not interfere, and the case continued.

The Lord Chancellor, in an address to the court, remarked on his past association with the accused: how he had lived with him in Gray's Inn; had served with him when he had been the Crown Attorney; had joined with him in legal endeavors; how the accused had been one who gave him "more attributes in public" than he "deserved," and was "a man of very good parts." Yet, as a judge, Bacon found himself compelled to regard the offence of the present Attorney-General as a very great one, for if officers of the Crown, entrusted with warrants, "shall practise the art of multiplication upon their warrants, the crown will be destroyed in small time. The great seal, the privy seal, signet, are solemn things." Bacon was far from satisfied with the statement in defence that the Attorney-General's "mistaking" was a mere error in judgment; rather, he was of the opinion that the "error" amounted to both a contempt and an excess of authority. He concluded his brief speech by recalling "the wisdom of the law of England, which termeth the highest contempts and excesses of authority, 'misprisions'; which, if you take the sound and derivation of the words, is but 'mistaken.' " Mistaking, in this sense, "is ever joined with contempt; for he, that reveres, will not easily mistake; but he, that slights, and thinks more of the greatness of his place than of the duty of his place, will soon commit misprisions." The accused was found guilty. Coke proposed a fine of £6,000, but the court reduced this amount. Yelverton was fined £4,000, given a nominal sentence to the Tower, and discharged from office.

Bacon's decision in the case, was, of course, both informed and just. There is no reason for supposing that Bacon on this, or any other, occasion "perverted justice." One instance, however, has been cited by E. A. Abbott, a biographer who pursues Bacon through every incident of his life, both private and public, with a "moral" guile that sometimes appears malignant, to prove that Bacon could subvert justice. Abbott calls this "the one case in which the Chancellor is apparently shown . . . to have been guilty of a deliberate perversion of justice." The action concerned a minor, eight years of age, who had been left a legacy of £800 and a share in his parents' property. The rents were to be collected by the executors, two uncles, a Dr. Steward and his brother, until the boy became twenty years of age. In the ensuing years the rents and profits, if any, became mixed with the uncles' own incomes and outlays. When the youth was twenty, in 1617, he filed a suit for the recovery of the money with profits. The uncles were unable to say whether they had "made any commodity out of the estate or not."

Bacon, having heard argument in the case, gave a formal order that the defendants "answer over to the point of the legacy," to show whether or not there had been profit on the estate. Indignant over what they considered an injustice in the circumstances, the defendants refused to answer for several months, claiming that they could not provide the particulars demanded. When half a year had gone by, the uncles made a statement of the amount of the estate due the heir, without providing an account of profit, this "being a thing by law not due to the plaintiff nor yet in equity, as these defendants verily believe any man will think that shall be truly informed of this case." The court's order was confirmed, but the defendants still refused to make further response. Dr. Steward could have asked for a rehearing before the decree was made final, but had failed to do so, either through ignorance of judicial practice or on the presumption that a further hearing would but lead to an accumulation of court costs.

After several new orders, of increasing severity, had been issued to force the defendants to comply with the court's decision, Dr. Steward made an appeal to Villiers as the accessible agent of the King. There was, of course, nothing unusual about a petitioning of the King through his immediate agent in a matter "concerning justice." Bacon in his second *Advice* to Villiers had mentioned this as one of the subjects on which he would receive "petitions."

Villiers first sent a letter to Bacon, saying, "I owe Dr. Steward a good turn which I know not how to perform but this way." This was the sort of note by which the approachable Villiers would terminate, so far as he was concerned, the solicitations of petitioners. On giving second thought to the case, however, Villiers began to suspect there might have been a miscarriage of justice through the Chancellor's being misinformed of circumstances by officers of court, who sometimes were not above withholding information which might prolong actions. The present case was complicated by the young plaintiff's "infirmity"; and during the proceedings the Solicitor-General had thought it just and proper to oppose the order being made. Villiers dispatched a second, less casual letter to the Chancellor, with a description of Dr. Steward—whom he called "a man of very good reputation, and a stout man that will not yield to anything wherein he conceiveth any hard course against him"—and the request: "If you can advise of any course how you may be eased of that burden and freed from his complaint, without shew of any fear of him or anything he can say, I will be ready to join with you for the accomplishment thereof." Villiers seemed to be of the opinion that, however correct the formalities of the case may have been, justice and equity had not prevailed.

On receiving Villiers' second letter, Bacon heard Dr. Steward *in camera*, had the litigants in the case brought together, ordered the defendants to pay £800—the amount of the original legacy—into court, and appointed a commission to investigate the conditions and circumstances surrounding any profits. There was nothing unconstitutional in Bacon's thinking about such a reopening after judgment had been made. He had addressed Chancery on first taking his seat there with these words: "I will say,

that the opinion, not to relieve any case after judgment, would
be a guilty opinion: guilty of the ruin, and naufrage, and perish-
ing of infinite subjects." On the same occasion the Lord Chancellor had said that, in certain cases respecting "revenue, or
treasure, or profit": "If . . . I do forsee inconvenience to ensue . . .
in respect of the King's honour, or discontent, and murmur of
the people; I will not trust mine own judgment, but I will either
acquaint his majesty with it, or the council table, or some such
of my lords as I shall think fit."

Abbott goes too far when he assumes that contemporary
practice precluded the reference of a "closed" case to an advi-
sory commission. The range of matters dealt with by committees
of the Privy Council in Bacon's day was very wide. Abbott is
also guilty of wrong judgment when he assumes that Bacon's
professions respecting justice were not consistent with his practice. The weight of biographical opinion, both critical and sympathetic, is in favor of Bacon and against Abbott. More than one
biographer has pointed out that had Bacon been guilty of a perversion of justice in this case, which had on several occasions
been before the courts, his wrongdoing would have been discovered and published before and during his trial when his
enemies—among them the energetic Edward Coke—resorted to
an examination of the proceedings in cases over which he had
presided.

England's affairs were now in the hands of Bacon, the Lord
Chancellor, Villiers, the favorite, and Sir Lionel Cranfield, a
"born financier." Through the skill of Cranfield the financial
worries of the King and Council had been abated. He was "a
London prentice," with a natural aptitude for casting accounts,
who had got his first start in the world by marrying his master's
daughter. Despite his lowly origin he had become Master of the
Wards. Cranfield introduced economies into the management of
the King's Household, the Wardrobe, the Admiralty, and the
Treasury, and increased the annual revenues from Customs and

wine duties from £90,000 to £156,000. He had impressed the King and Council as early as 1615 with his economic policy of decreasing levies on exports and increasing duties on imports. At that time Bacon had expressed his concurrence in this policy, and added a statement which he was to have cause to remember during his political tribulations in 1621. "I do allow well," he had said, "the proposition of Sir Lionel Cranfield, being more indeed than I could have looked for from a man of his breeding."

While the "base fellow" Cranfield—as Bacon called him because of his origin—was providing a bulwark for the Treasury, Bacon was sustaining the Royal Prerogative and all that this implied for the continuity of the unwritten constitution of England. In an address in the Court of Exchequer, Bacon told Sir John Denham, who had been called to be one of the barons of the Exchequer, that "above all you ought to maintain the King's prerogative, and to set down with yourself, that the King's prerogative and the law are not two things; but the King's prerogative is law, and the principal part of the law, the first-born or *pars prima* of the law; and therefore in conserving or maintaining that, you conserve and maintain the law. There is not in the body of man one law of the head, and another of the body, but all is one entire law."

In a speech in the Star Chamber, Bacon went even further when he admonished the judges before they set forth on their summer circuits. On this occasion he told his listeners: "You that are the judges of circuits are, as it were, the planets of the kingdom, I do you no dishonor in giving you that name, and no doubt you have a great stroke in the frame of this government, as the other have in the great frame of the world. Do therefore as they do, move always, and be carried with the motion of your first mover, which is your Sovereign. A popular judge is a deformed thing; and 'plaudites' are fitter for players than for magistrates." Bacon was now depicting the King, the primary source of law and justice, after the manner of James himself, as the *Primum Mobile,* the First Moved by God. In the Aristotelian cosmology the planet which is first moved, because closest of all to the Prime Mover, communicates its motion to the other spheres, to each according to its position in the planetary scheme; even as in the case of the political kingdom the initiative divinely bestowed upon the sovereign is passed on to each judge in turn according to his place in the judicial system. Bacon as Lord Chancellor naturally took great satisfaction in regarding himself as the planet nearest of all to the *Primum Mobile*!

XI

BACON'S POLITICAL DOWNFALL

O<small>N JANUARY</small> 22nd, 1621, F<small>RANCIS</small> B<small>ACON</small> celebrated his sixtieth birthday in the house of his birth, York House in the Strand. His guests included Ben Jonson who poeticized "the fire, the wine, the men," and sang of

> England's High Chancellor, the destin'd heir
> In his soft cradle of his father's chair,
> Whose even thread the Fates spin round and full
> Out of their choicest and their whitest wool.

Already a peer of the realm, the host was five days later to be created Viscount St. Albans, "with all the ceremonies of robes and coronet." This would be his "eighth rise or reach, or diapason in music," he told the King in his letter of thanks. Bacon could have been forgiven for any reflection of his on his extraordinarily good fortune: how he had risen in Court from "Learned Counsel, Extraordinary without patent" to Chancellor of the Realm; how he had been made a Privy Counsellor even while Attorney-General, a "kind of miracle," as he said, "that had not been in many ages." Now he had a court of his own at Gorhambury near St. Albans. His London mansion, York House in the Strand, was a dwelling fit for a king. He could still remember that occasion when, in 1618, he first took his seat in the

Court of Chancery. Then a reporter of news had been able to write that "to the Hall, besides his own retinue, did accompany him all the Lords of his Majesty's Council and others, with all knights and gentleman that could get horses and footcloths." "He was accompanied," as John Chamberlain said, "by most of the nobility, with other gallants, to the number of more than 200 horses, besides the Judges and the Inns of Court. There was a great deal more bravery and better show of horse than was expected in the King's absence; but both Queen [Anne] and Prince [Charles] sent all their followers and his other friends did their best to honour him."

This had happened three years before. Since then Bacon had been able to publish, only some months earlier, his *New Organon*, a nonpolitical and nonlegal writing in which he had been able to assert a dominion over nature. Bacon might have been excused, therefore, if he was now regarding himself (in Abraham Cowley's later words) as the one

> Whom a wise king and nature chose
> The Chancellor of both their laws.

Parliament would soon be assembled, because the Spaniards had invaded the Palatinate, of which the King's son-in-law, who had married James' daughter Elizabeth, was the "rightful prince." The King would be asking for money with the plea that Protestants on the Continent must be supported. Funds would be granted without opposition from the Nonconformists, because Frederick of the Palatinate was the leading Calvinist Prince of Germany. The Commons would again be voting supply. All the institutions of government would be in function. The Lord Chancellor was contemplating with great satisfaction the meeting of a new Parliament. He had always been a Parliamentary man. Recognition of his political capacity and the political trust of his peers had first been given him by the Lower House. At Parliament's next meeting he would not be in the Commons; yet he would address both Houses at the opening. His speech would follow upon that of the King. Already he had made notes of an address "intended to be spoken after the King's speech." It would include an admonition, in keeping with what he had said on earlier occasions, against meddling with *Arcana Imperii*. After Parliament had got under way he would be able to relax for study and recreation in the summerhouse which he had built near the fish ponds at Gorhambury. There he would meditate on problems in science and the law.

But nemesis in its ancient guise, as politico-social disapproval and pressure, was to intervene. Within four months the High Court of Parliament, having tried the Lord Chancellor on a charge of bribery, would adjudge:

1. That the Lord Viscount St. Alban, Lord Chancellor of England, shall undergo fine and ransom for forty thousand pounds.
2. That he shall be imprisoned in the Tower during the King's pleasure.
3. That he shall for ever be incapable of an office, place, or employment in the State or Commonwealth.
4. That he shall never sit in Parliament, nor come within the verge of the Court.

"There had been," as a biographer, R. W. Church, has said, "and were still to be, plenty of instances of the downfall of power, as ruinous and even more tragic. . . . But it is hard to find one of which so little warning was given, the causes of which are in part so clear and in part so obscure. . . . Every public man, in the England of the Tudors and the Stewarts, entered on his career with the perfectly familiar expectation of possibly closing it . . . in the Tower and on the scaffold. . . . So that when disaster came, though it might be unexpected as death is unexpected, it was a turn of things which ought not to take a man by surprise. But some premonitory symptoms usually gave warning. There was nothing to warn Bacon that the work which he believed he was doing so well would be interrupted."

This statement is not completely apt. There had been some "premonitory symptoms." Both Villiers and Yelverton had told Bacon of petitions against him to the King, and James himself had given intimation that this was so. There had been widespread discontent over Monopolies—whose warrants Bacon, as a certifying referee, had sanctioned—and over Proclamations, presumed to have the force of law, on the part of the Privy Council, of which Bacon had for several years been a member. The nation, said John Chamberlain in a correspondence, is already "much terrified with the Star Chamber, there being not so little an offence against any Proclamation but is liable and subject to the censure of that Court; and, for Proclamations and Patents, they are become so ordinary that there is no end, every day bringing forth some new project or other. In truth the world doth even groan under the burthen of these perpetual Patents; which are become so frequent that whereas, at the King's coming in, there were complaints of some eight or nine Monopolies then in being, they are now said to be multiplied by so many scores."

As early as October, 1620, a committee, with Bacon presiding, had been appointed by the Council for the perusing of Monopolies and other "grievances." This committee had selected for consideration some "that are most in speech, and do most tend either to the vexation of the common people, or the discontenting of the gentlemen and Justices." It had noted that there were "many more, of like nature but not of like weight, nor so much rumoured; which to take away now in a blaze, will give more scandal that such things were granted, than cause thanks that they be now revoked." The selected grievances were reported to the King and Villiers, who left their disposition to the Council. Members of the Council, still "irresolute," were not in agreement over what should be done. Coke, an opponent of the granting of Monopolies, as something which lay within the King's Prerogative, probably knew at this time what was in store for Bacon and therefore was not eager to mitigate circumstances by helping the Council decide on a course of action. The Lord Chancellor was inclined to think that some of the Patents should be cancelled, but he did not press the matter. He believed, of course, that if criticism were directed against him, or any of the other judges who had sanctioned the Patents, he would be able to make a good defence by showing that in certifying the Monopolies the referees had acted in the public interest. Monopolies had long been employed successfully as devices for strengthening the kingdom's economy. They had promoted invention through assuring discoverers of rewards for their ingenuity and labor. When the upholding of quality had been required of importers with Patents, the public had been protected from the sale of inferior foreign goods. Monopolies had served to encourage native manufacture by assuring sales until such time as English products were able to compete with those from abroad. When services had become lax and inferior, as in the case of inns, for example, these, it could be presumed, were improved through granting a Patent which entailed the meeting of a standard.

Parliament met on January 30th, 1621. In the Commons were Sir Edward Coke, Bacon's enemy of old, and Sir Lionel Cranfield, mindful of slights from the Lord Chancellor. In the Lords were Southampton, formerly a conspirator with Essex, and one whose imprisonment Bacon had helped secure; Suffolk, whom Bacon had recently fined and sentenced to the Tower; and Suffolk's son, another Howard. Members generally of the two Houses were already acquainted with or would soon be made aware of certain things which in recent years the Lord Chancellor had condoned, defended, or advocated: the Benevolence, to which most of those present had been called upon to contribute; Monopolies whose discussion in Parliament had been inhibited; the rendering of the courts consonant with what the King desired through his consultation with the judges. Other practices which Bacon had expressly opposed in "advices," in speeches in

Parliament, and in addresses to courts of law, would be wrongly associated with his name, as one given to defending the Royal Prerogative: the depriving of a people of their Parliament when it would not come to heel; the provision of supply for the Treasury without recourse to the Commons; the invasion of the consciences of subjects through the requirement of "one doctrine, one discipline, one religion," always the same "in substance and ceremony"; the excommunication and depriving of worthy ministers by prelates; the continuance of illegal Purveyance and outmoded Wardships and Tenures; the King's acting as if he thought that of all the inhabitants of the realm he alone possessed and would ever retain the power of political initiative, and that all the privileges of settled institutions and lawful subjects were revocable by him.

These many matters for grievance were not made the ground of an indictment or a move for impeachment against the Lord Chancellor; yet they were inherent within that political nemesis which had chosen him as the victim of its fury. If these matters had been made reasons for legal causes, Bacon could have answered them on grounds of fact or constitutional principle. Had the charge against Bacon been his part in the declaring of Proclamations, in that case Coke, as a member of the Council, would have been equally responsible with the Lord Chancellor, as would also several members of the House of Lords—the court before which Bacon was eventually to be tried. If the nature of Monopolies granted had been the reason for proceeding against the Lord Chancellor, then all the referees who passed on the Patents would have been equally involved. If the members of the King's ecclesiastical courts had been brought to trial, the accused would have included Lords Spiritual within the Upper House. If issues from the Prerogative had been made causes in law, then the King himself would have been tried by what he considered his own courts and his own Parliament. (This was to happen in the next reign.) Events, however, did not proceed in any of these ways. Punitive action was taken against one member of the Privy Council, one judge, one member of Parliament, one subject alone—Francis Bacon. He was to be fined, imprisoned, and put forever out of public life for having taken gifts from litigants in cases pending, when his judges knew that the giving and receiving of such presents was a conventional practice and, in Bacon's case, had never occasioned a departure from justice or legal rectitude.

By February 5th a committee on grievances had been set up by the Commons. A member of the House, Noy, moved, and Coke seconded, a resolution that Monopolies should be investigated. Coke, again a member of the Commons after his expulsion from the office of Lord Chief Justice, was an experienced Parliamentarian, and knew a great deal about courts of law. He would tell the Commons just when the court of the Lords was to be approached, and would meanwhile permit the Commons to act as arbitrarily as he himself had done in the ordinary courts over which he had earlier presided and in the Star Chamber, of which, as one of the Privy Council, he was also a member. The Monopoly on Alehouses was brought up for consideration. The committee discovered that, instead of curbing drunkenness, many licensed proprietors were encouraging violation of laws against this offense by collecting their own private penalties from the transgressors whom they harbored. Sir Francis Michell, who had administered the Patent, was summarily and arbitrarily condemned without any entertainment of a defence. Another Patent (for Inns) was held by Sir Giles Mompesson. After an investigation, it was found that this patentee had demanded perquisites before he issued licenses, and that of inns he had licensed in one shire alone some sixty had been closed as disorderly houses. Mompesson admitted in a petition that "so general a Patent cannot but be a great grievance to the subject." The committee at first decided, with Coke agreeing, that this Patent was good in law but not in execution, but later reported through Coke that it

was bad both in execution and in law—without an apposite defining of terms. Mompesson fled to the Continent and was
sentenced *in absentia* by the Lords to imprisonment for life.

The Monopoly for the manufacture of gold thread and laces
presented a special problem and in consequence occasioned a
resourceful tactic on the part of Coke and a denunciation by
James. In 1619, Bacon, in order to relieve the courts of law, had
this Monopoly put under the direct jurisdiction of the King,
who since then, along with the two Villiers—as former patentees
and now pensioners—had been receiving whatever profits the
Monopoly brought. It was no longer an ordinary Monopoly.
James took occasion to inform Parliament that in his opinion
any inquiry into such a "Monopoly" as this, and indeed into any
Patent granted by the King, was a presumption of a right which
Parliament did not possess. The Lower House was now, in effect,
attempting to revive an old and long-unused principle of Impeachment by Parliament, whose employment had had precedent only in former times of political anarchy. The Commons,
none the less, insisted on a discussion with the Lords on the
question of Patents. At the meeting which followed, when the
representatives of the Commons presented their case, the Lord
Chancellor was refused admission to reply to their charges.

Up to this point Bacon had regarded the recent conduct of
the members of the Lower House in a purely constitutional light.
He had not looked with favor on their debating the Monopolies
granted by the King and he had been appalled by their high-
handed action in the case of Michell. The latter was an indication
of what might follow from an assumption by Parliament of
sovereign power. By now, because of his treatment during the
conference between the two Houses, and from indications on
the part of Coke and Cranfield that the Commons were casting
their gaze in the direction of the Chancery—but not of the Star
Chamber, to which Coke belonged—Bacon began to realize that
not all of the members of the Privy Council nor all of the
judges who had certified the Monopolies, but only *one* council-

lor and *one* judge, the Lord Chancellor, would soon be called upon to bear the brunt of an attack. Bacon warned James that "those that will strike at your Chancellor, it is much feared will strike at your Crown."

Soon the committee of the Commons began an inquiry into the proceedings of the Chancery. Bacon who, as an upholder of the King's Prerogative, had been distressed by their attitude towards the whole question of Monopolies and their treatment of Michell, welcomed this turn of events. He was willing "that any man might speak freely anything concerning his court." However, at this juncture, to the Lord Chancellor's disquiet, a former Deputy Registrar of the Chancery, John Churchill, who some time before had been cashiered for exacting fees for forging documents, came upon the scene, bearing "revelations." Before long, the investigating committee was reporting that it had also received "divers petitions, many frivolous and clamorous," but also "many of weight and consequence," against practices in the Chancellor's court. So far, the petitions seemed to be complaints against real or imagined incivilities and inattentions by court officials. But by the middle of March, information was received and evidence provided of two cases in which the Chancellor had accepted gifts from suitors while their causes were still pending in his court. Bacon, on being informed of a report on the first of these, wrote to Villiers that he was in "Purgatory"; "but," he added, "I know I have clean hands and a clean heart. . . . And if this be to be a Chancellor, I think if the great seal lay upon Hounslow Heath, nobody would take it up." A third complaint was advanced by a habitual litigant, Lady Wharton, who had had three husbands and was now having trouble in her attempt to prove the deed of the property of the second of these. She had lost a case—as had the others—after she had presented the Chancellor with a purse of gold. Earlier, Lady Wharton had successfully bribed an official—John Churchill, who had been dismissed—to change a court record.

The inquiry into the actions of the Lord Chancellor was now

transferred to the House of Lords, on the assumption that the
Viscount St. Albans should be tried for his crimes by his peers.
Bacon, now ill, wrote the Lords to regard his absence from the
Upper House rightly, and to allow him, when his present in-
disposition had passed, to examine witnesses. He also wrote to
James:

> When I enter into myself, I find not the materials of such a
> tempest as is comen upon me. I have been (as your Majesty
> knoweth best) never author of any immoderate counsel, but al-
> ways desired to have things carried *suavibus modis*. I have been
> no avaricious oppressor of the people. I have been no haughty,
> or intolerable, or hateful man, in my conversation or carriage. I
> have inherited no hatred from my father, but am a good patriot
> born. Whence should this be?

The King had already attempted, and failed, to have the pending case brought before a select body of commissioners, twelve
from the Commons and six from the Lords. The day after he
received Bacon's letter, James went in person to Parliament. He
acknowledged the authority of the Lords as a criminal court,
undertook to impress the Upper House with the seriousness of
their present undertaking, and promised the Commons that he
would "strike dead" obnoxious Monopolies in return for grants
in equivalence and a cessation of the present attack on his judges.
Villiers urged the King to dissolve Parliament and thus bring
the present commotion to an end. The Scottish King, fool as he
often showed himself to be in his constitutionl dealings with the
English, was sufficiently wise to reject Villiers' advice. The
favorite then wavered in his loyalty to Bacon, and for a time
seemed to take the side of the Lord Chancellor's accusers. He
remarked that "with so bad a case he could have no sympathy."
The King was aware that members of the Commons were now
assuming an authority over things which they never before had
dared debate, except as subjects for petition. One of their number, Coke, had even introduced a bill to the effect that all things

which had previously lain under the King's grant of Monopoly were henceforth to be placed within the disposing of the Lower House. Things were on the march, and no one could say what the end would be. The present Parliament wanted a greater sacrifice than Mompesson in exile, and had chosen as a scape-goat none less than the King's Chancellor. James, who wept over Bacon's plight, knew that Parliament was now seeking something more than the punishment of "bribery." He had already been apprised (through the rejection of his request for a commission of judges) of the fact that the case of his Lord Chancellor would be one in which the trying court would definitely not subscribe to his strongly affirmed principle that judges should consult with their King.

While definite charges were being prepared against him, Bacon remained at Gorhambury in a state of great physical depression. For many years far from robust, he now feared that death was at hand. On April 10th he prepared a draft of a will, beginning with the words:

I bequeath my soul to God above, by the oblation of my Saviour. My body to be buried obscurely. My name to the next ages and to foreign nations.

In this will he left a symbolic token to Prince Charles (1600-1649, Prince of Wales in 1616) as one of a succeeding age. The Prince was to have the offer of Gorhambury. It was at this time that Bacon wrote the prayer or psalm which, according to Joseph Addison, is composed in the style of an archangel, and which, in the view of another critic, is "rather like a passage for a nation's liturgy than the outpouring of a broken spirit." The prayer or psalm ran—to quote a part of it:

The state and bread of the poor and oppressed have been precious in mine eyes: I have hated all cruelty and hardness of heart: I have (though in a despised weed) procured the good of all men.... Besides my innumerable sins, I confess before thee, that I am debtor to thee for the gracious talent of thy gifts and graces, which

I have neither put into a napkin, nor put it (as I ought) to ex-changers, where it might have made best profit; but misspent it in things for which I was least fit; so as I may truly say, my soul hath been a stranger in the course of my pilgrimage.

Within a week the Lords had prepared a list of specific charges. The Lord Chancellor, in the meantime, had been ex-amining law and precedents in "cases of bribery," in preparation for a meeting with the King. He set down in writing the follow-ing conclusion:

There be three degrees or cases of bribery charged or supposed in a judge:—

1. The first, of bargain or contract for reward to pervert justice, *pendente lite*.

2. The second, where the judge conceives the cause to be at an end by the information of the party, or otherwise, and useth not such diligence as he ought to inquire of it.

3. And the third, when the cause is really ended, and it is *sine fraude* without relation to any precedent promise.

For the first of them I take myself to be as innocent as any born upon St. Innocent's Day, in my heart.

For the second, I doubt, in some particulars, I may be faulty.

And for the last, I conceived it to be no fault, but therein I desire to be better informed, that I may be twice penitent, once for the fact, and again for the error. For I had rather be a briber than a defender of bribes.

I must likewise confess to your Majesty, that at New Year's tides, and likewise at my first coming in (which was as it were my wedding), I did not so precisely, as perhaps I ought, examine whether those that presented me had causes before me, yea or no.

And this is simply all I can say for the present concerning my charge, until I may receive it more particularly. And all this while I do not fly to that, as to say that these things are *vitia temporis*, and not *vitia hominis*.

On April 21st, four days after the charges had been formally presented by the Lords, Bacon wrote to the King that he hoped his accusers would be satisfied with a "submission" and his sur-render of the Great Seal, for "if it be reformation that is sought, the very taking away the Seal upon my general submission, will be as much an example, for those 400 years, as any further severity." The following day he sent a "humble submission and supplication" to the Lords, where this was presented by Prince Charles. The Lord Chancellor acknowledged technical guilt of some of the charges, and continued with this statement:

For after the clear submission and confession which I shall now make unto your Lordships, I hope I may say and justify with Job in these words; *I have not hid my sin as did Adam, nor concealed my faults in my bosom.* This is the only justification which I will use.

It resteth therefore, that, without fig-leaves, I do ingenuously confess and acknowledge that, having understood the particulars of the charge, not formally from the House, but enough to inform my conscience and memory, I find matter sufficient and full, both to move me to desert the defence, and to move your Lordships to condemn and censure me.

Neither will I trouble your Lordships by singling those particulars which I think may fall off.

As a reason for his decision not to defend his case, the accused said, "In the midst of a state of as great affliction as mortal men can endure, honour being above life," he would "take no small comfort in the thought that, hereafter, the greatness of a judge or magistrate shall be no sanctuary of guiltiness, which in few words is the beginning of a golden world." He also reminded the Lords that he was confessing conformity to a general practice among judges, which would now be made judicially culpable. He wrote:

Neither will your Lordships forget that there are *vitia temporis* as well as *vitia hominis,* and that the beginning of reformations hath the contrary power of the pool of Bethesda; for that had strength to cure only him that was first cast in, and this hath commonly strength to hurt him only that is first cast in. And for my part I wish it may stay there and go no further. . . .

And therefore my humble suit to your Lordships is, that my penitent submission may be my sentence and the loss of the Seal my punishment; and that your Lordships will spare any further sentence, but recommend me to his Majesty's grace and pardon for all that is past. God's Holy Spirit be amongst you.

This statement was read in the House of Lords on April 24th and "no Lord spoke to it, after it was read, for a long time." The silence was broken by the Lord Chamberlain, who inquired "whether this submission be sufficient to ground your Lordships' judgment for a censure, without further examination." Suffolk demanded that the accused be required to appear in person before the bar of the House. Villiers and Prince Charles favored the acceptance of the submission as sufficient. Southampton, of a different mind in the matter, moved that "the House could not proceed without particular confession" from the accused. "He is charged by the Commons with corruption," said this former conspirator in treason and rebellion, "and no word of confession of any corruption in his submission. It stands, with the justice and honour of this House not to proceed, without the parties' particular confession; or to have the parties to hear the charge, and we to hear the parties' answer."

The court determined that since the accused was not entering a defence he should be permitted an expeditious answer to particulars without personal appearance. This Bacon provided by letter on April 30th. He admitted twenty-eight charges. Six of these had to do with the acceptance of monies from suitors with cases pending. To the twenty-eighth charge—that "The Lord Chancellor hath given way to great exactions by his servants, both in respect of private seals, and otherwise for sealing of Injunctions"—the Lord Chancellor, who had issued two thousand orders a year, replied, "I confess it was a great fault of neglect in me that I looked no better to my servants." On May 3rd, after Southampton had suggested banishment and Suffolk's son had moved unsuccessfully for degradation of title, sentence was passed, Villiers alone dissenting.

The cause for Bacon's trial was not the perversion of justice;

that was never seriously entertained, even by his most ardent accusers. The charge against the Lord Chancellor was aimed at an official *persona*, a destructible representative and symbol of a regime. Constitutionally speaking, the trial was the first major assault against a position to which Bacon, acting on principle, had given his support. It had been Bacon's firm belief that in the political circumstances of his time there could be no middle ground between that position and anarchy. James, had he been a wise monarch, could have brought about a constitutional development which would have met the reasonable desires of his people. But since this development could not be brought within the orbit of a Stuart king's mind, a dedicated public servant, whose political endeavor had extended over two reigns, had to take the consequences. The action taken by Parliament had meant disgrace for the Lord Chancellor, but it had also brought defeat to the King. There had been a free debate in Parliament of the whole question of Monopolies; James had been forced to capitulate to the Commons in an offer for their discontinuance so far as the Prerogative was concerned. The Sovereign had found himself in a condition of duress; for once he had not dared to dismiss Parliament. He had been denied a commission of selected judges who could have been persuaded to consult with their King before and during the hearing of the case. There had been a final trial before the High Court of Parliament, which Coke had long been maintaining was the highest court of the kingdom, and James had been unable to interfere. Even the Chancellor's expressing the hope that his trial might mark the ushering-in of a golden age of justice had been a reflection on James' management of his kingdom. Bacon had accepted bribes; but so had every other officer in the kingdom, including many who tried him. Those who received bribes ranged from servants in the royal household, through administrative officers and favorites, up to the King himself. James once told the Spanish Ambassador that if he dismissed all those in his service who took bribes, there would be no one left to carry on the work of the kingdom. James himself sold public offices; but the bribes involved in the transactions of the King, his Secretary of State, and his favorites were not comparable in character to those "gifts" which since the days of the Magi had been offered in homage to great persons in high office, including judges and Lord Chancellors. The complaining litigants whom Coke and Cranfield had employed as witnesses during Bacon's trial had mistaken traditional homage for contractual "consideration" in a business deal. Even the dull Coke, as well as the bishops and other members of the Lords, was aware that such was the case. There could be *vitia temporis* even among the Lords Spiritual. The most vocal of those among the Lords Temporal who tried the case had been criminals earlier sentenced, for proper reasons, to the Tower.

Of the three persons against whom Parliament's action had been directed—James, Villiers, and Bacon—only the third was named in an indictment. He only, as things were, could have been brought before the court of Parliament—and Bacon had an Achilles' heel, a conformity with an accepted practice among judges. James would never have permitted a trial or an impeachment of Villiers. The time was not yet when Parliament would undertake the destruction of a king. His accusers could only strike at his deputy. James kept his throne and lived out his natural life. But his son Charles would be beheaded. In the same Charles' reign it would be the fate of the favorite, James' beloved George, to be declared in a Remonstrance by the Commons "the cause of all our miseries." King Charles I (1625-1649) would thereupon prorogue Parliament, and one John Felton would quote the Remonstrance, and then use an assassin's knife to terminate the career of George Villiers.

After a verdict had been rendered at his trial, Bacon's sentence proved to be light in effect. Having asserted its right to sit in judgment without consultation with the King and to move within areas of government which James and his Lord Chancellor had reserved to the Royal Prerogative, Parliament was not interested in punitive measures against one of its most notable and memorable members. (What Coke, Cranfield, Southampton, Suffolk, and Howard felt in this regard was another matter.) Bacon's fine was remitted to trustees named by himself. By this disposing of the fine, which was never exacted, and whose payment took precedence over the discharge of all other debts, Bacon was given a relief from creditors he had never since the days of his youth enjoyed. After two days in the Tower he was released through Villiers' intervention. At the end of two years (1623) he was permitted to dwell in London, and given a full pardon. The King ordered the payment of arrears in his pension of £1,200. For his part in easing the lot of the condemned Chancellor—at least, so it seemed for a time to Bacon—Villiers exacted the price of the conveyance, if not to himself, then to Cranfield, of York House, Bacon's mansion by the Thames. By this act the favorite, whether intentionally or unintentionally, did his old friend, who complained bitterly over the transfer, a favor. Bacon's failure to compute his financial assets and expenditures had long been notorious. With his now greatly reduced income —from pensions from the state and rents at Gorhambury—he might still have attempted to keep up both his country estate and his elegant establishment in the Strand.

In Bacon's opinion the verdict of the Lords and his own sentence to the Tower had not been tantamount to future political disablement. Elizabeth herself, and Burghley too, had been confined in the Tower. Coke had been disgraced, and then brought back to the Privy Council. Persons whom he had fined and sentenced to the Tower, when a judge, were among his triers in the Lords. The sting had been removed from the charge of bribery through the awareness on the part of those who had judged him that the accused was speaking the truth when he affirmed that he had no "bribe or reward in his eye or thought when he pronounced any sentence or order." His peers had discerned his sincerity when he called his conviction "the beginning of reformations." They could understand what he meant when he told Villiers in a letter that he had been "(howsoever I acknowledge the sentence just, and for reformation sake fit) the justest Chancellor that hath been in the five changes since Sir Nicholas Bacon's time."

Soon Bacon was contemplating a return to the King's confidence and service. He wrote to James and to persons of influence, seeking political offices. None was forthcoming, yet for a time the King thought of employing his former Chancellor as advisor on the reform of the courts of the realm. When approached in the matter, Bacon, always a Parliamentarian and a defender of Parliament's privileges, told the King to "pursue the reformation which the Parliament hath begun." In enforced retirement from politics, Bacon pursued his literary and scientific works for the remaining five years of his life. With these he soon became content—although he tried unsuccessfully to obtain the provostship of Eton. It seemed now that politics had been an intrusion into the main current of his thought and desire. Within five months he completed his *History of Henry VII*. He began the writing of a history of the reign of Henry VIII and the preparation of parts of a "Digest of the Laws of England." The political histories were designed for the instruction of Prince Charles, the King-to-be. By 1622, Bacon had presented the Prince with the first part of a *Natural and Experimental History for the Foundation of Philosophy*, and promised a "particular history" each month thereafter. He was now hoping that his philosophic design might be looked upon with favor by a succeeding sovereign and the members of a succeeding Court. Before long the author was forced to admit that the furnishing of an "experimental" history in sufficient variety and detail for the instauration of the sciences would be an impossibility during his lifetime. In feverish haste he compiled a thousand short histories from whatever sources he could lay his hands on—largely from ancient and modern books—and assembled the components of a very inadequate *Sylva Sylvarum* (*Forest of Materials*). These, he thought, would at least help to indicate the range of the materials required for the third of the six parts of his Great Instauration. In 1625, now ill, Bacon wrote to the Venetian Father Fulgentio saying he could not complete his natural history; and, as if consigning the task to others in the future, he described it as clearly the work for a king, a pope, or some college or religious order. Most of his last days were given over to labor on the *Sylva Sylvarum*.

Bacon came to his death through an experiment in refrigeration. On a sunny day he set out for Highgate to dine with the King's physician. There was snow on the ground and, according to Thomas Hobbes—who for a period had been a secretary to Bacon—it occurred to him that flesh might be preserved in snow as well as in salt. Bacon alighted from his coach and "went into a poor woman's house at the bottom of Highgate Hill, and bought a hen, and made the woman exenterate it, and then stuffed the body with snow, and my Lord did help to do it himself." He became suddenly ill with a chill and, unable to return to Gray's Inn where he was now living, he "went to the Earl of Arundel's house at Highgate"; there "they put him into a good bed warmed with a pan, but it was a damp bed that had not been lain in about a year before, which gave him such a cold that in two or three days he died of suffocation."

Not knowing that he was on his deathbed Bacon wrote a note of apology to Arundel for the enforced visit to his house, and remarked, "I was likely to have had the fortune of Caius Plinius the elder, who lost his life by trying an experiment about the burning of the mountain Vesuvius."

Verulam was buried, as he had desired, near his mother, in the Church of St. Michael in St. Albans. In his last will he remembered his servants generously, left a legacy to Lady Hatton, and designated sums for endowment of two lectureships in either of the Universities and twenty-five scholarships for needy students. Although he had lived at the rate of £12,000 a year while Lord Chancellor, Bacon's liabilities at his death amounted to £22,371 and the assessed value of his estate to £7,000. The Universities were not to reap the profit of his good intent. For "just and great causes," as he said, he left nothing beyond her legal "right" to his wife, an alderman's daughter with a modest income, whom he had married in 1606. Lady Bacon's mien and manner of living had not kept pace with her husband's rise in station. She had never been at ease in the miniature court at Gorhambury and could not cope with York House, the mansion in the Strand. She had sought her company, some of it more physically masculine than her husband, outside her home and Court circles. She had not been content in the days of her husband's prosperity and had made his life miserable by incessant complaining after the reduction of his circumstances. A clause in the will was her husband's reminder that it would be appropriate for Lady Bacon to return to her earlier station.

Regarded as an event in Stuart history, Bacon's downfall was the climax of a tragedy within a greater political drama of heroic dimensions, which would reach its climax in the beheading of Charles I. Of Bacon it could be said: "If ever a man was fitted by nature and study to be the leader of a great nation it was he," for he "was not one man as a thinker and another as a politician." This thinker had postponed a revolution through his sway over Parliament and his informed and authoritative ordering of the juridical affairs of a kingdom. Now tragedy had come. If soon a greatness of mind and character was to reassert itself in full endeavor without repining, still there had been tragedy, personal as well as political. The motion of the political planet nearest the First Moved by God had been brought to an absolute stop. The most active agent in the constitutional life of the kingdom had been rendered completely inert. The King's deputy, devoid of injustice in motive or deed, had been put out of place as a disgraced creature. The undaunted Parliamentarian whose effort and pride had been the preserving of Parliament's privileges had been sent to the political scaffold through the self-deception of Parliament's members. The man of the age who had placed his memory and merit in the keeping of "times succeeding" was entreating the King "to the end that blot of ignominy may be removed from . . . my memory with posterity." Magnificence had been reduced to straits. The victim now "cast for means" was being forced to sell his furniture to "spread," as he said, "upon poor men unto whom I owed, scarce leaving myself bread." A fallen Lord Chancellor was imploring his peers in words—as E. A. Abbott remarks—King Lear himself might have uttered: "I am old, weak, ruined, a very subject of pity." He was writing in lamentation to a correspondent, "I do not think any except a Turk or a Tartar would wish to have another chop out of me."

The scenes of Bacon's political life were thronged with characters, plots, and subplots which sustained a single dramatic action. In the midst of these was a man whose "immensity" of "genius" was, as S. R. Gardiner has said, to be "a sore trouble to his biographers"—as all heroes of great tragedy are bound to be. The cause of the hero's downfall had not been the acceptance of "bribes"—that had merely provided the tragic occasion—but his belief that what the Greeks had called *arche*, political initiative, issued from the King as *persona*. In this tragedy Nemesis was comprised of the opinions and actions of men less constitutionally informed than he, and less forbearing towards a determined monarch intent on keeping everything political, including all privileges and power, within his own disposing.

Bacon's trial by his peers as a legal cause ended in 1621; his trial by biographers and commentators on grounds of political philosophy and ethics has continued ever since. It has not uncommonly been maintained, in a late-seventeenth-century manner, that Bacon, when he thought politically, disregarded the Law of Nature on which were founded the "rights" and the "liberty" of subjects. E. A. Abbott, who usually goes further in condemnation of Bacon than any of his other critics, says that this Parliamentarian and administrative officer "deliberately espoused the cause of despotism." The reason for this extreme accusing on Abbott's part is Bacon's upholding of the Royal Prerogative in conflicts between the King on the one side and his Parliament and courts of law on the other. With this much misunderstood constitutional problem on the part of "ethical" commentators we have already dealt. As for the conception of natural rights, as stated by John Locke (1632-1704): this was not current in Bacon's time, nor was the doctrine of natural law conjoined with that of an historical state of nature on which the liberty of subjects was premised in the manner of late-seventeenth-century thinking. Whether the concepts employed in enunciating a doctrine of natural rights and a universal law of nature are philosophically sound, or merely so many "fictions," is a question which need not concern us here. Bacon's political principles were derived initially from his interpretation of Scripture. He separated three kingdoms: the kingdom of Saving Grace, whose works God keeps within the "mystery" of his own dispensing; the political kingdom established within the same "mystery" by God on the giving of power, initiative, and rule to temporal monarchs; and the kingdom of nature, created by God and placed under the dominion of man. These three kingdoms were not united by the bond of natural law. As a participant in each of the three kingdoms, man had, according to Bacon, specific stations and duties. In his religious, political, and moral thinking, faith and its issue of charity belonged to God, and justice flowed from the King, as an agent divinely endowed with sovereign initiative. Man's first duty was to God; then came his obedience to the sovereign; and from these followed his just dealings with his fellow men and fellow subjects.

The divine endowment of kings remained for Bacon as great a "mystery" as the salvation of man through Divine Grace. Kings were "ordained" by God's "secret providence." This ordination was certified by Scripture—not to mention its attestation by acceptance and use in English history. According to the statements of Scripture, political sovereignty lies within the prerogatives of God alone: "*Solvam cingula regum;* I will loosen the girdles of Kings," says the Scripture; "He poureth contempt upon princes"; "I will give a king in my wrath, and take him away again in my displeasure"; and the like. When such prerogatives as these were made the claims of mere men they became, in Bacon's opinion, the iniquities of mortal creatures who now placed themselves on an equality with God. Bacon read Scriptural statement quite literally. It was his opinion that "as wines which flow gently from the first treading of the grape are sweeter than those which are squeezed out by the wine-press; because these last have some taste of the stones and skin of the grape; so those doctrines are very sweet and healthy, which flow from a gentle pressure of the Scriptures, and are not wrested to controversies or commonplaces."

The alternative "pagan" theories of sovereignty, which did not impress Bacon, were several. One, which went back to the ancient Sophists, was to the effect that selfish subjects created a sovereign for their protection, one against the other, by entering into a contract mutually to abstain from lawlessness. This was obviously fanciful history. Establishment by contract is not in keeping with sovereign majesty, power, rule, and justice. No one in his senses could imagine how justice could issue from non-justice, rule from lawlessness, sovereignty from subjection, and God's-anointed from creatures without power to anoint. After the Sophists in time, Plato and Aristotle had founded the state on the basis of human needs, desires, and powers. The former, in a refutation of the proposition of contract, made some men deserving of rule through their recognition of forms in a non-

accessible domain; while the latter made men politically capable
through a desire for an abstract being equally remote. Plato and
Aristotle gave men a dialectic when they needed a Creator. The
Stoics, in turn, propounded a law of nature which, with Cicero,
became the natural light of reason, a reason within the whole of
man, within nature, and within human judgment. On this, the
theologians seized, making it a binding principle on the mind
and will of God, kings, bishops in council, judges in court and
legislators in assemblies, and ethical agents. These thinkers were,
of course, wise in at least one regard: rulers must respect reason
as the ruling part—but far from all—of their nature and the nature
of their subjects, if they would escape monstrosity and barbar-
ism. But escape from such evils is not the establishment of sovereignty. To hold with Stoically inspired philosophers that the
source of human justice, the sanctity of human law, the authority of the ruler, and the rights of subjects are consequent on an
impersonal law and not upon the will of a Creator, is, especially
when regarded in the light of God's Revealed Word, to promote
wrong opinion, superstition, and great presumption. Such a con-
travention and theoretical enfeeblement of Scriptural truth
through philosophical argument is an example of the principle
that "the more you recede from your grounds the weaker do
you conclude." The operation of this principle is found in natural
philosophy, where "the more you remove yourself from particulars the greater peril of error do you incur, so much more in
divinity the more you recede from the Scriptures by inferences
and consequences, the more weak and dilute are your positions."
Bacon, without a doubt, looked upon the king under whom he
served as a weak vessel of divine power. But James was still, as
king, such a vessel. In the case of the sovereign, as in the case of
bishops, Bacon believed that it was not the person of an incumbent that determined kingly rule as such, but the *persona* of
the office. This had been so from the beginning of the human
race: "Neither," said Bacon, "did Adam's sin, or the curse upon
it, deprive him of his rule."

What Gardiner calls the "immensity" of Bacon has far too often been reduced and dissipated by the embroidering on the main theme of his tragedy pointless and formless moralistic cacophonies. In saying this, we are not now contending—after Aristotle—that there are better ways of interpreting tragedy than through ethical precepts; nor are we merely maintaining that there are more things in life's drama than moral consequences; rather, we are affirming that, when judged by principles fit for reasoned ethical criticism, Francis Bacon's character is one of the most virtuous to be found among men of great political renown. Bacon was eminently virtuous in that distinctive part of man which is called the human reason, and in that distinctive virtue which is called charity and said by moralists and, certainly, by theologians to be best of all moral attributes. Bacon displayed in his life Aristotelian magnanimity, Plato's four cardinal virtues, justice, wisdom, fortitude, and temperance, and the three theological virtues, faith, hope, and charity, not to mention the attribute of honor whose source, in tradition, was the King. For these virtues Bacon provided a foundation in his philosophical thinking. Surely all this should be enough to satisfy any ethically critical biographer. Certainly, no devious interpretation of motive, no malignancy of minds filled with "vapours and fumes," no sentimental rhapsodizing on pseudo-honorable themes, no assumption by clerics of man's right, and not God's, to judge the secrets of the human heart, should ever be allowed to dissipate or impair the political consistency, moral vigor, and ethical virtue of a man of Bacon's stature.

Even such a highly censorious biographer as E. A. Abbott has had to admit that Bacon was held in reverence by his chaplain, friends, and servants. Persons who knew him best saw in him a temperate, religious, charitable man, no "less gracious with the subject than with his sovereign," consistent through good and ill fortune. Bacon's secretary and domestic apothecary, Peter

Boener, hoped that a statue might be put up not only in cele-
bration of his master's learning—which time could never efface—
but "as a memorable example to all, of virtue, kindness, peace-
fulness, and patience." Dr. William Rawley, his chaplain,
rendered Bacon the following tribute, among many other
praises, after his death: "When his office called him, as he was of
the king's counsel learned, to charge any offenders, either in
criminals or capitals, he was never of an insulting and domineer-
ing nature over them, but always tender-hearted, and carrying
himself decently towards the parties (though it was his duty to
charge them home), but yet as one that looked upon the *example*
with the eye of severity, but upon the *person* with the eye of
pity and compassion." Tobie Matthew could write of the man
he had known intimately for years: "I never saw any trace in
him of a vindictive mind, whatever injury were done him, nor
ever heard him utter a word to any man's disadvantage which
seemed to proceed from personal feelings. . . . It is not his greatness that I admire, but his virtue. It is not the favours I have
received of him . . . that have thus enthralled and enchained my
heart, but his whole life and character; which are such that, if
he were of an inferior condition, I could not honour him the less,
and if he were my enemy, I should not the less love and endeavour to serve him." Ben Jonson said in sincerity of the fallen
Lord Chancellor: "What I feel for his person has never been
augmented by his place. I hope his disgraces will only serve to
show his virtue in a clearer light . . . greatness could never fail
him."

   With the "theological" and the four "cardinal" virtues in
mind, consider for a moment Bacon's conduct. Of his faith and
Christian hope there can be no doubt. These, acquired early, he
never relinquished throughout his life. Bacon was "God-
conscious" in doctrine and in practice. Reared a Calvinist, he
yet became Arminian enough to believe that faith would manifest itself in moral endeavor. From the days when he first sought
aid for scientific means to relieve mankind, until the end of his

life, the love of man and desire for his relief pervaded Bacon's thoughts and deeds. His instauration of knowledge was conceived and nurtured for the easing of human misery and the cure of human ills. His legal reforms, attempts to repeal "snaring" statutes and reduce penalties for minor offenses, his readiness to reconsider legal cases already determined when considerations of equity required, his pleas for the joining of mercy to justice, these were all the outward guarantees of an inner charity. The same was true of his designs for religious toleration, frustrated by the parties who might have reaped benefits therefrom; his efforts with the Queen on behalf of the unfortunate Essex; his loyal endurance of his cousin, Robert Cecil; his patient forbearance with King James and George Villiers to the end of maintaining constitutional continuity; his acceptance of many things as they were because nothing better could then conceivably have been attained in the circumstances of what Bacon himself called Time.

Never strong in body, Bacon was almost abstemious in his habits. His deportment in and out of office, in gatherings with his friends, in courts of law and Parliament, when presenting Remonstrances of the Commons to the Lords and King, throughout magnificent living—as Aristotle had understood the term—on a scale which befitted his station, was seasonable, appropriate, and apt—as Plato would have said—always within the bounds required by what Plato found "temperance" to be. Bacon's courage became manifest when he opposed Burghley in Parliament and endured the Queen's displeasure while refusing to retract or retreat. It continued when he told a contending Commons time after time what they could and could not constitutionally debate; when he acted as the spokesman of a remonstrating Lower House in compounding matters with the Lords and with the King; when he pointedly told James to cease trading and put on Majesty, and many things in like vein; when he faced the days of his political disgrace.

Bacon's exercise of legal justice can never be seriously

questioned. It was continual from the time he entered the Commons and the courts of law as a young man, through years on the Bench, to the day when he heard the verdict of the Lords on his own case. He accepted this verdict as just, even as he had thought just the judgments pronounced upon Essex, Suffolk, Yelverton, and lesser persons who had appeared before the tribunals over which he had presided. Bacon left the precedents of the law and the courts of England without any of the "vapours and fumes of law, which are extracted out of men's inventions and conceits." As for the fourth cardinal virtue, wisdom: Bacon's "immense" mind encompassed the principles of theological, philosophical, scientific, legal, and literary knowledge. By the age of forty his learning was vast in detail, and to the end of his days it continued to increase. He could justly be called the most universally informed man in the England of his time. He was, as Rawley said, "the glory of his age and nation, the adorner and ornament of learning."

XII

EARLY PHILOSOPHICAL WRITINGS

Francis Bacon was by nature and nurture a reformer. Always he desired to make things "better," as he said. In his parents' home he had imbibed religious "reform" from the time of his birth. As a constitutional lawyer, he had taken a firm stand in upholding the Royal Prerogative; yet, had circumstances permitted, he would have enlarged the power of Parliament as a legislative body and made the courts of law independent of the King's will. Had the Puritans not made the government and rituals of the Church matters of faith, and of politics as well, Bacon might have succeeded in moderating the contemporary rule of the bishops in the Established Church. Had James provided his Solicitor and Attorney with leisure and means for the purpose, outmoded statutes and conflicting precedents would have been removed from English law. In these several conjunctions political conditions had worked against Bacon. There was one area of endeavor, however, in which, as he said himself, circumstance could not interfere. This was the realm of philosophy. Nothing short of an Inquisition could militate here and, thanks to the defeat of the Spanish Armada, there was no longer any possibility of an English Inquisition.

Bacon's bent towards philosophical reform showed itself before the age of sixteen. While at Cambridge he rebelled against Aristotelian doctrines and Peripatetic instruction, as "unfruitful" things. After he had left the University and continued with his reading in modern as well as ancient authors, his opinions, as the thoughts of one who would rebuild, became firmly set in an opposition to all the philosophical systems of past and present. A piece written in his middle twenties showed a predisposition towards the experimental investigation of nature. This unfinished treatise was designed to promote a new "formula" or method of scientific discovery. The young author called the writing in which this method was announced *Temporis partus maximus* (*The Greatest Birth of Time*). Later on he changed the title to *Temporis partus masculus* (*The Fertilizing Birth of Time*).

This, Bacon's first philosophical treatise, takes the form of a trial in court of a number of past and present philosophers, who are known to the presiding judge as "phrenetics"—persons out of their senses in more ways than one—and of their followers, whom the court regards as a company of professional hirelings. Of these phrenetics, commands the author in juristic fashion, let Aristotle be summoned first, because of all those now accused he is probably in the worst condition, having a mind utterly confused with useless subtleties—a laughingstock of words. Aristotle is the person who, when the human mind had arrived, as by chance, at some truth, put the intellect under an insane logic, and thus delivered it over to verbiage. He then became the sire of many artful babblers who, on their cessation from Peripatetic ramblings, make up, through the agitation of their own wits, from the stuff of his foolish precepts and propositions, the endless trash of the schools. Aristotle, as their progenitor and instructor, is more deserving of accusation than they. At one stage of his life this founder of a contentious line was able to face the open facts of nature; but he was not satisfied with the observation of these. He would weave constructions on the histories of particulars like a spider spinning a web. These fabrications he would then take as actual causes—such makeshifts, indeed, as one, Jerome Cardan, in our own age produces. But, Bacon continues, now addressing his remarks to a prospective disciple among the listeners in his court, do not divine that we are in agreement with that modern rebel against Aristotle's teachings, Peter Ramus by name. We will have no traffic with that producer of handbooks. Ramus binds together empty and arid trifles. Aquinas, Scotus, and their associates were given to fashioning a variety of things out of nonexistent objects, but this rhetorician produces the nonexistent out of what actually is. He is indeed worse than a sophist.

Let Plato be called next—Plato the cultivated scoffer, the elated poet, the theologian out of his natural wits. When this writer merged popular opinions in a system and at the same time loosened and stirred men's minds by use of some vague inductions, he might well have been content with providing grace and charm for the *noctes* of literary persons. Instead, he must go on to disguise facts. Plato turned the human understanding inward, upon itself, and made it ponder, in the guise of a contemplator of things, blind Idols or phantoms of the mind. Plato's disciples, under the spell of their master's verbal subtlety, have occupied themselves with that pleasant ruminating upon delicate notions which brings to ruin the severe investigation of truth. Among Plato's followers are Cicero, Seneca, Plutarch of Chaeronea, and many others of lesser stature.

Let the court deal next with the physicians. Galen is here, narrow in mind, the vainest of pretenders, the deserter of experience. He has composed a complete system, and by this he banishes all ignorance from medicine, puts its practitioners into a place of false security, and brings their art to a standstill. By pronouncing incurable all diseases which do not conform to his rules, Galen dooms mankind to suffer endless ills and casts a malignant blight on human capacity.

Let us not overlook old Hippocrates, whose disconnected utterances all physicians still quote—because once upon a time he set down some narratives of cases of diseases. Hippocrates still seems to be taking in particulars through his senses; but actually his gaze is wandering. His mind is obsessed by the phantoms of theory, and when he is under their influence he behaves as if he considered himself an oracle.

Over there is a troop of chemists, and one of them, Theophrastus Paracelsus, is vaunting himself. This physician and chemist, for his very impudence, deserves correction separately from the rest. Let him be summoned. You, Paracelsus, charges the judge, by putting together your false images, have turned man into a mummer. We can more easily endure Galen weighing his so-called elements than you when you embellish your fantasies. By mixing the divine with the natural, the profane with the sacred, the heretical with the fabulous, you have corrupted truth, both human and divine. The light of nature, whose sacred name you often appropriate to your impure speech, you have not concealed, as have the Sophists, but have quenched. They have been the deserters of experience, you its betrayer. Among your disciples is a man of capacity, Peter Severinus. He deserves a better occupation than the translation of your falsehoods into fables, however delightful to the ear his tales may be.

Unlike Paracelsus, the empirical chemists occasionally do hit upon, as by chance, some useful things. But, alas, these burners of charcoal will attempt to build a whole philosophy on a few experiments in distillation. Speaking of the fabrication of systems from meagre materials, Telesio has recently been holding the stage with a new philosophic play of no sound argument and, we may add, without any reward of applause. In astronomy, where system-building has long been a vogue, the contrivers of eccentrics and epicycles, on the one side, and the modern wagoners who move the earth about, on the other, are employing exactly the same evidence to support diametrically opposed theories. There is something wrong there, for quarrels among scientists betoken not truth but error.

At this stage of our proceedings someone may think it appropriate to ask the question, whether among all those who have thought and written in mankind's past about nature, have there not been some persons who have discovered some truth. Is it not possible that the river Time, which has brought down many light and inflated imaginings, has carried beneath its surface some solid and weighty things? What of the ancient Heraclitus, Democritus, Anaxagoras, and Empedocles, whose records have disappeared but whose doctrines are still available in the writings of others? Our opinion, replies the judge to his own question, is that in the surviving fragments of some of these early philosophers there is evidence of diligence and ingenuity, and of an auspicious scientific beginning. The number theory of Pythagoras, too, is of good omen. At this point, however, we must utter a caution—and this is intended for investigators in prospect: any inquirer who desires to bring benefits to mankind had better seek truth by the light of nature, and not in the darkness of antiquity. What the past has done will be seen to matter little when this is placed in a comparison with what the future may achieve through the employment of a new method of inquiry. Fortuitous discovery, which has characterized the past, is not science. To use a rustic metaphor, it is not unlike the chance upturning by a digging animal—say, a sow. If by empirical chance such a creature, endowed with senses as it is, were to form the letter *A* by its uprooting, one would not suppose that it could by the same token compose a whole literary tragedy! An empirical item in discovery is solitary and not germinous. Only a procreative activity, in which sense and reason are united and in which one discovered item is conjoined with another, will produce a family of scientific works. Certainly a single finding or several unrelated discoveries, even when upheld by observation and experiment, can never serve as sufficient means for the founding of a philosophy of nature. The thinker who attempts to make a philosophy out of such meagre materials must either have recourse to the Idols of the Marketplace, mere words, or rely on the Idols of the Theatre, stageplays. As things now are, an immense sea flows around the island of truth, and everywhere are to be found scatterings of systems strewn about by the winds of Idols.

We have entertained charges against past and present thinkers, including some of the tallest scions of the theoretical sects. Their indictments have been more moderate in statement than their deeds warrant. While we condemn them, we would not act like Vellius, that literary rhetorician who touches hastily on the opinions of Cicero merely to cast them away; nor like the modern Agrippa, that trivial buffoon, who in reviewing the opinions of Aristotle and others distorts for purpose of mere ridicule. O miserable me! who, because I have taken it upon myself to condemn the follies of the past, am compelled to compare myself with the jackasses of the present!

This early statement by Bacon, which reads like the animadversions of a very censorious judge in court, is a rhetorical preamble to a major philosophical undertaking. The nature of this enterprise is indicated by its author in 1592. Then Bacon asks Burghley for an office to "carry" him because, he says, "I have taken all knowledge to be my province, and if I could purge it of two sorts of rovers (whereof the one with frivolous disputations, confutations, and verbosities, the other with blind experiments and auricular traditions and impostures hath committed so many spoils) I hope I should bring in industrious observations, grounded conclusions, and profitable inventions and discoveries." The two "rovers" are, on the one hand, the rationalists in a tradition from Plato to Bruno and, on the other, the contemporary experimenters and their empirical kind.

Two years later (1594), in a masque presented at Gray's Inn for the entertainment of Elizabeth, Bacon, in the person of "The Second Counsellor, Advising the Study of Philosophy," addresses the Queen as follows: "I . . . will wish unto your Highness the exercise of the best and purest part of the mind, and the most innocent and meriting conquest, being the conquest of the works of nature; making this proposition, that you bend the excellency of your spirits to the searching out, inventing, and discovering of all whatsoever is hid and secret in the world. . . .

"And to this purpose I will commend to your Highness four principal works and monuments of yourself. First, the collecting of a most perfect and general library. . . . Next, a spacious, wonderful garden, wherein whatsoever plant the sun of divers climates . . . either wild or by the culture of man, brought forth, may be, with that care that appertaineth to the good prospering thereof, set and cherished; this garden to be built about with rooms to stable in all rare beasts and to cage in all rare birds, with two lakes adjoining, the one of fresh water, the other of salt, for like variety of fishes. And so you may have in small compass a model of universal nature made private. The third, a goodly huge cabinet, wherein whatsoever the hand of man by exquisite art or engine hath made rare in stuff, form, or motion; whatsoever singularity, chance, and the shuffle of things hath produced; whatsoever nature hath wrought in things that want life and may be kept, shall be sorted and included. The fourth, such a still-house, so furnished with mills, instruments, furnaces, and vessels as may be a palace fit for a philosopher's stone. Thus, when your Excellency shall have added depth of knowledge to the fineness of your spirits and greatness of your power, then . . . when all other miracles and wonders shall cease, by reason that you shall have discovered their natural causes, yourself shall be left the only miracle and wonder of the world."

After a lapse of eleven years these early attempts to obtain aid from the Court for the founding of a new sort of learning are to be followed by another, when Bacon addresses to James, as a learned Sovereign and Visitor to the Universities, a full work called *Of the Proficience and Advancement of Learning* (1605). By this writing Bacon hopes to bring about a change in university practices or, failing in this, to have the ruler of the kingdom provide helpers and means for a suppliant who would collect natural histories and labor industriously in the sciences and arts of nature—even as another king, the father of Alexander the Great, gave similar aid to Aristotle. The author brings under review the uncultivated areas of knowledge; provides a new classification of the sciences—which is to supersede that of Aristotle; announces a new instauration of learning with a new method of inquiry; and finds great fault with the exercises, anciently begun and still continued, within the Universities.

About the same time, partly before and partly after the preparation of the *Advancement of Learning*, Bacon prepares some chapters of an unfinished work in which he treats of certain aspects of his new philosophy which are not stressed or mentioned in the completed work. This treatise he calls *Valerius Terminus of the Interpretation of Nature: with the Annotations of Hermes Stella*. The latter half of the title is a memento of Bacon's early hope that the scholarly King would join with an enterprising subject in a publication dealing with a new learning. Another work of Bacon's written a little later (1606-7), *Partis instaurationis secundae delineatio et argumentum (Outline and Argument of the Second Part of the Instauration)*, exhibits in a preliminary way a new scheme of scientific inquiry. These three pieces and, probably, two sets of jottings, *Cogitationes de scientia humana (Thoughts on Human Knowledge)* and *Cogitationes de natura rerum (Thoughts on the Nature of Things)*, are written before the author is made Solicitor-General (June, 1607). While holding the Solicitor's office, Bacon produces twelve more philosophical writings. Of the seventeen pieces written by the time he becomes Attorney-General, only two are completed and published: the *Advancement of Learning* and *De sapientia veterum (Concerning the Wisdom of the Ancients)*. In the remainder of this chapter we shall indicate some of the contents of the *Advancement of Learning* and the *Valerius Terminus* and sketch the *Outline and Argument of the Second Part of the Instauration*.

The first part of the *Advancement of Learning* is an exposure of what the author calls the "vanities and errors" of present learning. His attack is directed in the main against the Universities, which, the author says, are not reservoirs of truth but houses of relics. Learning, contends Bacon, lies in the keeping of grammarians who render it bookish, of editors who make it textual, and of logicians who reduce it to disputation. Its professors are aspirants for "second prizes," such as befit the commentator, compounder, abridger, and adder of glosses—all scholarly debasers of generative thinking. The disputers, who include all persons within the Universities, assume that tumbling up and down in intellectual conceits produces sublime philosophers. These arguers equate scientific inquiry and proof with the art of deductive logic. By this art they have hedged every division of learning with a set of determining, yet unproven, axioms, and then have put the several parts into a system complete in structure and detail. To demonstrate a truth, they cite a text, define the terms of their citation, add objections, and finally frame solutions which prove on examination to be no more than additional verbal distinctions. Disputation, with its adduction of authorities and its citation of their theses, with its cavillings, its "breeding" of many questions for the solution of one, is practised by schoolmen of several persuasions. But, in the main, peripateticism, as a method, prevails. The earlier schoolmen undoubtedly possessed "sharp and strong wits, and abundance of leisure, and small variety of reading; but their wits being shut up in the cells of a few authors (chiefly Aristotle, their dictator) . . . and knowing little history, either of nature or time; did out of no great quantity of matter, and infinite agitation of wit, spin out unto us those laborious webs of learning which are extant in their books. For the wit and mind of man, if it work upon matter, which is the contemplation of the creatures of God, worketh according to the stuff, and is limited thereby; but if it work upon itself, as the spider worketh his web, then it is endless, and brings forth indeed cobwebs of learning, admirable for the fineness of thread and work, but of no substance or profit."

Science and philosophy, despite the immense speculation of schoolmen, have undergone but slight advance since the days of the ancient Greeks, while the arts, through mere chance discovery, have progressed—witness modern printing, instruments of navigation, and gunpowder. The names of the great innovators of antiquity, Plato, Aristotle, Hippocrates, Euclid, and Archimedes, are still being invoked, not so much to promote inquiry as to provide cause for doubt that anything not already discovered can ever be found out. Aristotle's divisions and descriptions of the sciences are presumed to be established forever, as if no new branch or kind of science could ever again be developed. Such provisions by the Universities as might conduce to observation and experiment—small botanical gardens, some anatomical dissection, globes, spheres, and astrolabes— even these are designed not for scientific discovery, but as aids to immediate practice in the professions.

Having made a protracted attack on the Universities in the above vein, Bacon goes on to announce plans for a new learning. These include a reclassification of the sciences and a reorganization of such knowledge as may be discovered through the use of the natural faculties. Excluded from Bacon's new classification of the sciences and reserved to that wisdom which is given in the inspired Scriptures are the knowledge of the truths of revealed theology, the derivation of a supreme rule of ethical conduct and of the discovery of the "nature and state" of the part of man which is made in the Divine Image. "The soul in the creation," writes Bacon, "was not extracted out of the mass of heaven and earth by the benediction of a *producat*, but was immediately inspired from God; so it is not possible that it should be (otherwise than by accident) subject to *the laws of heaven* [i.e., heavenly bodies] *and earth*, which are the *subject of philosophy*; and therefore the true knowledge of the nature and state of the soul must come by the same inspiration that gave the substance."

Bacon classifies the parts of natural knowledge initially according to the dominant faculties concerned—for the reason functions in all three parts. History depends on memory, poetry on imagination, philosophy on reason. History and poetry treat of particulars circumscribed by place and time, while natural philosophy—which is generalized physics—dismisses or discards individuals and operates by means of general notions and general axioms. History is of two main sorts, natural and civil. Natural history comprises the history of generations, of pretergenerations, and of the arts; that is to say, it is a record of nature in "ordinary" course, of nature when it "strays" from this and produces what are called "monsters" or "marvels," and of nature when "vexed" by the hand of man for the production of works of art. The main function of natural history is to provide materials for the inductions of natural philosophy.

Philosophy has three objects: God, nature, and man. It accordingly has three main branches, but like a tree, which has a trunk, natural philosophy includes a universal part which nourishes and sustains the several parts. Bacon calls this *philosophia prima*. This "first philosophy" is concerned with such axioms as are common to several sciences. It also, according to the later Latin version of the *Advancement of Learning*, brings under reckoning "adventitious" or accidental "conditions of essences," such as much and little, like and unlike, possible and impossible, being and not-being. Bacon's *philosophia prima*, he informs us, is quite distinct in conception from traditional "first philosophy," or metaphysics, called by Aristotle theology. It is not based, like Aristotle's "first philosophy," on the abstract Principle of Identity—What is, is; it is not concerned with being as such; and it is not independent of all lesser sciences. Its axioms, common to several sciences, are derived through inductive inquiry into particulars in such fields as physics, ethics, and politics. It operates in the area of the adventitious—or what may or may not be—and not in the realm of the necessary. It does not include a doctrine of a "first cause." It provides no knowledge of the being, mind, or operation of God.

Philosophy, concerned with nature, is divisible into a speculative part, the inquiry into causes, and an operative part, the production of effects. The speculative part is to be further divided, according to the causes investigated, into physics, which deals with "material" and "efficient" causes, and metaphysics, which inquires into "formal" and "final" causes. While making these distinctions Bacon is aware that he is using old terms in new senses. In the Latin translation of the *Advancement of Learning*, the *De augmentis*, the author criticizes Aristotle for his "undertaking . . . to coin new words of science at pleasure," and then goes on to say: "But to one on the other side . . . it seems best . . . to retain the ancient terms, though I often alter their sense and definitions; according to the moderate and approved course of innovation in civil matters, by which, when the state of things is changed, yet the forms of the words are kept." Soon, in his dealing with causes Bacon will, in effect, discard the four traditional sorts, except one, the material, which for him will become also an efficient cause.

Physics investigates what is more relative and variable—the same fire, for example, can produce opposite effects on diverse materials—while metaphysics studies what is more general and determined. Conjoined with these two divisions of speculative natural philosophy are two operative parts: mechanics, which is accordant with physics; and "magic," in its early sense of "wisdom," which is accordant with metaphysics. Mathematics, dignified by Aristotle as an independent "theoretical" science along with physics and metaphysics, Bacon classifies as an agent of metaphysics and an appendix to physics. "Knowledges," writes the author, "are as pyramides, whereof history is the basis: so of Natural Philosophy the basis is Natural History; the stage next the basis is Physic; the stage next the vertical point is Metaphysic. As for the vertical point, *Opus quod operatur Deus a principio usque ad finem* [the work which God worketh from the beginning to the end], the Summary Law of Nature, we know not whether man's inquiry can attain unto it. But these three be the true *stages* of knowledge; and are to them that are depraved no better than the giants' hills [Pelion, Ossa, and Olympus, piled upon each other] . . . but to those which refer all things to the glory of God, they are as the three acclamations, *Sancte, sancte, sancte* [Holy, Holy, Holy]; holy in the description or dilatation of his works, holy in the connexion or concatenation of them and holy in the union of them in a perpetual and uniform law. And therefore the speculation was excellent in Parmenides and Plato, although but a speculation in them, That all things by scale did ascend to unity. So then always that knowledge is worthiest which is charged with least multiplicity; which appeareth to be Metaphysic; as that which considereth the Simple Forms or Differences of things, which are few in number, and the degrees and co-ordinations whereof make all this variety."

Human philosophy, concerned with man, Bacon divides into two parts: the study of "man segregate" and the study of "man congregate" in society. The first part he subdivides into three more studies; one treating of man's body, another of his mind, and a third of human nature as a whole. The study of "man congregate," or civil science, includes three parts which deal respectively with three activities of society: "conversation," or the dealings of individual with individual; "negotiation," or business; and government.

The *Valerius Terminus*—a compiled set of papers—is less erudite in presentation and more strictly philosophical in character than the *Advancement of Learning*. It contains an early statement of the major principles and concepts of the author's systematic philosophy. There is definite indication in this writing that Bacon's philosophical scheme is to be both naturalistic and materialistic in character.

The "troublesome" title of the present writing, *Valerius Terminus of the Interpretation of Nature: with the Annotations of Hermes Stella*, applies specifically to the first, the only full chapter of the treatise, which has been assembled from fragments of writing. In this chapter the author contends that the province of natural philosophy does not include divine "mysteries," since God "is only self-like, having nothing in common with any creature," and no "light for the revealing of the nature of God" can be obtained by "inquiry into . . . sensible and material things." The name "Valerius" is one which belongs to ancient Roman consuls or highest magistrates or to praetors or senior magistrates during consulates; as in the case, for example, of P. Valerius Publicola, consul, 508 B.C.; L. Valerius Flaccus, consul—with Marius, 100 B.C.; L. Valerius Flaccus, praetor during Cicero's consulate, 63 B.C. Bacon observes that "the names of the Roman magistrates are the same" even "when the status of things changes." "Terminus" in the title means boundary or limit; "Valerius," here employed as an adjective, means authoritative; hence, the first part of the title of the work, when translated, becomes "the authoritative limit of [natural science, or] the interpretation of nature." Of the words in the second part of the title, "stella" (star) is a symbol employed by the author to designate the sovereign, as in his early device, or masque, for Elizabeth's entertaining—the *Gesta Grayorum* in the

Advancement of Learning, and in the *De augmentis.* As for "Hermes": in the *Advancement of Learning* the author compares James with this ancient god to whom, he says, was ascribed in veneration "the power and fortune of a King, the knowledge and illumination of a Priest, and the learning and universality of a Philosopher." Apparently during the period in which Bacon assembles the *Valerius Terminus* he is entertaining the hope that James, who long has been drinking at the "fountains of learning," may be prevailed upon to annotate a subject's writing. But on reflection, he thinks it imprudent to make such a request, for the present at least, of this learned sovereign and very considerable author. He writes on the title page of the compiled document, "None of the Annotations by Stella are set down in these fragments."

In the compiled work, especially in the first chapter, whose content occasions the title of the whole, a sharp distinction is drawn between the respective areas of revealed theology and philosophy. The former of the two is not to encroach in any degree upon the province of the latter, which is to be pursued through inductive inquiry by natural human powers. While philosophy is to be limited by religion, the scientist, as a religious man, will put his natural philosophy, with whose findings revealed theology is never to interefere, into the service of a charity prescribed through Divine Revelation. Natural science is not to provide a bridge—like the natural theology of the Peripatetics—for the making of an ascent from the causes, operations, and structures of nature to God, as First Cause, Prime Mover, or Being *qua* Being. Indeed, for Bacon these three modes of description of God, either in metaphysics or in theology, are gratuitous and inept.

The subject matter of the philosophy which Bacon sketches in the *Valerius Terminus,* and develops in his later works, is to be limited to physical nature. Between this philosophy and revealed theology a definite boundary is fixed. Physical nature, as one body, is to be understod within one limited system of truth. In the investigation of nature there is to be no enfranchisement of independent, mutually exclusive sciences to the weakening of all, in the manner of Aristotle, through the use of mutually exclusive basic axioms. All axioms, whether newly proposed or in process of establishment, will, as investigation proceeds, receive their authority and draw their strength from a unified body of physical science, within which they are to be intimately conjoined. "Without this intercourse the axioms of sciences will fall out to be neither full nor true; but will be such opinions as Aristotle in some places doth wisely censure, when he saith, *These are the opinions of persons that have respect but to a few things.*" "I mean," writes Bacon, "not that use which one science hath of another for ornament or help in practice, as the orator hath of knowledge of affections for moving, or as military science may have use of geometry for fortifications; but I mean it directly of that use by way of supply of light and information which the particulars and instances of one science do yield and present for the framing or correcting of the axioms of another science in their very truth and notion ... for sciences distinguished have a dependence upon universal knowledge to be augmented and rectified by the superior light thereof, as well as the parts and members of a science have upon the *Maxims* of the same science, and the mutual light and consent which one part receiveth of another. And therefore the opinion of Copernicus in astronomy, which astronomy itself cannot correct because it is not repugnant to any of the appearances, yet natural philosophy doth correct. On the other side if some of the ancient philosophers had been perfect in the observations of astronomy, and had called them to counsel when they made their principles and first axioms, they would never have divided their philosophy as the Cosmographers do their descriptions by globes, making one philosophy for heaven and another for under heaven, as in effect they do."

Care must be taken, however, to make certain that, through a desire for immediate unity, the results of investigation in limited areas do not dominate all other divisions of knowledge. With such an unfortunate consequence, Plato mingled his whole philosophy with theology, Aristotle his with logic, and Plato's followers of the Second Academy theirs with mathematics. At present the alchemists are prone to produce a full philosophy out of the results of a few chemical experiments, while Gilbert makes a whole universe from his observations of the loadstone. These are examples of thinkers who elevate what actually applies to "a few things" into something which supposedly pertains to all.

Bacon now names some of the objects which are to be investigated by a new inductive method. These are the "natures," "motions," and "appetites" of bodies. The "natures," "few and permanent," are "as the alphabet or simple letters, whereof the variety of things consisteth; or as the colours mingled in the painter's shell, wherewith he is able to make infinite variety of faces or shapes." As for "motions" and "appetites": philosophers of the past have written too much and badly about the first "beginnings or principles" of things and have neglected to inquire into the "motions, inclinations, and applications" of matter here and now. Actually there can be no "beginnings" in a philosophy of nature. Doctrines respecting a First Cause are groundless and invalid, "impertinent and vain." Among other "conceits" and "mere nugations," which have appeared in past interpretations of motion, Bacon lists the views of Aristotle, certain Platonists, Parmenides, Anaxagoras, Empedocles, Leucippus, Democritus, and Epicurus: "shift or appetite of matter to privation; the spirit of the world working in matter according to platform; the preceeding or fructifying of distinct kinds according to their proprieties; the intercourse of the elements by mediation of their common qualities; the appetite of like portions to unite themselves; amity and discord, or sympathy and antipathy; motion to the centre, with motion of stripe or press; the casual agitation, aggregation, and essays of the solid portions in the void space." Of the three best known of the thinkers who have treated of the subject motion Democritus is to be preferred to Aristotle and Plato. "There is no great doubt," he says, "but he that did put the beginnings of things to be *solid, void, and motion to the centre*, was in better earnest than he that put *matter, form, and shift*; or he that put the *mind, motion, and matter*."

The author inveighs against the deference which is being paid by investigators to "antiquity and authority; common and confessed notions; the natural and yielding consent of the mind; the harmony and coherence of a knowledge in itself; the establishing of principles with the touch and reduction of other propositions unto them; inductions without instances contradictory; and the report of the senses." Such things as these fall within sorts of "idols" or "false appearances that offer themselves to the understanding in the inquisition of knowledge." Bacon has already mentioned Idols in the *Fertilizing Birth of Time* and the *Advancement of Learning*. Here they are specifically named and their number stated as four: "the Idols of the *Tribe*, the Idols of the *Palace*, the Idols of the *Cave*, and the Idols of the *Theatre*." (The word "Palace" is, presumably, the result of a scribe's slip, the original having been "Place," or "Market Place.")

In the *Valerius Terminus*, unjustified conclusions in science, over-hastily arrived at, are called "anticipations," as opposed to "interpretations," of nature. The necessity of a natural history for the founding of philosophy is reasserted and stress is laid on particulars, especially those of a "vulgar and ignoble" sort which, the author observes, are at present being put to use mainly by "persons of mean observation." Definite indication is now given of the role of the senses, the reason, and the axiom —occasionally called "hypothesis" by Bacon—in philosophic inquiry. The senses are said to have their own distinctive "sufficiency," not because they do not err, but because of their contribution—which is not, for the most part, "immediate"—to knowledge. "It is the work, effect, or instance," says Bacon, "that trieth the Axiom, and the sense doth but try the work done or not done." Scientific truths are general in character; their objects are universals available to reason. Particulars are infinite and transitory. Truths are to be sought through reducing particulars "by exclusions and inclusions to a definite point." Reason provides the axiom; sense tries the exemplification of the axiom in the operation of the particular which the axiom governs. After particulars have served in the establishing of the axiom, "the axiom found out" by reason "discovereth and designeth new particulars." The axiom, through intercourse with other axioms, also begets axioms of a more general character. These begotten axioms are either established or disproved by the evidence of particulars in causal operation within works available to sense. "In deciding and determining the truth of knowledge ... the discovery of new works and active directions not known before, is the only trial to be accepted of ... you may always conclude that the Axiom which discovereth new instances is true, but contrariwise you may safely conclude that if it discover not any new instance it is in vain and untrue." Here, the active direction is the axiom in operation. "The fulness of direction to work and produce any effect consisteth in two conditions, certainty and liberty. Certainty is when the direction is ... infallible. Liberty is when the direction ... comprehendeth all the means and ways possible. ... If therefore your direction be certain, it must refer you and point you to somewhat which, if it be present, the effect you seek will of necessity follow, else you may perform and not obtain. If it be free, then must it refer you to somewhat which if it be absent the effect you seek will of necessity withdraw, else you may have power and not obtain." These things are so because the nature—or cause, or form—which the axiom defines is convertible, through identity, with the object in operation.

Most of what Bacon writes in the *Valerius Terminus* will be incorporated in some form or other within his *Novum organum* (*New Organon*, 1620). Much of the author's next philosophical treatise is so similar to portions of the *New Organon* that it may be regarded as an attempt to produce a draft of the later work. The main subject of the present, unfinished treatise, *The Outline and Argument of the Second Part of the Instauration*, is a new logic or method of investigation. This is to constitute the second of six parts of Bacon's Great Instauration of the sciences, which will be formally announced in the *New Organon*. In the *Outline and Argument* the author mentions five "books," which, he says, belong to the instauration of the sciences. The second of these is concerned with method, and the third, fourth, and sixth with the "interpretation of nature." The fifth book deals with "anticipations" of nature, findings not yet attested by the requirements of the new method. These, after subjection to full inquiry, may, if not then rejected, be incorporated in the sixth book. Nothing is said about a first book because, presumably, the author has not yet decided on the specific character of its content.

The purpose of the second book of the instauration, says the author, is to expose a use of reason more thorough than any hitherto known to man, to the end of exalting the human understanding as far as "this mortal state permits" and thus enabling man to assert his rightful dominion over nature. To achieve this aim, the surface of the mind must, first of all, be levelled and cleared of those impediments which have hitherto encumbered it. Next, the mind must be turned in the direction of the proper subject for investigation. Finally, information is to be imparted to the understanding, now rendered capable and ready to receive it.

The obstructive—and scientifically destructive—part of the human understanding is multiplex, in keeping with the several sorts of Idol which frequent the mind. Some Idols are old inhabitants, "settlers" long in occupancy, of the intellect. These include notions which have been received from the systems and sects of philosophers, who derived them originally through use of false rules and wrong methods of demonstration. Other Idols are native to the mind itself, inherent within its very constitution. Even as an uneven mirror distorts the real shape of objects, according to the curvature of its surface, so the understanding on receiving impressions through the senses mingles its own nature with what comes before it. The first task, then, is the dispersal and banishment of the host of theories which have been argued in the schools. Next will follow the job of freeing the intellect from the bondage of perverse methods of demonstration. Then will come a third undertaking, the holding of the mind's own seductive influence in check, either by uprooting its native Idols or, if this is not feasible, by indicating what these are, so that they may be recognized and, where possible, controlled. It will be fruitless, even harmful, to demolish and destroy prevailing errors in philosophy if new offshoots of error, conceivably worse than those which they supplant, are encouraged to proliferate.

Some readers, continues the author, will perhaps object to the delay we are inflicting on scientists by the tedious experimentation we are about to invite. Others may argue that by the entertainment of the immense number of particulars which we require for observation and study, the intellect will be thrown into a "*tartarus*," or hell, of confusion, far removed from the high serenity and calm of abstract wisdom—as if the latter were a godlike state. Those who, having abandoned themselves to a passion for contemplation, find our constant reference to "practical" achievements harsh and offensive, as something appropriate to mechanics, will now be shown how, in fact, they are working against the attainment of their own desire; because clarity in theoretical reflection on nature and the invention of practical works can only be achieved together, and by a common dependence on the same means. If someone demurs, because in his caution he regards our scheme for the regeneration of the sciences as a proceeding without any finality, we tell him with assurance that our instauration will mark the end of prevailing error and desolation. We hope to make it evident to all that a full and proper investigation of particulars and the concepts derived from these will amount to something more finished, manageable, intelligible, sure of itself, and better informed than any number of abstract speculations and meditations, such as at present prevail in science and philosophy.

Some sober critic—as he may think himself—will perhaps regard our whole undertaking with a reserve befitting a prudent man of affairs, and say that our statements are but "prayers"—and overly optimistic prayers at that. He may form the opinion that our transformation of philosophy will effect nothing but a change in dogma, by which the human situation would be improved in no way whatever. In that case, we shall persuade this critic that we are doing anything but establishing a dogmatic system or sect; that our method differs completely from any hitherto employed in philosophy and the sciences; and that a harvest of practical results is quite certainly assured, that is, if "practical" men do not in their hurry and haste attempt to reap the crop while it is still green, or grasp with childish impatience at what can be but promises of results to follow. The true interpretation of nature, the project in which we are engaged, is, of course, an arduous undertaking, but the greatest part of its difficulty does not depend upon anything that is placed beyond our capacities, but rather on what lies within our own power, and can therefore be overcome. One thing we would have our readers believe at the outset: we are not starting on a journey into a wilderness without reconnaissance. Our strategy is devised according to a formulated method or art.

The art of discovery which we are now introducing belongs

to the same family as ordinary logic, for that too prepares aids and constructs defences for the understanding. But ours differs from the common logic in various respects, and in three especially: the starting point of investigation, the order of demonstration, and the end and nature of proof. Our inquiry starts at a deeper level, by subjecting to examination things which the ordinary logic takes on trust, such as first principles, the basic axioms of the several sciences, and the evidence of the senses. Our method departs utterly from the old order of demonstration. It develops and elicits propositions and axioms cautiously, moving in a gradual ascent from recorded observations of particulars, as both positive and negative instances, to general truths, instead of jumping immediately from what is given in sense to "first" principles and large generalities, and from these speculatively deducing intermediate propositions. The end of the logic we profess is not the invention of arguments but the discovery of the natures of real things, a discovery which will be established by operations within particulars.

The new logic is an instrument which controls and, at the same time, aids human faculties or powers. Aristotle, whose teachings still prevail, acknowledges sense, memory, and reason as three instruments of knowledge. But he provides no assistance for the first of the three and disregards the particulars to which they are exposed. His account of the second is indefinite. He permits the third to range and soar at will. The new logic, on the contrary, both controls and supplies aids for the senses, aids for memory, and aids for reason.

In presenting helps for the senses, we shall attempt to show how a good notion (comparable to what the Peripatetics in the context of their logic call the middle term) may be elicited and established, and how the senses, whose testimony is ever proportionate to man, may be brought into adjustment through axioms with the scale of the universe of nature. Actually, we do not attach great weight to the senses when operating by themselves, however necessary they may prove themselves to be in the trying of experiments which establish axioms. In cases where things escape the faculty of sense because of the smallness of their bodies or of their parts, or through their distance, the slowness or quickness of their movements, or in other ways, we shall show how such objects may be brought within the scope of sense. We shall also indicate what may be done where objects cannot be presented immediately to sense. To this end we shall emphasize, for example, the employment of instruments, the skilled observation of gradual processes, and the drawing of such evidence from what is perceptible in bodies of size and character proportionate to the senses as may be related to bodies or parts of bodies which cannot be made available for immediate observation. Finally, we shall examine the question of natural history, including experiments, and shall designate the sort of history which can be made to serve as a foundation for philosophy. We shall also indicate what kind of experimentation should be made when other natural history is not available. At this point we shall introduce remarks on the stimulating and the retaining of attention, for many things which belong to natural history and scientific experiment have long been within the field of our vision, and yet have never become part of our scientific experience.

Our second sort of aids, those to memory, will further the extraction of a specific set or sort of observations from the mass of particulars, the accumulation of serviceable natural history in general, and the arrangement of this material of philosophy in a manner which permits the understanding to make use of it. The capacity of the understanding does not allow a ranging over the infinity of nature. Memory, too, can embrace only a limited number of objects. When unaided, the memory is not fitted to select matters relevant to definite inquiry. The best means, generally speaking, of overcoming its incapability in these two regards is a single, simple remedy: the rule that no result of investigation is to be accepted unless presented in a written record with properly ordered tables. To pursue the interpretation of nature in any field by relying upon memory unaided by such tables is like trying to retain and recite the content of an astronomer's almanac.

The selective function of memory requires special attention. Once the subject for research has been decided upon and placed within limits, so that it stands isolated from other matters and freed from any confusion with them, aids to memory can provide three services. To illustrate these we shall first indicate the kind of questions which are to be asked when the natural history of the subject concerned has been accumulated and considered —here we are reminded of what the logicians call "topic." Secondly, we shall explain in what order particular histories are to be marshalled into tables. We do not expect, of course, at this stage of investigation to hit the actual "veins" of the subject under study; all we can hope for is its tentative partitioning. We shall bear in mind, too, that truth emerges more readily from error than from confusion, and that reason can rectify a wrong division more easily than it can penetrate a heap of jumbled evidence. Thirdly, we shall show how and when an investigation should be started afresh; when the charts of previously compiled tables are to be transformed, and how often the inquiry should be repeated, as the case may require. We think that the first series of charts or results should be mounted upon adjustable axes, because they can represent only trial phases of investigation. The senses and the memory by themselves cannot, of course, establish axioms, but only simple notions and ordered histories for their placing at reason's disposal.

When considering our third group of helps, those to the reason, we must bear in mind the fact that, while the scientific reason is essentially a single thing, its aim is twofold: knowledge and contemplation on the one hand, and action and achievement

on the other. Accordingly, we shall have regard for both the
understanding of causes and the ability through means to produce effects. These two objectives, on close examination, will
prove, like the reason itself, to be one thing. They can be
separated only for the purpose of separate inquiry. What in
reflection counts for a cause is in operation a means. If every
means required for any purposes were available to man at his
wish, there would be little or no point in treating theory and
practice separately. But man finds that his action is confined
within much narrower limits than his knowledge and that
sometimes he can act experimentally in works without employing a scientifically established axiom. These are among the
reasons why we treat the theoretical and practical aspects of
reason separately. So far as the theoretical part is concerned,
everything turns upon a single problem, that of establishing
true notions and axioms. The established axiom contains a solid
portion of truth, while a plain motion is, so to speak, only
truth's surface.

There are three procedures which can especially further
investigation in its theoretical aspect: the maintenance, the
adaptation, and the abridgement of investigation. When we
come to describe the first of these we shall have to explain how
axioms may be used to suggest and to establish other axioms of
a higher order and of greater generality, so that by a firm and
unbroken ascent the investigator may eventually arrive at a
unity of system. We shall also find it necessary to provide a
way for testing and verifying these higher axioms by natural
history and experiments, so that the user of our method may
not lapse at any stage of inquiry into conjecture and mere
probability.

The adaptation of investigation depends on the sort of cause
being sought and the nature of the subject under investigation.
Setting aside final causes, which have thoroughly corrupted
natural philosophy, our search may be restricted to formal,

efficient, and material causes. When we speak of efficient or of material causes, we do not mean "ultimate" agents or indeterminate matter—common topics in scholastic disputations—but proximate agents and formed matter. Lest the search for these be pursued through pointless refinements, we shall annex a method of discovering what may be called hidden processes. This is the name we give to the series and successions of change which result from the actions of efficient causes and the fluctuations of materials affected by them.

As for the abridgement of inquiry: this can help in two ways, to blaze a trail through trackless areas and to make a short cut across paths already worn. In these regards a certain kind of experiment and a certain kind of question have prerogative power. We shall accordingly indicate questions of a definite and comprehensive sort, queries by which an inquirer can early "take the auspices" of an investigation. Such questions, when placed in the vanguard will bear a torch, so to speak, for those which are to follow. We shall also indicate some experiments which can furnish more information than a multitude of others less outstanding and less enlightening. (A large section of the *New Organon* is given over to the illustration of "prerogative instances.")

Reason's second office, which has to do with operation in works, may be disposed of with a threefold thesis. As a preparative to this thesis, we must make an observation or two. When inquiry is conducted according to the requirements of our new induction, whatever is found to concern the practical reason should be interspersed with considerations which relate to the theoretical. Again, the fact should be borne in mind that in practical inquiry the procedure is by a ladder of *descent*, for here operations involve particular matters, which occupy the bottom of the scale of investigation—whose top is the most universal axiom—and must therefore be descended to, step by step, from general axioms.

The threefold thesis itself is, in effect, a prescription of three special parts or rules of method. One of these is appropriate to investigation where the desideratum is not so much a cause or an axiom as a practical achievement. Another concerns the compilation of such records as may further and hasten the production of works; and a third, an admittedly imperfect part of inquiry—an appendix as it were to scientific method—provides aid for the disclosing of operative possibilities by proceeding from experiment to experiment without the establishment of an axiom.

Having given this outline of what he intends to provide as principles and specific rules for a new method of inductive investigation, Bacon expresses the hope that he has prepared the way for the marriage of the "Human Mind and the Universe, if divine goodness will be their bridesmaid." It is his trust that the supplication of the "prayer of their nuptial hymn" will be for the begetting from their union of a line of heroes who may, in some degree at least, conquer and subdue man's necessities.

XIII

PHILOSOPHICAL WRITINGS
WHILE SOLICITOR-GENERAL

Bᴇᴛᴡᴇᴇɴ 1607 ᴀɴᴅ 1612—ᴛʜᴇ ʏᴇᴀʀ ɪɴ ᴡʜɪᴄʜ ʜᴇ was called upon to assume heavy responsibilities of state—Bacon wrote some twelve philosophical pieces. Many of these were brief, some were of considerable length, some had hardly been begun; only one, *De sapientia veterum (Concerning the Wisdom of the Ancients)*, was completed. One can hardly imagine what the results would have been had this thinker been denied public office in the reign of James I. This much is sure: a stream of impressive writings would have flowed from his pen. The implications for philosophy of the doctrine of the three separate kingdoms (of nature, politics, and Divine Grace), of a new classification of the sciences, of the concepts and principles of a new naturalistic philosophy, of an inductive metaphysics hitherto unknown, and of a new method of inquiry, would have been worked out. There would have been exposition of the eight aids to investigation which are merely announced in the *New Organon*. A man of genius would have illuminated the field of induction which has remained to this day an area of philosophic obscurity. As it was, Bacon wrote more fully and more impressively on this subject than any other philosopher was to write for more than three hundred succeeding years.

Bacon's philosophic writings while Solicitor-General include: *Filum labyrinthi, sive formula inquisitionis (Thread of the Labyrinth, or Rule of Inquiry); Cogitata et visa: de interpretatione naturae, sive de scientia operativa (Thoughts and Impressions: Concerning the Interpretation of Nature, or Concerning Operative Science); Redargutio philosophiarum (The Refutation of Philosophies); De sapientia veterum (Concerning the Wisdom of the Ancients); Phaenomena universi (Phenomena of the Universe); Filum labyrinthi; sive inquisitio legitima de motu (Thread of the Labyrinth; or the Legitimate Investigation of Motion); Calor et frigus (Heat and Cold); Historia et inquisitio prima de sono et auditu, et de forma soni, et latente processu soni; sive sylva soni et auditus (History and First Investigation of Sound and Hearing, and Concerning the Form of Sound, and the Latent Process of Sound; or the Material of Sound and Hearing); Descriptio globi intellectualis (Description of the Intellectual Globe);* and *Thema coeli (Theory of the Heaven).* Either in this period or soon thereafter he wrote *Scala intellectus sive filum labyrinthi (Ladder of the Understanding or Thread of the Labyrinth)* and *Prodromi sive anticipationes philosophiae secundae (Forerunners or Anticipations of the New Philosophy).*

Bacon's publication of the *Advancement of Learning* (1605) had not produced the effect which its author had desired it to have on the King, the Court, Universities, clergy, and laymen of consequence. James and the frequenters of his Court had showed no interest in the establishment of either a new learning or a new science. Members of the Universities were resentful of the author's attack on their opinions and practices, and regarded his alternative for traditional logic as an unworthy thing, fit only for the training of mechanics and apothecaries' clerks. Clerics who read the book were appalled by its identification of metaphysics with universalized physics. The author's separating the principles of ontology from the placets of revealed theology did not appeal to those among the reading public who were sure that they knew what they intended when they thought that "truth is one and not many."

In 1608, Bacon, now intent on making a stronger and a better impression on his readers, conceived the plan of writing "scornfully" of the pagan Greek philosophers and respectfully of the "ancient poets"—as authors whose sayings contained in the form of parables some of his own most cherished opinions. Bacon began to prepare the *Redargutio philosophiarum (Refutation of Philosophies)*, two other similar pieces, and the *De sapientia veterum (Concerning the Wisdom of the Ancients)*. In the following year he was able to send a copy of the first of these to Tobie Matthew. Within an accompanying letter he included the statement, "I send you at this time the only part which hath any harshness. . . . it doth more fully lay open that the question between me and the ancients is not of the virtue of the race, but of the rightness of the way." He also sent, about the same time, a copy of another writing, *Cogitata et visa (Thoughts and Impressions)*, to his friend Bishop Andrewes. This piece had been composed for distribution to a few persons so as to invite comment and criticism before the author embarked on his large undertaking, the preparation of the *New Organon*. In *Thoughts and Impressions* Bacon repeats with increased emphasis arguments he has already employed in earlier treatises, and introduces topics which are to become prominent in writings to come. The piece is an enlargement of another written in English under the Latin title *Filum labyrinthi, sive formula inquisitionis (Thread of the Labyrinth, or Rule of Inquiry)*. This *Filum labyrinthi*—the author composes another on Motion—is one of the very few philosophical pieces which Bacon writes, or leaves, in English; the *Advancement of Learning* and the *Valerius Terminus* are two others. At the top of the last page of its incomplete manuscript is written, in Bacon's hand, "The English as much as was parfited." In the same hand is added to the first page "*ad filios*," as if the author were communicating with an audience of disciples in prospect. The writing is probably the preliminary draft of the Latin *Cogitata et visa (Thoughts and Impressions)*.

There is, says Bacon in the *Thread of the Labyrinth, or Rule of Inquiry*, neither magnitude nor certainty in the knowledge now possessed and professed. Men strive by argument to save the credit of ignorance and to make themselves satisfied with their poverty. The good opinion of their store is the cause of their want. The physician has his set rules of practice and pronounces diseases incurable which are not encompassed by his prescribed art. The alchemist makes his experiments according to the recipes of auricular tradition, and explains his failures as the misunderstanding or misuse of the same. The aspiring magician is bent on finding what he deems to be breaches in the operations of nature. The mechanic refines what has been come upon by chance. The learned man regards the sciences as bodies of truth forever settled, and not as pursuits of examination and discovery. The succession of knowledge is from master to disciple, and not from discoverer to advancer.

In the course of learning, since the days of the ancient Greeks, natural science has been given the least attention of any part of philosophy. After Socrates taught, Grecian thinkers became concerned with moral instruction, as a sort of applied philosophical divinity. Able men among the Romans, because of the large problems posed by the extent and complexity of their Empire, confined their reflections to political and legal questions. Among the Greeks natural philosophy flourished but a very short time, for soon it became disputation among competing sects. Never since has science possessed a man wholly, except a rare monk in a cloister or an unusual gentleman at his country estate. At present it receives only casual recognition in the Universities, and that by raw wits in passage to professional studies.

Whenever the investigation of physical nature showed signs of producing results, religious authorities intervened. Greek thinkers who gave a naturalistic explanation of thunder were condemned for impiety. Fathers of the Church censured cosmographers who had discovered and described the roundness of the earth and told of the Antipodes. After scholastic philosophers "almost incorporated the contentious philosophy of Aristotle into the body of Christian religion," learning became a matter of texts, glosses, and disputations. The level of knowledge could go no higher than the source of its flow, the works of the defining, determining, magisterial Stagirite. In addition to a continuing authoritarianism which issues ultimately from Aristotle, other hindrances to science have appeared in a religious guise. Clerics argue that the desire to probe the secrets of nature is akin to the temptation of Adam which—as they understand it—brought about man's original sin and fall; that the more men know of second causes, the less they depend upon the First Cause; that innovation in philosophy leads to the subversion of orthodox theology. Such contentions are, of course, foolish and unsound. The occasion of the Fall was not a knowledge of the creation which is nature, but the assumption of a moral knowledge of God's will and intention and a refusal to obey His commands. Natural inquiry, which has nothing to do with a First Cause, is both sanctioned and required by God of men for the exercise of their dominion over the lower creatures, a dominion granted them by the Creator at Creation. Adam, accordingly, gave a name to every living creature, and Solomon wrote "a natural history of all verdor, from the cedar to the moss, and of all that breatheth." True Religion, so far from restraining natural inquiry and promoting submission to ignorance, requires diligent investigation of such of God's works as are put under man's dominion, works which show the Creator's power, but not His essential nature and will. This dominion will never be reclaimed by means of theological studies or through a continuance of the past and present practices of learned Christians.

In *Thoughts and Impressions* the author repeats several of his earlier observations. The science of the present possesses no certainty, magnitude, or promise of increase. Medicine, alchemy, and magic are filled with impostures. Mechanics is not sustained by a general philosophy of nature. Chance, and not design, is the discoverer and inventor. The preoccupation of thinkers with theology and ethics, the devotion of the Universities to narrow and retrograde studies, the despair of would-be inquirers, the contempt by the learned of "works" and of the "vulgar" things in nature, the common reliance on the opinions of the ancients—these have served to bring science to a standstill. There are, however, some grounds for hope. Age is wiser than youth and, opinion to the contrary notwithstanding, to the modern and not to the ancient times belongs the adulthood of the human race. There is a general weariness of religious controversy. The discovery of the new world has occasioned some expectation that the intellectual globe may be correspondingly enlarged. Recent inventions, acquired through groping and chance, have led men to expect greater discoveries from planned inquiry. Some investigators are professing a reliance on observation and experiment, if still continuing in the persistent vice of system-building.

From the contemporary builders of systems we can expect nothing of consequence for science. Like the ancient Greeks, the modern Bernardino Telesio, Giordano Bruno, Thomas Campanella, Jerome Cardan, and even William Gilbert have constructed large fictions, like so many stageplays, out of a few observations. Certain of these thinkers have discovered through experimentation some limited causes extending to limited observable effects. But with patient inquiry they cannot be satisfied. They must turn from this and assert axioms which imply great causes generally operative; yet causes, alas, of which no one can discern commensurable and corresponding effects. Their more general principles are not accordant with observable or proved operations in nature, as inductively established comprehensive axioms must be.

Science should make a new beginning. Natural philosophy must be purged of those methods and theories which have traduced it. Inquirers must again become like little children and approach nature with wonder and awe and without prejudice. Through experience and induction, they can learn its alphabet. A strict method of induction would bring guidance and furnish helps for the senses and the understanding. As the human hand by itself fails when it attempts to draw an exact circle without a compass, so the human mind wavers and wanders when without proper direction it would discover and comprehend the system of natural causes. Science must be provided with a new method. If renown accrues, as it does, to the maker of a discovery of a single cause in nature, how much more deserving of honor would be the discoverer of the method of all discovery of all causes. The immediate consequences of his invention would be nothing less than the purification and control of the human faculties. From this would issue the recapture of man's dominion over the kingdom of nature. Such a discovery would be so productive of results that it might well be called the "Fertilizing Birth of Time." Such a discovery would surely be more worthy of recognition than any deed of any conqueror, lawgiver, or founder of empire, since it would make man the ruler over the whole realm of nature.

The new method of science (the Second Part of the Great Instauration) is not to be confused with the modes of demonstration employed and taught by Aristotle, namely, induction and deduction. Aristotle's induction consists of a simple enumeration of agreeing particulars without the salutary employment of any negative instance, which might invalidate the principle asserted. In his deduction, the middle axioms are obtained not through observation of particulars but through derivation from more general propositions previously established by initial precluding definitions. Whatever fits these definitions is by the definitions determined; what fits them not is from demonstration excluded. This traditional method when compared with what is now proposed is as water to wine. As a vintage of discovery, the principles of the new science will not be a raw product rudely and hastily fermented, but a yield slowly produced from select particulars carefully gathered, mildly pressed, and well-purified.

In addition to a method, the new science requires an accumulation of a "forest" of particulars, the material on which the method may operate (the Third Part of the Great Instauration). In this collection particulars will not be thrown together as in a heap, but arranged and tabulated. When the material thus ordered will have been interpreted according to the rules of the new method, Tables of Discovery will be prepared in exemplification of the preliminary results of induction (the Fourth Part of the Great Instauration). Next, a scale or ladder of ascent to more general comprehensions must be undertaken. At this stage the investigator will be assailed by the temptation to proceed without inductive warrant to the enunciation of most general comprehensions—after the manner of Cardan, William Gilbert, and Telesio. Care must now be taken to make certain that at every step of ascension no instance contrary to an asserted axiom is overlooked.

For its scientific ratification, an axiom at any stage of inquiry must submit to two tests. First, it must meet the basic requirement of induction: proof by observable positive instances and disproof by observable negative instances. The latter sort of instance is not to be accommodated, in the manner of Aristotle, by the introduction of new verbal definitions to meet their cases. Secondly, no general principle is to be made a party to intellectual negotiation or let at large unless it give earnest, or bail—to use a figure from the courts—by indicating new particulars, and not merely principles, beyond those from which it has itself been derived. At this point of his exposition, Bacon is about to enter upon the Sixth Part of his Great Instauration.

The writing, which is said by its author in the quoted statement to Tobie Matthew to contain "harshness," is called by Bacon *Redargutio philosophiarum (Refutation of Philosophies,* 1608). This takes the form of an address to disciples in prospect by a wise man who bears on his countenance—like the Head of Solomon's House in the *New Atlantis* (1627)—a look of kindly pity for mankind. He speaks not from a pulpit or dais, but on a level with his hearers. His address is, in dramatic supposition, reported verbatim to the author, who is engaged in a discussion of his philosophic plans with a friend in Paris. The speech has been delivered in that city before an audience of some fifty persons eminent in church and state. The address in substance is as follows:

God has made you, my sons, not beasts in subjection but free men capable both of receiving by faith a knowledge of your Creator and also of attaining through your own faculties an understanding of the material world which the Creator has placed under your dominion. In what you consider your knowledge of nature, you think yourselves very rich, while in fact you are extremely poor. All your income of the present and the prospective future consists of reduced revenues from the labors of some six of your intellectual forebears, Aristotle, Plato, Hippocrates, Galen, Euclid, and Ptolemy. Yet your Maker requires, in addition to your allegiance to Himself, your own effort and toil in the study of His created works. The God who has endowed you with trustworthy faculties for search into the nature of His creation will hardly be satisfied with a blind faith in the opinions of six men. The conversion of your minds to what I am about to say will not be an easy undertaking, because all your theological and political treatises assume the sufficiency of the thought of the aforementioned persons. Your language and literature have been set in their terms and maxims. Their thoughts have been confirmed within you by the training received at colleges, by your social inheritance, and, one may almost say, by your national endeavor.

I am not asking you to surrender your learning; keep that for your dealing with those who speak and think in its terms. Have one way of communicating with the public, but employ another for dealing with nature. Give yourselves to the ignorant for a time, but beware lest they hold you captive forever. If you would understand and control nature you must first acquire a new method of inquiry, one hitherto untaught and unused. This you will not be ready to employ, or even to entertain, until your minds are prepared through a deliverance from much that is false. It is to make a beginning in the effecting of this deliverance that we are assembled today.

The people from which the old philosophy has come belonged to the boyhood of the race. The Egyptian priest in Herodotus wisely said, "You Greeks are ever children," for those whom he censured were like boys, given to much talking but incapable of generation. In the matter of time, the Greeks had not even a thousand years of history to look back upon. In the matter of place, they knew only a small portion of the world; their travels, in comparison with the voyages of modern discoverers, were merely suburban jaunts. Their foremost teachers, Plato and Aristotle, were men of capacious, and in a way sublime, intellect; yet by pretension to authority in everything, they became contending sophists, ignorant of most things. If Aristotle, who was to draw into his train men of learning in every age, is still regarded as chief among teachers, his continued eminence is the token of the indolence and pride of those who follow him; of indolence that retards the search for truth, of pride that conceals ignorance. So far is the common consent which prevails among Aristotle's disciples from the betokening of truth, it is the worst of all signs where the intellect is concerned. Nothing wins universal consent unless it is either commonplace, ostentatious, or superstitious. Phocion, when he was applauded by all the Athenian populace, properly suspected his past conduct, and asked, "What error have I committed?"

In the new philosophy there is to be no dictator; he who is least in the new kingdom of learning will be greater than the greatest in the old. Eminence will be measured according to the fruitfulness of inductive inquiry. The produce from former philosophical tillage has consisted of idle disputations, without a single discovery. While the mechanical arts have progressed, the sciences have remained stationary, lifeless images to be adored in idle contemplation. The chief defect of the philosophy of the past, the one which has dominated all the rest, has been the lack of a valid method. In this regard, let no one be misled by the common assumption that Aristotle employed induction and relied on experience. His so-called induction was an imposture. So opposed was Aristotle to consulting with experience, he dragged her along as a captive chained to the wheel of his chariot.

Train yourselves then, my sons, to study the ways of God's creation, and not the behavior of Aristotle. Pursue the subtleties of things themselves and not those of the Peripatetics. And be not like the empirical ant, who only collects, or like the weaving spider, who fills the air with the cobwebs of theory; rather use your senses and your reason in the manner of the bee, who first collects and then produces means for life and growth. Do not fear the "nothing beyond" which has been written on the Pillars of Hercules to mark the boundary of the charted Mediterranean Sea. Let your own cry be "further yet." Dare to pit your strength against imaginary perils. With Jove's ancient "non-imitable thunder" match a greater thunder of your own,

devised by art. Let the voyages of daring men who discovered
unimagined places and areas be your encouragement to chart
the whole intellectual globe, ever bearing in mind the words of
the prophet, "Many shall run to and fro, and knowledge shall
be increased."

The philosophical work which Bacon publishes while Solicitor-General, *De sapientia veterum* (*Concerning the Wisdom of
the Ancients*, 1609), contains two dedications, one to Robert
Cecil, Lord Salisbury, Chancellor of the University of Cambridge, the other to the University of Cambridge itself, in the
"hope," as the author writes, "that the inventions of the learned
may receive some accession by these labours of mine." The
work, written in Latin, proves to be popular, and is reprinted
and translated into English and Italian. The *Wisdom of the
Ancients* presents a philosophy both naturalistic and materialistic, and yet in such a manner that not even a member of the
Spanish Inquisition, as the author says, could find fault with
any of its contents. Bacon in this writing interprets pagan parables only, yet in all his thinking he never finds reason to dis-
tinguish a "Christian" natural philosophy—something quite
independent of revealed theology—from a "heathen" philosophy of nature. Here he presents in a disarming manner some of
those major principles of his naturalism which most of the
clergy and laity consider an erroneous or a disturbing philosophy.

In the Preface, Bacon affirms the opinion that the ancient
fables have "hidden and involved meaning." He tells Salisbury
in a dedication that "parable has ever been a kind of arc, in
which the most precious portions of the sciences were de-
posited." The author has already esteemed the fable, as a vehicle
of philosophic thought, sufficiently to incorporate in a short
writing, *Cogitationes de scientia humana* (*Thoughts on Human
Knowledge*), the myths of the Sisters of the Giants or Fame,

Coelum or the Origin of Things, Proteus or Matter, and Metis or Counsel. Later, in his *De augmentis*, he will employ for philosophical purposes the fables of Pan, or Nature; Perseus, or War; and Dionysus, or Desire. One of his last writings, *De principiis atque originibus (Concerning Principles and Origins)*, will include a treatment of the myths of Cupid, or Eros, and Coelum, or Uranus.

The *Wisdom of the Ancients* contains philosophical readings of thirty-one fables. Some of these interpretations are as follows. Pentheus, according to poetic myth, climbed a tree in order to observe the secret mysteries of Bacchus. In punishment, he became frenzied and saw everything double. Then, as he journeyed to the city of Thebes, he saw in his madness one Thebes in front of him and one behind, and knew not whither to proceed. The calamity of Pentheus, says Bacon, is a poetic representation of that perplexed, vacillating state of mind which is to be found in those who have aspired to penetrate what God keeps within his own curtain, through mistaking the light of nature for divine wisdom. Similarly, the punishment of Prometheus for his attempt on the chastity of Minerva signifies the plight of those who, having failed to keep faith free from incursions by human sense and reason, are doomed to perpetual struggle with fictional philosophies and heretical religions.

Another story concerning Prometheus singles out man's creation from other events, because the intellectual part of man, as the poets teach, is not the product of matter and is not brought forth by natural generation. The fable of Proteus makes clear that matter, and not man, is the oldest of created things. Matter spans the past, the present, and the future. Like Proteus, matter assumes all shapes, from fire and water to organic bodies. While Proteus himself represents matter, his flock represents the species of animals, plants, and minerals. Proteus may be put in chains and can be made, as matter can be made by art, to assume more shapes than those found in the recognized species of things. Proteus is also a knowing prophet. If one were to understand, as Proteus does, the "sum and general issue" of nature one would also comprehend both the composition of the whole world and the constitutive forms of individual things.

Coelum, according to poetic story, was the most ancient of the gods. His generative parts were removed with a scythe by his own son, Saturn. This son also devoured his own children, of whom only one, Jupiter, escaped. Jupiter in turn overpowered Saturn, cast him into Tartarus, and removed his generative parts. The teaching of this fable, says Bacon, is in agreement with the philosophy of Democritus, which asserts the eternity of matter and denies the eternity of the world. The deprivation of further power to create indicates allegorically that the totality of matter remains fixed and the *quantum* of nature undergoes neither increase nor decrease. The devouring by Saturn and his treatment by Jupiter represent the shaping and reshaping of the fabric of nature, and its perturbations and changes.

The fable of Pan has to do with the universal frame of things. To Pan are ascribed horns, broad at the base and narrow at the tip. The teaching in this case is clear: nature, when understood, is seen to be like a pyramid. At its base are infinite particulars, farther up numerous species, higher still genera, and at the top a single principle. Pan's horns ascend to heaven, but only touch it, because what is beyond nature pertains to God and is reserved to God's own Revelation. Pan is also given a biform nature, brute in the lower part and human in the upper. By this is signified the mixed nature of natural species. Strictly speaking, there are no simple species in nature. Man has in him something of the brute, the brute something of the vegetable, the vegetable something of the mineral. Again, the imputing of but few amours to Pan is not without meaning. Pan, who represents the natural universe, married Echo. Echo, who represents science, reflects nature as it is.

The story of Vulcan's forced attentions on Minerva shows how art, here figuratively portrayed by Vulcan, cannot subdue nature except through an understanding of her ways through patient and diligent research. Atalanta, who represents art, lost her race by turning aside to seize the fruit—in her case an apple —before the full course of her trial was undergone. The Sphinx's riddle and its solving in the myth which bears her name, makes a similar point. Those who attempt a hasty solution of the riddle of nature are certain to end with nothing more than false promises and pretensions.

Many of the stories associated with the name of Prometheus contain good counsel for scientific inquirers. In the contests held in his honor, when the light of a torch went out its bearer stepped aside to let the one who came after proceed in pursuit of the victory. The application of this fable to scientific endeavor is obvious. Aristotle, Euclid, Ptolemy, and some others made lively beginnings, but their successors were not to carry the torch.

Prometheus is said to have stolen fire from heaven and given it to mankind. Men, far from grateful for the gift, arraigned the giver before Jupiter. Jupiter in return rewarded the human race with the present of perpetual youth. Man put this gift on the back of an ass. The ass became thirsty on his way home and sought relief at a spring guarded by a serpent, which demanded as the price of the water the object the ass was carrying on his back. The price was paid, and mankind lost its gift of perpetual youth. In this parable perpetual youth signifies man's achievement in medicine and other arts and sciences. The slow pace of the ass, his turning aside on his way, and his surrendering of a precious gift for an immediate satisfaction all shadow forth those events which are to be found in the history of human inquiry.

The accounts given by the poets of Cupid, or Love, involve not one person but two, the elder Cupid, the oldest of the gods, and the younger Cupid, the son of Venus and youngest of the gods. The elder Cupid is said to be without parents. Both are represented as blind, naked, given to archery, and perpetually in a state of infancy. The infancy of Cupid represents "the appetite or instinct of primal matter; or to speak more plainly, *the natural motion of the atom*; which is indeed the original and unique force that constitutes and fashions all things out of matter." One Cupid's lack of parentage signifies the fact that matter, which contains causal agents, cannot be regarded philosophically as having any cause outside itself. There can be no First Cause in natural philosophy, Bacon argues, because if there were, the line of causes would be broken, and causation as such rendered incomprehensible through the adduction of an uncaused cause. The blindness of Cupid is a poetic representation of the the truth that God's created works are not to be interpreted as so many continued acts of Providence but as the operations of the parts of matter in motion.

Bacon now interrupts his reading of the parable, and turns to history. The investigation of motion, "wherein lies all vigour of operation," has, he says, been "negligent and languid." There are those who take a leap beyond nature and ascribe all motion to the immediate operation of God. Another account, by the Peripatetics, in terms of privation is the naming of a problem and not the explanation of a fact. The Epicurean opinion that motion is a fortuitous agitation of atoms is an example of trifling and ignorance. Democritus does better than the others, because having attributed to the atom dimension and shape, he assigns it two motions: a primary motion to the centre, where all atoms gravitate; and a secondary motion engendered in conflict whereby that which has less matter is forced away from the center by what has more. This limited doctrine of Democritus will not, however, explain either the movements of the celestial bodies or the phenomena of rarefaction and condensation.

To return to the parable: Cupid is described as an infant always, for the reason that the atoms, of which all things are composed, remain eternally what they are. He is said to be naked because only atoms can, in the last analysis, be so described. Cupid's skill in archery represents the action of matter through distance in space, for any doctrine of atoms and the void, or vacuum, must imply the action of the atom at a distance. The younger Cupid is called the youngest of the gods because he cannot operate until the species of things have been brought into existence, when he brings the appetition within matter to bear on particular objects. His mother, Venus, appropriately represents the general "appetite" of things for production and conjunction through locally contiguous causes.

The rest of Bacon's philosophical writings between 1607 and 1612 are mainly of two sorts, drafts of parts of the *New Organon* and pieces having to do with local motion, as the dominant factor in the explanation of the operations of nature and art—as befits a materialistic philosophy. Motion is the subject of the author's first attempt, presaged in his *Commentarius solutus* (1608), to furnish a "table" of inductively discovered knowledge. His second *Thread of the Labyrinth*, in which the author undertakes to provide a clue to the maze which is nature, includes within its title "the legitimate inquiry concerning motion." This short writing treats of variants of local motion. The several types of change, or "motion," traditionally recognized in the schools as generation and decay, increase and decrease, alteration in quality, and transference in place are all regarded by Bacon, a materialistic naturalist, as variants of local motion, the contiguous operation of the constituents of matter. Causation is not allowed a teleological pattern. There are to be no final causes in natural philosophy. Local causation is to prevail in the sphere of art, which, contrary to what Peripatetics teach, is not to be sundered from nature. In the *Descriptio globi intellectualis* (*Description of the Intellectual Globe*), a work concerned mainly with the motions of the heavens, Bacon declares that "things artificial differ from things natural, not in form or essence but only in the efficient; that man has in truth no power over nature except that of motion—the power, I say, of putting natural bodies together or separating them—and that the rest is done by nature working within. Whenever, therefore, there is a possibility of moving natural bodies towards one another or away from one another, man and art can do everything; where there is no such possibility, they can do nothing."

XIV

THE NEW ORGANON

During the years between Salisbury's death, in 1612, and the end of his own political career, in 1621, while he carries heavy burdens of state, Bacon's philosophical writings are few. Between 1614 and 1617 he composes the first draft of the *New Atlantis*. This work in design is to include two constitutions, one for an ideal commonwealth and another for a scientific brotherhood, or order. Only the second is written, however, and that merely in outline. During the same period, Bacon prepares one scientific history, *De fluxu et refluxu maris* (*Of the Ebb and Flow of the Sea*), and before 1620 draws up a set of rules for the collecting and sorting of observations and experiments. The latter he calls *Parasceve ad historiam naturalem et experimentalem* (*Preparative toward a Natural and Experimental History*). The author is also working between 1613 and 1619 on several pieces obviously intended for incorporation in some manner within his *New Organon*. These include *De interpretatione naturae, sententiae XII* (*On the Interpretation of Nature, XII Judgments*) and *Aphorismi et consilia, de auxiliis mentis et accensione luminis naturalis* (*Aphorisms and Counsels, concerning the Mind's Aids and the Kindling of Natural Light*).

In 1620, Bacon is in his sixtieth year, and he has not yet published any work in representation of his instauration, as he now conceives it to be. There is still no lessening of his public labors. Now, in order to put some parts of the instauration "out of peril," he decides to publish his *Novum organum sive indicia de interpretatione naturae (The New Organon or True Directions concerning the Interpretation of Nature)*. This is the most philosophically comprehensive of all his writings to date; to its preparation all of his previous philosophical pieces have, in one way or another, been either preparatory or contributory. As a book on scientific direction it is far from complete. Readers will be made to understand that the cause of his haste in publishing it now, is "not ambition for himself, but solicitude for the work; that in case of his death there might remain some outline and project of that which he had conceived, and some evidence of his . . . inclination towards the benefit of the human race." The author calls the work the Second Part of the Great Instauration. To this major treatise he adds a proem; an epistle dedicatory to the King, saying that its contents are "totally new in their very kind"; a preface to the Great Instauration; the plan of the Great Instauration; and the argument of its six parts. The author attaches to it in publication the *Parasceve ad historiam naturalem et experimentalem* and also *Catalogus historiarum particularium secondum capita (A Catalogue of Particular Histories by Title)*. This catalogue lists one hundred and thirty topics for investigation. The *Preparative* will serve to show something of the Third Part of the instauration, as will certain experiments included within the Second Book of the *New Organon;* the *Catalogue* will indicate the range of subjects requiring investigation. The First Book of the *New Organon* will present, too, something of the First Part of the instauration, which is now to include an account of Idols, in a partial "refutation" of the doctrines and the methods of past and present philosophies. The deficiencies of these old and new systems and the mode of their support and continuance by learned men and institutions have already been exposed in another manner in the *Advancement of*

Learning (1605). A Latin translation of this early work can be prepared, with some textual additions and deletions to make the whole more palatable to Continental readers. The amended and translated treatise will not be fully adequate for the purpose, but since there is no other appropriate writing at hand or in prospect, it will have to do as a representation of the First Part of the instauration. The translation will be published, as soon as it has been made ready (in 1623), under the title *De dignitate et augmentis scientiarum* (*Of the Dignity and Advancement of Learning*).

In the Proem, attached to the *New Organon*, Bacon states that by this treatise he intends to inaugurate "a total reconstruction of sciences, arts, and all human knowledge, raised upon the proper foundations." By the method which it contains he hopes to restore "to its perfect and original condition, or if that may not be . . . to a better condition" than at present, "that commerce between the mind of man and the nature of things, which is more precious than anything on earth, or at least than anything which is of the earth." In the Plan of the Work, the author explains that the Great Instauration consists of six parts:

1. The Divisions of the Sciences.
2. The New Organon, or Directions concerning the Interpretation of Nature.
3. The Phenomena of the Universe, or a Natural and Experimental History for the foundation of Philosophy.
4. The Ladder of the Intellect.
5. The Forerunners, or Anticipation, of the New Philosophy.
6. The New Philosophy, or Active Science.

The First Part of the instauration exhibits the knowledge at present in possession of the human race and indicates those areas of the intellectual globe which still remain unknown and uncultivated. The scientific cultivation of the latter will proceed, the author says, within those newly transformed and newly classified sciences which have been described already in the *Ad-*

vancement of Learning. A new classification of the sciences is required for the present instauration because "in adding to the sum total you necessarily alter the parts and sections; and the received divisions of the sciences are fitted only to the received sum of them as it stands now." The Second Part of the instauration is given over to a new method. This method differs from the old logic in end, order of demonstration, and point of departure. Its aim is the invention not of arguments but of arts, not the bringing of things into agreement with principles and definitions already assumed by the inquirer but the discovering of axioms which conform to nature's operations. The starting point of the new logic is not, then, a fixed position of argument, seized upon after a hasty flight of the intellect to a first notion or principle. Its demonstration proceeds from particulars, ordered according to their agreements and disagreements as affirmative and negative instances, to lesser axioms, and then gradually through middle axioms of greater generality to the highest axioms of the greatest possible comprehension. Each axiom, of whatever degree of generality, will be tried by the observation of the particulars which it presumes to include within its range. There is to be no setting down at the outset of certain axioms as so many determining principles, things which, according to the thinking of members of the traditional schools, underlie and separate the several sciences. The foundations of knowledge must be sunk deeper than these, into things themselves, where no such separation can be found.

The Third Part of the instauration will consist of a large body of natural history. This history, which is to be collected and ordered to meet the requirements of the method of the Second Part, is indispensable to scientific investigation. "What I have often said," Bacon writes in the *Preparative*, "I must here emphatically repeat, that if all the wits of all the ages had met or shall hereafter meet together; if the whole human race had applied or shall hereafter apply themselves to philosophy, and the whole earth had been or shall be nothing but academies and colleges and schools of learned men; still without such a natural and experimental history, such as I am going to prescribe, no progress worthy of the human race could have been made or can be made in philosophy and the sciences."

The Fourth Part of the instauration will consist of exemplary results obtained through the employment of the new inductive process, while the Fifth Part, which is only for temporary use, will embrace conclusions reached through incomplete observation and experiment not as yet under the control of a rigorous induction. Such inferences, somewhat like the inventions of chance, will serve as wayside inns for temporary rest. To vary the metaphor, they will be like interest given before the principal is returned. Eventually, as many of their number as can be proved will be incorporated within a system of axioms. The Sixth Part of the instauration, to which all the rest is subservient and ministrant, is a philosophy to be established according to the rules of a severe, legitimate, inductive interpretation of natural history.

In the First Book of the *New Organon* proper, discussions of questions contained in the author's earlier published and unpublished writings reappear in aphoristic summary. Criticisms of past and present philosophers become, in the main, examples of the Idols of the human mind. Bacon has entertained a doctrine of Idols for some thirty-seven years, ever since he began to write the *Fertilizing Birth of Time*. He has derived the meaning of the term Idol, as false phantom or image, from a statement of Democritus to the effect that in the act of perception *eidola*, or images, on entering the human soul, produce conventional, and not true or genuine, opinions. Idols, Bacon now explains, are either adventitious, coming from without the mind, or innate, within the mind's constitution. The sources of the adventitious sort are the doctrines of sects of philosophers and traditional methods of demonstration. These Idols may be eradicated with difficulty. The inherent kind can only be controlled.

Idols may be classified according to four kinds: those of the Tribe, of the Cave, of the Market Place, of the Theatre. The Idols of the Tribe have their foundation in human nature itself. The human understanding is like an uneven mirror which distorts and discolors objects by mingling its own nature with what it receives. The understanding is prone, for example, to find in the world an order and a regularity not in keeping with facts. It sees "parallels and conjugates and relatives" which do not exist; hence the fictional opinions of Aristotle and his followers that the motion of the heavenly bodies, as "perfect," is circular, and that a fourth element, "fire," must be added to three others, the cold, the moist, and the dry, to make a quaternion.

Once the human understanding has adopted an opinion agreeable to itself, it tends to bring everything it can muster to this belief's support. Negative instances of particulars which might prove embarrassing are disregarded, or taken care of by a new definition, or set aside as so many "monsters"—as the writings of Aristotle and his followers make manifest. The human understanding, again, cannot rest in what it comprehends; it must press on to what it cannot know. The treatment of causes is a case in point. Thinkers who deal with natural causes will have it that beyond these lies a further cause which itself cannot be part of a causal order, but must be an uncaused cause, or "first cause." After unsuccessful attempts to describe this agent remotely, the rationalists fall back on what is closest to hand, their desires and volitions, and crown their thinking with a doctrine of final causation.

The human understanding is not a "dry light," but ever "receives an infusion from the will and affections." What a man prefers, that he takes to be true. He shrinks from difficult questions because of his own impatience and their narrowing of his hope. He avoids the deeper problems of nature because of religious superstition; neglects the examination of mean and vulgar things because of pride; and refuses to entertain new opinions from fear of public disapproval. The intellect and the senses, man's enabling faculties in inquiry, can both produce grave misrepresentations of fact. The senses can be dull, incompetent, and deceptive. The inner workings of organisms, subtle changes in inorganic bodies, very slow and very fast motions, and comparable phenomena lie beyond their range. Instruments such as microscopes and telescopes, devised for their help, are not sufficient to overcome their inherent weakness. In the interpretation of nature the evidence they supply may be taken as crucial only in the trial of experiment; it is never sufficient for the establishment of an axiom. The intellect, for its part, is given to reliance on abstractions of its own making. It confers reality and stability on things which are nonexistent. In its speculation, without stopping for investigation, tedious or otherwise, it will soar, like a bird in flight, to "first" notions of the mind and what it takes to be the first or most general principles of things.

The second sort of Idols, those of the Cave, are several and varied. Their sources, which are many, include the mental and bodily constitutions, the habits, the trainings, and the accidental circumstances of the individuals concerned. Some investigators become attached to certain studies, more especially those with which they have taken great pains, or in which they deem themselves authorities, or of which they consider themselves the authors. Such inquirers adjust their findings to their special preoccupations. Aristotle, for example, puts his natural science under the rule of his logic of abstractions, and Gilbert makes the philosophy of nature accord with his theory of magnetism. Some inquirers are given to the admiration of antiquity, others to a desire for novelty. Some are strong on differences, distinctions, and minutiae; others find resemblances everywhere and readily compose comprehensive systems. The atomists, like

Leucippus and Democritus, are so absorbed with particles that they forget the structure of things; other philosophers of many sorts are so lost in admiration of nature's complexities that they fail to regard her simplicities.

Of all Idols, those of the Market Place are the most troublesome. These have to do with words. It is a common supposition that the reason controls words; but the truth is that words, having been put into commerce, lay hold on the understanding and place it in bondage. When an honest observer would alter his thoughts to bring them into conformity with the structures of investigated things, resistant words stand in his way. Definition does not ease the situation, as some philosophers suppose—except, of course, in mathematics, where the beginning and the end lie in definition of terms—because definitions consist of words, and beget new words. This fact accounts for the disputations among philosophical sects, which are concerned, not with things, but with the meanings of terms. The Idols which words set up and perpetuate are either names for things which do not exist or false names for things which do. Among the former sort are Fortune, Prime Mover, Planetary Orbits, Element of Fire. False names, which are commonly the result of hasty and confused abstracting, differ in degrees of error. The names of common substances, such as chalk and mud, are the least faulty. Examples of greater confusion and error are the Peripatetic Generation, Corruption, Alteration, Augmentation, and Diminution. Perhaps the most faulty of all terms in natural philosophy are those which stand for the so-called qualities of terrestrial bodies, Heavy, Light, Rare, Dense.

The Idols of the Theatre consist of philosophical systems which, like the fictions of the stage, are more elegant and compact than things themselves are. To produce these, some philosophers make a great deal out of a few things, and other philosophers take a little out of each of many things. The productions of the empirical schools are as mixed and disordered in content as their experiments are aimless and dark in conception. The combining of pieces taken from disparate things is most evident, however, in the corrupting of philosophy by mixing it with theology. This has been going on since the time of Pythagoras. In recent years it has shown itself in the raising of a natural philosophy on the first chapter of Genesis and the Book of Job, to the production of fictional philosophy and heretical religion. The ambition to draw too much out of a few things, however diligently and laboriously examined in the beginning, as in Gilbert's case, say, and perhaps that of Telesio, too, has in age after age brought science and philosophy to a standstill, sometimes to ruin.

"To what purpose are these brain-creations and idle displays of power?" Bacon is to ask in his *Historia naturalis et experimentalis* (*Natural and Experimental History*, 1622). "In ancient times there were philosophical doctrines in plenty; doctrines of Pythagoras, Philolaus, Xenophanes, Heraclitus, Empedocles, Parmenides, Anaxagoras, Leucippus, Democritus, Plato, Aristotle, Zeno, and others. All these invented systems of the universe, each according to his own fancy, like so many arguments of plays. . . . Nor in our age, though by reason of the institutions of schools and colleges, wits are more restrained, has the practice entirely ceased; for Patricius, Telesius, Brunus, Severinus the Dane, Gilbert the Englishman, and Campanella have come upon the stage with fresh stories, neither honoured by approbation nor elegant in argument. . . . There is not and never will be an end or limit to this; one catches at one thing, another at another; each has his own favourite fancy; pure and open light there is none; every one philosophizes out of the cells of his own imagination, as out of Plato's cave; the higher wits with more acuteness and felicity, the duller, less happily but with equal pertinacity. And now of late by the regulation of some learned and (as things now are) excellent men (the former variety and licence having, I suppose, became wearisome), the sciences are confined to certain and prescribed authors and, thus restrained, are imposed upon the old and instilled into the young; so that now (to use the sarcasm of Cicero concerning Caesar's year), the constellation of Lyra rises by edict, and authority is taken for truth, not truth for authority. Which kind of institution and discipline is excellent for present use, but precludes all prospect of improvement. . . . I know not whether we more distort the facts of nature or our own wits; but we clearly impress the stamp of our own image on the creatures and works of God, instead of carefully examining and recognizing in them the stamp of the Creator Himself. Wherefore our dominion over creatures is a second time forfeited, not undeservedly; and whereas after the fall of man some power over the resistance of creatures was still left to him—the power of subduing and managing them by true and solid arts—yet this too through our insolence, and because we desire to be like God and to follow the dictates of our own reason, we in great part lose. If therefore there be any humility towards the Creator, any reverence for or disposition to magnify His works, any charity for man and anxiety to relieve his sorrows and necessities, any love of truth in nature, any hatred of darkness, any desire for the purification of the understanding, we must entreat men again and again to discard, or at least set apart for a while, these volatile and pre-posterous philosophies, which have preferred theses to hypotheses, led experience captive, and triumphed over the works of God; and to approach with humility and veneration to unroll the volume of Creation, to linger and meditate therein, and with minds washed clean from opinions to study it in purity and integrity. For this is that sound and language which went forth into all lands, and did not incur the confusion of Babel; this should men study to be perfect in, and becoming again as little children condescend to take the alphabet of it into their hands, and spare no pains to search and unravel the interpretation thereof, but pursue it strenuously and persevere even unto death."

Portions of the First Book of the *New Organon* and the first part of the Second Book are given over to an account of the present state of scientific inquiry and to arguments for its reform. These are mainly amplifications of statements already made by the author in other writings. The remainder of the present work deals with a new method of induction. This, Bacon again takes pains to inform his readers, is not to be confused with mere empiricism, or with the practices of the past which are said to be inductive. The author is not an empiric who collects a heap of observations and experiments without a definite cause, nature, or form in mind. He does not rely merely on senses and particulars for his hypotheses or his proof. He begins with a nature, a form, or a cause, to be defined through an examination of agreeing and disagreeing instances of particulars under observation and experiment. The senses, to which these particulars are for the most part available, can try the experiment, but only operation can establish the axiom which scientific definition becomes.

Bacon does not attempt to explain knowing in terms of its "logical" content, like Plato; or as process initiated by the organism's contact with external objects and ending with the "informing" of the rational soul, like Aristotle; or as physical impact, like Democritus. He does not say where sense, reason, forms, and axioms "come from." He finds these four factors available like the planets in the heavens and like verdure and heat on the earth. He does not "make" them in the manner in which an epistemologist makes them to be what an epistemologist wants them to be for an explanation. Bacon is aware that the attempts in philosophy to explain the origin of concepts and axioms and the acts of sense or reason have resulted in one or other several unsatisfactory things: the scepticism of persons like Pyrrho, the "image" theory of Democritus, the assignment by Plato, Aristotle, and the Stoics of a rationale to nature—a device for putting "mind" into material things. In any event, Bacon's own placing of reason within the province of revealed theology precludes a turning from the method of science and its employment in physical inquiry into the byways of an epistemology of sense or of reason, or of a mixture of the two. Bacon thinks that by his new method he has brought about "a true and lawful marriage between the empirical and the rational faculty, the unfortunate separations ... of which" by those who have advanced theories of knowledge "have thrown into confusion all the affairs of the human family." Having done this, Bacon draws the curtain on their bedchamber and refuses to interrupt or impede their nuptial activities by epistemological descant.

Bacon asserts that his method of inquiry is not to be confused with a "wandering" Socratic induction which in Plato's case becomes the definition of essences unavailable to sense and removed from particulars. Nor is it to be identified with the induction discussed by Aristotle. Aristotle in the beginning recognized two sorts of induction. The first of these was a "perfect" kind which imposed an impossible task on the inquirer by requiring the examination of every particular of the species of thing under investigation. This was soon put aside by the author, who proceeded to employ induction by definition, which made every object that failed to conform to his own definitions an exception. Some of these exceptions Aristotle was able to accomodate by shifts of definition; the others remained for him "monsters." Aristotle also cut off his sciences, one from the others, through axioms which defined several independent and mutually exclusive areas of inquiry. After doing this he made deduction by syllogism the method of demonstrating whatever lay within each separate science. This deduction was based on the first notions of the mind, gained by intuition; on first principles, or axioms, of the several sciences, gained by intuition and secured by definition; and on the middle terms of demonstrating syllogisms, secured by definition. Aristotle provided no satisfactory means for establishing the middle term of the syllogism on which his deduction depended. The main objection, then, to the whole business of Aristotle's deduction—still regarded as the proper method of scientific discovery and proof by learned persons within and without the Universities—is the obvious fact that his syllogism did not apply to the "first notions" of the mind nor to the "axioms" of the sciences, and consequently could never establish a lesser proposition with a true middle term, except in a purely formal and, as far as scientific discovery is concerned, a fruitless way.

In academic demonstrations of "truth," argument by syllogism hangs on the defined middle term. Here, this term is "elected at the liberty of every man's invention." Such a practice will not serve, however, in the investigation of nature, whose end is not the defeat of an opponent in verbal argument but the discovery of actual forms, causes, or laws. Aristotle, after he had discarded his "perfect" induction, which involved the examination and enumeration of every particular instance of the form under examination, and therefore was not feasible, attempted to compensate himself for his loss by bringing induction under syllogism. His classic statement in the matter, which Bacon most likely knew first- or second-hand, is this: "Man, horse, and mule [i] are long-lived animals [ii]; man, horse, and mule [i] are bileless animals [iii]; therefore all bileless animals [iii] are long-lived animals [ii]." In this case the validity of the argument obviously rests on the assumption that [iii] is no wider than [i]. Such a demonstration as this exemplifies three of what Bacon regards as great defects in Peripatetic proof: first, induction by simple enumeration of particulars or species; second, induction by positive instances only; and third, the too hasty and arbitrary definition of terms, without a full citing, sifting, and aligning of instances. Proof with these defects leaves the conclusion in the realm of extreme probability or, if you would have it, of mere improbability.

There can be, reflects Bacon, but two ways of philosophizing about nature. The first of these is to fly speculatively from sense and particulars to the most general axioms—with all that this practice entails—and, after taking these as settled truths, to deduce from them "middle" axioms. This is the proceeding now in fashion. In the other way, as yet untried and untrodden, axioms are derived from sense and particulars by gradual ascent until the most general axioms are reached. Here the senses are guarded and made subject to rule and correction; that mental operation which is said by Aristotle to follow upon the perception of sense is for the greatest part discarded; and the intellect will be controlled at every step. If the rules of a new sort of logic do not intervene from the beginning, and the intellect is allowed to soar suddenly to high abstractions and great generalities, as the old logic permits and encourages, then no logic will ever be able to set matters right again. Certainly, if the syllogism is to enter the picture at either an early or a late stage in inductive progression, it will probably do nothing more than confirm error. The new inquiry will proceed by gradual stages—except, of course, in purely mathematical thinking—and at every stage will bring such universalities as the intellect may provide back to particulars for proving. Thus, it will always both ascend and descend.

The new induction begins with experience duly sifted, prepared and digested, and from this educes axioms. These axioms suggest more universal axioms and, in turn and consequence, new experiments. At every stage of the procedure the axiom must descend to particulars for verification, in order to show that whatever it asserts as principle is operative as cause in nature. No axiom is worthy of the name unless its representation of the schematisms and the processes of nature can be established by the operations it elicits from nature when bodies are put together according to its formula. Nothing obscure, then, nothing occult, nothing general that cannot be shown through particulars directly or indirectly available to the senses, will do at any stage of search for the truth of nature. Care must be taken, therefore, to see that each axiom proposed by the intellect is framed to the measure of the sort of instance it is presumed to cover. As it goes beyond these in hypothesis, suggesting other experiments and axioms, both it and the axioms which it suggests must be brought back to particulars for proving and demonstration by operative causes. A wider hypothesis, when it has been proved, will manifest the possibility of great "clusters" of discoveries. If such an hypothesis transcends the boundaries of any one of the traditional sciences, so much the better. It has already put that science on the way to drawing sustenance from a larger body of scientific truth than its own. Any "profound and radical alteration" of nature will depend on general axioms. The same is true of the knowledge of things on which man cannot experiment as, for example, the heavenly bodies. A full knowledge of these bodies can result only from comprehensive discoveries respecting motion and such "natures" as magnetism, attraction, and "spontaneous" rotation.

The tasks confronting the scientific investigator are of two sorts, one speculative and the other operative. "Of a given nature to discover the form, or true specific difference, or nature-engendering nature, or source of emanation (for these are the terms which come nearest to a description of the thing), is the work and aim of Human Knowledge." "On a given body to generate and superinduce a new nature or new natures is the work and aim of Human Power." The form of which we speak may be regarded as a nature, a cause, a law. These four terms are all convertible, one with the others. The choice of a term in a particular instance is determined by use in context. "The form of a thing is the very thing itself." "Forms are the laws of pure act." "When I speak of forms," Bacon writes, "I mean nothing more than those laws and determinations of absolute actuality which govern and constitute any simple nature, as heat, light, weight, in every kind of matter and subject which is susceptible of them." The forms of the new philosophy, then, are not to be confused with Plato's Ideas, which are not materiate or within particulars, nor with Aristotle's abstract forms, nor with the atoms of Democritus. Democritus does affirm, however, something of great worth and consequence when he asserts that formed matter and its configurations and changes are the proper objects of inquiry, because "forms are figments of the human mind" unless they be regarded as "laws of action." Aristotle, on the other hand, employs one of his abstract forms to mark *wherefrom* the operation of his formless matter proceeds and another to mark *whereto* this proceeds, but he fails to provide an explanation of the process itself which is brought about by cause within formed matter.

Aristotle is content with the supposition, which readily follows the slight observation of things, that nature contains primary forms which she seeks to educe as species. He separates the members of these natural species, not only from "monsters" —so-called because his ordinary definitions cannot accommodate them—but also from works of art. He maintains that in the case of the last an artificial "form" is added to one already in nature. Bacon cannot countenance Aristotle's segregation of species, monsters, and works of art, each from the others, nor his separation of matter and form even in conception. Matter, for Bacon, is not something deprived, formless, indeterminate, and inert, but a formed and active entity. It has within it causes and laws of lesser and greater generality, from which issue, as components of one body or system, without segregation of parts, all the particulars in nature, all so-called "marvels," and all works of art. The form is the law of actual operation in matter. Even as a civil measure has its clauses, so the more general laws of nature have subsidiary laws confined to lesser areas of natural things. By the same token, some forms are more inclusive in operation than others. Here the reader should be cautioned, says

Bacon, lest he imagine that a greater form—which is always the very nature of the object concerned—is composed of lesser forms. Such is not the case. The more general form has a more general authority in operation, and this authority cannot be divided, any more than one law, one nature, one cause can be divided into part laws, part natures, or part causes. "Every body contains within itself many forms of natures." These natures, which constitute bodies, are to be regarded—to use terms from the old logic—as predicates of which complex bodies are subjects. In the new logic, however, the "predicates" are fully explanatory of the subjects, and themselves come under more general forms or laws or causes. To take an example: motion in the case of the nature of heat is one thing; motion in the case of the nature of celestial bodies is another thing; yet, and as science progresses, we may hope to have an account of the nature of motion which includes a nature common to the motion of heat and the motion of the heavens. Then we shall have knowledge of a higher law, a more inclusive cause, a greater form.

The object pursued in science is not, then, the form of what the Peripatetics call a substance, but the forms, or laws, of matter. "To inquire the form of a lion, or of an oak, of gold," writes the author, "nay, even of water or air, is a vain pursuit; but to inquire the form of dense, rare, hot, cold, heavy, light, tangible, pneumatic, volatile, fixed, and the like . . . which (like the letters of the alphabet) are not many and yet make up and sustain the essences and forms of all substances:—this, I say, it is which I am attempting." The subject matter of inquiry becomes the more "disentangled . . . the nearer it approaches to simple natures . . . the business being transferred from the complicated to the simple; from the incommensurable to the commensurable; from surds to rational quantities; from the infinite and vague to the finite and certain, as in the case of the letters of the alphabet and the notes of music. And inquiries into nature have the best result when they begin with physics and end in mathematics."

Here Bacon is showing the influence of Plato's *Philebus*. Among the four "concauses" of the intelligible world, Plato lists the infinite, or indeterminate, and the finite, or determinate—the other two being the "mixture" of these and the *nous*, or Reason. Knowing, according to Plato in this dialogue, proceeds by bringing what is indeterminate under determination.

When an object undergoes change, a form previously present is superseded by another form—a doctrine in Plato's *Phaedo*. The object changes; the form does not. Forms, however general, remain simple and fixed. They are not transient or efficient causes in the old meaning of these terms. The cause does not precede the effect in time, for it is the object in actual operation. The form is the "very thing itself" within operative, material nature. Forms are materiate, and not abstract, or separate, or separable from matter. Matter is subject to inherent causation, but the cause itself is not caused. The only authority beyond any cause is a more general cause; to this it stands not in the relation of effect but as a species to a genus.

Having dealt with these general questions, Bacon proceeds in the remainder of the Second Book of the *New Organon* to provide specific examples of induction in use. These examples prove disappointing for several reasons. In the first place, they are lacking in full and precisely detailed and determined experiment and observation, because natural history of a "new kind" collected according to a "new principle" is simply not available in sufficient quantity or variety for the author's purpose. Secondly, Bacon pursues his investigation only as far as the preliminary stages of induction. Thirdly, of the eleven aids to the understanding which are promised, the author expounds by example only three. The other eight are presumably not ready for description and exemplification in 1620—nor will Bacon ever have or find time to make them ready.

The chief example of induction, in its preliminary stages, which the author now employs concerns the form of heat. For the investigation of this—and any other form—there should, says Bacon, be mustered from a natural history, assembled and sorted, particular instances which agree in possessing the nature in question. The author lists some twenty-seven instances of heat and indicates that others may be added. These instances include the rays of the sun—especially at noon in midsummer, rays of the sun when "condensed"—as on walls and in burning-glasses, eruptions of flames in volcanoes, ignited solids, boiling liquids, substances rubbed violently, quicklime sprinkled with water, natural baths, animal bodies, and so on. Such affirmative instances will constitute a Table of Essence and Presence. Next, a Table of Deviation or Absence in Proximity is to be prepared. This will contain examples from which the nature under investigation is absent. Such cases, Bacon observes, are of the greatest consequence, because even one contradictory example can render nugatory an axiom founded only on positive instances. The instances chosen for this second Table should be those which agree in as many ways as possible with those in the first, and yet disagree in one regard, the absence of the nature under investigation. Of such cases the author provides some thirty-two examples, among them the rays of the moon, the rays of the sun in the middle air, unheated liquids, oil mixed with quicklime. A third Table, Degrees of Comparison, will exhibit recorded observations of the increase and decrease of heat in the same subjects, and also in different subjects under comparison. There can be more or less heat in an object at one time than at another, because the operation of this species of form, or cause, may at times be restrained in degree by the operations of other forms or causes. Bacon provides some forty-one examples for use in the third Table: increase of heat in animals by motion and exercise, striking repeatedly on anvils, fires progressing against a strong wind, the sun's approaching the zenith, alternating coldness and heat in persons with intermittent fevers, air in process of losing heat, and so on.

After a lengthy examination of the instances presented in the three Tables, with special emphasis on negative instances, Bacon states the conclusion that the form, cause, or nature of heat is motion of a sort. That is not to say, he warns the reader, that heat generates motion, because heat itself, its quiddity, its essence, its nature, is motion. The motion which is heat is a species within the genus motion, set apart from other species of motion by certain differences. These differences are part of the definition of heat which, as the First Vintage or Commencement of Interpretation, may be stated thus: *"Heat is a motion, expansive, restrained, and acting in its strife upon the smaller particles of bodies."* However, expansiveness must be further qualified within the definition, because heat's motion, *"while it expands all ways, it has at the same time an inclination upwards."* Strife upon particles also must be qualified; in the case of heat this *"is not sluggish, but hurried and with violence."* Since the definition we are concerned with belongs to the operative part of physics as well as to the theoretical, it may be stated as a direction thus: *"If in any natural body you can excite a dilating or expanding motion, and can so repress this motion and turn it back upon itself, that the dilation shall not proceed equably, but have its way in one part and be counteracted in another, you will undoubtedly generate heat."*

Having provided the foregoing example of what he calls the Presentation of Instances to the Understanding and the Commencement of Interpretation, Bacon goes on to list nine more aids to the understanding. These are, Prerogative Instances, the Supports of Induction, the Rectification of Induction, the Variation of Inquiry according to the Nature of the Subject, Nature's Prerogative with Respect to Investigation—what should be investigated first and what afterwards, the Limits of Investigation or the Synopsis of All Natures in the Universe, the Bringing Down to Practice, the Preparations for Investigations, and the Ascending and Descending Scale of Axioms.

Prerogative Instances are so named because they deserve priority for their outstanding assistance to the senses and reason and their striking promotion of operative works. The author lists twenty-seven kinds. Of these, five sorts of Instances of the Lamp serve especially to enlighten the senses. Solitary Instances aid the reason by hastening the exclusion of the form; Migratory, Striking, Companionship, and Subjunctive Instances by indicating more clearly than others the affirmative of the form; Clandestine, Singular, Constitutive, Conformable, Alliance, and Bordering Instances by leading the intellect more immediately to genera. Other instances help to guard the reason against false forms and causes, to indicate aims for practice, to measure operation, and generally to facilitate the production of works by which axioms must ultimately be tried.

After an exposition in considerable detail of his twenty-seven sorts of Prerogative Instance, Bacon brings the *Novum organum* abruptly to a close. No account of the eight remaining aids to induction is given. The *Novum organum* of 1620 is incomplete, and destined to remain so. In the remaining years of his life, the author's philosophical writing is to consist almost wholly of works in representation of the Third Part of his Great Instauration.

XV

BACON AND NATURAL HISTORY

Between 1621 and 1626, the year of his death, Bacon composes an almost unbelievable number of works. Among these are a *History of the Reign of King Henry the Seventh;* in dialogue form, an *Advertisement touching an Holy War;* a *Preface to a Digest of the Laws of England;* the *Beginning of the History of the Reign of King Henry the Eighth;* a third edition of the *Essays;* the *Translation of Certain Psalms into English Verse.* The philosophical writings of this period include a revision of the *New Atlantis; De principiis atque originibus, secundum fabulas cupidinis et coeli: etc. (Concerning Principles and Origins, according to the Fables of Cupid and Coelum: etc.); Historia naturalis et experimentalis ad condendam philosophiam; sive phenomena universi (Natural and Experimental History for the Foundation of Philosophy; or Phenomena of the Universe); Abcedarium naturae (The Alphabet of Nature); Historia vitae et mortis (History of Life and Death); Historia gravis et levis (History of Heavy and Light); Historia sympathiae et antipathiae rerum (History of the Sympathy and Antipathy of Things—*preface only); *Historia sulphuris, mercurii, et salis (History of Sulphur, Mercury, and Salt—*preface only); *Sylva Sylvarum (A Forest of Materials); Historia densi*

et rari: necnon coitionis et expansionis materiae per spatia
(*History of Dense and Rare: or the Contraction and Expansion
of Matter in Space); Topica inquisitionis de luce et lumine* (*A
Topic of Inquiry Concerning Light and Illumination*).

By 1621 Bacon has become rather desperate over the problem of supplying a natural history sufficient in scope and variety
for the illustration of the Third Part of his instauration. Ever
since he began to entertain a philosophy of his own he had
always thought of its foundation in terms of natural history.
When this philosophy became definite in design the author
engaged himself in entreaty to members of the Court for aid
towards the collecting and ordering, under his own direction,
of a record of nature on a large scale. By the time he composes
his *Outline and Argument* (1606 or 1607), Bacon's thinking has
become certain about the characteristics of this natural history.
Some six years thereafter he wrote in his *Description of the
Intellectual Globe*: "I consider myself bound not to leave the
completion of this history which I pronounce deficient to
others, but to take it upon myself; because the more it may
seem a thing open to every man's industry, the greater fear there
is that they will go astray from my design; and I have therefore
marked it out as the third part of my instauration." In the same
vein he will write in the introductory part of his *Natural and
Experimental History* of 1622: "It has occurred to me . . . that
there are doubtless many wits scattered over Europe, capacious,
open, lofty, subtle, solid, and constant. What if one of them
were to enter into the plan of my Organum and try to use it?
He yet knows not what to do, nor how to prepare and address
himself to the work of philosophy. If indeed it were a thing
that could be accomplished by the reading of philosophical
books, or discussion, or meditation, he might be equal to the
work, whoever he be, and discharge it well." The author will,
therefore, provide examples of the sort of history required. He
will tell Prince Charles, to whom the present history is ad-

dressed: "I have bound myself as by a vow every month that the goodness of God (whose glory is sung as in a new song) shall add to my life, to complete and set forth one or more parts of [natural history]. . . . It may be also that others will be stirred by my example to a like industry; especially when they shall fully understand what it is that we are about."

Bacon's entreaty for aid actually began in 1592 with the request to Elizabeth's Lord Treasurer for a place to "carry" him, so that he might have more "wits" than his own for the pursuit of "industrious observations." It was continued in a request of a similar sort to Elizabeth within a "device" for her entertainment, the *Gesta Grayorum* of 1594. Eleven years later Bacon reminded another sovereign of the support given to Aristotle by the ruler of Macedon for the compiling of "an History of Nature," and told James, after reviewing learning's defects, that the improvement in prospect were *opera basilica*, works for a king. What is now required, he then said, "may be done by many, though not by any one . . . may be done by public designation, though not by private endeavour." In 1608, James' Solicitor-General conceived the plan of acquiring a "place to command wits and pens, Westminster, Eton, Winchester, especially Trinity College in Cambridge, St. John's in Cambridge, Magdalene College in Oxford, and bespeaking this betimes with the King, my Lord Archbishop, my Lord Treasurer."

Within a few years Bacon began to prepare a constitution, under the title *New Atlantis*, for a scientific foundation which he called Solomon's House. This college or brotherhood of benign, beneficent, assiduous inquiries would be dedicated to the "interpreting of Nature and the producing of great and marvellous works" for the benefit of mankind. This college Bacon described as "the noblest . . . upon the earth." It was to contain among many other resources for scientific inquiry, a mathematical house, with instruments for the study of the planets; horticultural gardens for the examination of soils, trees, shrubs, and herbs; enclosures for the observation of beasts, birds, insects, and fishes; theatres for anatomical dissections; laboratories for the study of diseases, medicines, foodstuffs, refrigeration, minerals, gems, the effects of natural and artificial baths, motions of sounds, tempests, earthquakes; houses for the production of new species of animals, birds, and plants; facilities for producing magnifying glasses, telescopes, gunpowder, instruments of war, silks, dyes, wines, boats which might travel under the seas and others which might fly in the air. Certain Fellows of the House would engage in experiments; others would travel abroad to obtain scientific information; others would concentrate on the production of operative works; some would draw experiments into "titles and tables"; still others would direct such new inquiries as might be indicated by earlier experiments, observations, and axioms; and some would raise discoveries by experiments "unto greater observations, axioms, and aphorisms." All members of the House would praise God daily for His marvellous works, and pray for His blessing on labors designed for "good and holy uses."

On presenting a copy of the *New Organon* to James, in 1620, the Lord Chancellor told his sovereign, in language befitting an address to this monarch, that one part of the instauration, "namely the compiling of a Natural and Experimental History . . . is but a new body of clay, whereinto your Majesty, by your countenance and protection, may breathe life." In simpler speech, he called upon his readers "to come forward and take part in what work is to be done." In the *Preparative Toward a Natural and Experimental History*, Bacon again reminded the King of what he had "said elsewhere," that the history, which "cannot be executed without great labour and expense; requiring as it does many people to help . . . is a kind of royal work." "My own strength," he continued, "is hardly equal to such a province"; the materials "on which the intellect has to work are so widely spread, that one must employ factors and merchants to go everywhere in search of them and to bring them in." After three more years had gone by, in 1623, Bacon, in the *De augmentis* (the Latin translation of the *Advancement of Learning*), was again addressing James, in complaint, with the words: "I often advisedly and deliberately throw away the dignity of my name and wit (if such be) while I serve human interests; and being one who should properly perhaps be an architect in philosophy and the sciences, I turn common labourer, hod man, anything that is wanted; taking upon myself the burden and execution of many things which must needs be done, and which others shun through an inborn pride."

Two years later, in 1625, Bacon would write Father Fulgentio that the Third Part of the instauration, the *Natural History*, "is plainly a work for a King or a Pope, or for some college or order, and it cannot be done as it should be by a private man's industry." In 1627, a year after Bacon died, Rawley, in preparing the *Sylva Sylvarum* for publication, would include in an epistle to the reader the following note: "I have . . . heard his lordship discourse that men (no doubt) will think many of the experiments contained in this collection to be vulgar and trivial, mean and sordid, curious and fruitless. . . . I have heard his lordship speak complainingly, that his lordship (who thinketh he deserveth to be an architect in this building) should be forced to be a workman and a labourer, and to dig clay and burn the brick; and more than that (according to the hard condition of the Israelites at the latter end), to gather the straw and stubble over all the fields to burn the brick withal. For he knoweth, that except he do it, nothing will be done; men are so set to despise the means of their own good."

In the *Preparative* of 1620, Bacon calls natural history "the nursing-mother" of active science or philosophy. Two years later, he writes in the preface to his *Natural and Experimental History*: "My Organum, even if it were completed, it would not without the Natural History much advance the Instauration of the Sciences, whereas the Natural History would advance it not a little. And therefore, I have thought it better and wiser by all means and above all things to apply myself to this work." The histories of the past, Bacon observes, are filled with fabulous experiments, fabricated "secrets," and frivolous records. No author except Pliny has dealt with nature in her threefold manifestation, that is, in her ordinary courses, her constraint by art, and her production of prodigies through her so-called "erring." Extant natural history is bulky, pleasingly varied, and often diligently prepared, yet when its fables, antiquities, quotations, "reported" opinions, controversies, philology, and ornaments are removed, it shrinks into very small compass. As a record, it fails almost entirely to meet the requirements of a "legitimate interpretation" of nature. Its content is better fitted to table talk than to the foundation of a philosophy. A new natural history, collected and arranged according to the rules of the new inductive method, must therefore be compiled.

In the *Preparative*, Bacon calls for a natural history free of mere antiquities, citations by doubtful authors, everything purely philological and ornamental, all superstitions, and tales by old wives and empirics. He invites histories of the arts, of those, in the first instance, which "exhibit, alter, and prepare" materials, such as cookery, agriculture, freezing, and the making of commodities, including glass, enamel, gunpowder, fires, and clocks, because these can provide needed information about nature's motions. The collecting of these and other natural histories is not to be a haphazard business because, when properly done, it involves the bringing of the infinity of particulars within determinate investigation. To this latter end, topics or points of inquiry should be noted, and tabulations and written records of the results of observation and experiment set down with exactitude. All natural history is to be carefully, even reverently, compiled, since it is the record of God's works and, therefore, is a second kind of Scripture. As such, it will include within its scope the movements of every sort of thing, including objects which learned men of the present think too "illiberal" and commonplace for inquiry, even childish, base, or filthy. Let the motions and virtues of all bodies, then, says Bacon, from the largest planet to the smallest terrestrial object, be determined; and let these be numbered and measured, so far as circumstances permit, because the combination of physics with mathematics engenders the most fruitful knowledge of causes, a knowledge which leads directly to the production of operative works.

Bacon's precipitancy in turning out "histories" of his own compiling resulted inevitably in a failure to produce any that were worthy of a place in his Great Instauration. Those written between 1608 and 1612 were definitely excluded by the author from the Third Part. Their contents were too "mixed" with general philosophical problems. Of the several histories prepared betwen 1622 and 1626, that of *Dense and Rare* is especially interesting because it contains the only extant record of the author's considerable application of mathematical quantity to experiment. This work includes some tentative hypotheses respecting rarefaction, condensation, and the vacuum. The *History of Winds* and the *History of Life and Death* are comprised of topics, observations, and provisional or hypothetical conclusions *(canones mobiles)*. The *Sylva Sylvarum* consists of a thousand paragraphs dealing with phenomena in the fields of inquiry even more varied than those indicated in the *New Atlantis*. The work contains some observations and results of experiments of the author's own, but, taken as a whole, the compilation is "bookish." The author has drawn, in great haste, on the writings of authors from Aristotle to the contemporary George Sandys. No one writer or investigator, nor even a thousand, could have prepared within a period of five years adequate histories of the subjects specified in the *Sylva Sylvarum*.

One can hardly avoid the question why the author, who was to produce a "Bacon-faced generation" less than two scores of years after his death, failed to acquire during his lifetime support and help for his inductive enterprise. An answer would include many factors. Burghley looked upon his nephew's philosophical preoccupation as a weakness in an aspirant for political place. Elizabeth took Bacon's mention of scientific gardens and the like as a compliment rather than a request. The learned James, whose mind was full of theology and learning of traditional sorts, thought little of the proposed philosophy of nature. The Universities disdained the "new learning." The author, notwithstanding his public career as Parliamentarian, judge, and administrator of state, was by nature an individualist —as, no doubt, every genius is. Bacon's political, legal, literary, historical, and philosophical concerns left him little time to frequent the company of others. What he did in these several regards he could in the main do too well to require, or to suffer, cooperation with others. Bacon had devoted friends, but their interests were chiefly political or literary. While he conceived his Great Instauration as a common effort under the principle of universal charity, he always looked upon himself as its one sufficient intellect, its architect, and its supreme director. When he sought aid from the Court, he saw himself either as the magnanimous superior of a foundation, or the employer of a large number of secretaries and factors who would carry out his benign bidding.

Bacon's instauration of knowledge and learning had inherent within its philosophy a great difficulty—the education, learning, and habitual mentality of his contemporaries considered. Its metaphysics was naturalistic and materialistic, nothing more or less than a generalized physics. The author had asserted that Democritus should be set above Plato, Aristotle, the Augustinians, and the Peripatetics; and required that philosophy, as something attained by the use of natural faculties, be completely

sundered in source and establishment from the truths of revealed theology. Had Bacon been less of a systematic thinker
and, as a scientific naturalist and not a philosophical materialist,
more of a recorder of nature, his enterprise might have fared
better from the beginning. His systematic philosophizing became a warning to his followers in the philosophical college
which became the Royal Society. They prudently excluded
questions of theology and metaphysics from their transactions,
and found a supporter in Charles II, who granted them a Royal
Charter.

Bacon, as an exponent of a materialistic metaphysics, enjoyed,
of course, one great advantage over contemporary Continental
thinkers: he could not be condemned before an Inquisition of
either a Romanist or a Genevan sort. He could not be sent to
the stake, like Giordano Bruno. The Reformation in England
had engendered ecclesiastical conflict, but it had produced a
considerable tolerance for theologico-philosophical speculation. James, to his discomfort, knew that his kingdom had
within its borders, his Church among its clergy, and his Privy
Council among its members, Aristotelians disposed toward and
Calvinists opposed to the mingling of philosophy and theology,
High Churchmen who were Aristotelians or Platonists and yet
maintained a belief in the Real Presence, and Puritans who professed no philosophy at all and thought the High Churchman's
belief idolatrous. But Bacon's scheme of reform was very extreme. The author was supplanting the prevailing Platonic and
Aristotelian ontologies with a universalized physics and was
seeking to transform academies of learning into laboratories designed for the production of "works." It was with such aims as
these that Bacon confronted a sovereign schooled in traditional
learning, prelates of Platonic and Aristotelian training, clergy
and laity who regarded a materialistic metaphysics as the work
of the devil, and heads, fellows, and graduates of the Universities whose exercises were based on the medieval trivium, and

whose books of study were largely the works of classical authors or writings derived from these. It can hardly be a subject for wonder, then, that Bacon's philosophical undertaking was to receive its initial support not from the Head of the Established Church, nor from members of the King's Council, nor from the clergy, nor from the Universities, but from a detached band of independent thinkers and experimenters.

Within a generation after his death, experimenters and Nonconformists of the Enthusiastic persuasion, who completely separated the revelation of saving faith from natural and "depraved" knowledge, were to disregard Bacon's materialistic metaphysics and to accept his inductive inquiry. That scientific regimen which promised best to promote "useful" knowledge and attendant prosperity in the temporal world was acceptable to Puritan Enthusiasts, whose "carnal" thought and business affairs did not impinge on their Revealed Wisdom. Oliver Cromwell, one of their number, prompted by such Baconian agitators as John Webster and Samuel Hartlib, showed a readiness, at one stage, to convert the Universities into scientific academies. After the Restoration, when the rule of the "Saints" was over and done with, Bacon's philosophy would be associated with Enthusiasm, Cromwell, Puritans, and Nonconformists generally, in a public damnation and consignment to Hell by a senior Oxford divine in the Oxford Theatre. The association would be accurate, if the condemnation would be excessive.

XVI

BACON'S ORIGINALITY

Bacon is an original and originating philosopher. He propounds, in the first place, a distinctive pluralistic philosophy by which the science of nature is rendered free from overt invasions by revealed theology and from covert incursions by the same in the guise of theologico-metaphysics. Secondly, Bacon puts "mind" out of metaphysics. Thirdly, he reorganizes natural knowledge by assigning its recognized divisions new places and functions in a new classification of the sciences. Fourthly, he sets down the principles of a distinctive metaphysical naturalism, materialistic in character. Fifthly, he undertakes to establish metaphysics through a purely inductive procedure. Sixthly, he attempts to do for induction what Aristotle did for deduction, namely, to describe in detail its principles and to exemplify its operation. Seventhly, he regards logic, not as reason in operation, not as the alignment of terms in propositions, but as a "machine" for controlling the human faculties, including both sense and reason—an instrument which operates in exacting fashion between the empirical collecting of particulars and the asserting of general axioms. Eighthly, without a lapse into deduction, he makes the observation of induced causal processes in nature, that is, of operative works, including those of art, the test of every axiom or scientific principle, from the

318

highest—erroneously called "first" in traditional logic—to the lowest.

Let us consider, partly by way of review, some of these achievements, omitting what has already been elaborated in detail. It is Bacon's opinion that the "Prerogative of God comprehends the whole man." Man's lot, under God's dispensing, lies within the three kingdoms: the Kingdom of God—known through Revelation—in which through Divine Grace man is saved from his sin and receives his moral rule of charity; the civil kingdom, where God—as the Scriptures teach—bestows political initiative upon rulers, who are the creatures of His own making; and the kingdom of nature—known through inductive science—whose dominion has been given to man by the Creator. These three areas of knowledge are not brought by Bacon under a single classification of sciences. They have no common categories. They cannot become parts or aspects of one integrated system. Bacon's philosophical thinking—to use this phrase in a most comprehensive sense—remains pluralistic in character. The author will not permit the weakening of the placets of Revelation by any accommodation to a "unity of truth" in which the several truths of theology, metaphysics, politics, ethics, and natural philosophy are made components of a system organized either according to a principle of equality or to a scale of ascent in a hierarchy.

Attempts by thinkers of the past to bring differing kinds of truths into a single system have, in Bacon's opinion, resulted in the reduction of all. Plato made knowledge and virtue dependent on the contemplation of abstract forms divorced, beyond reconciliation, from the world of particulars. As these abstract entities became the more removed from matter and actualities, they became for this author, in an absurdity, the objects of inquiry in natural philosophy, the ends of dehumanized human desire in ethics, the foundation of rule and sovereignty in politics, the components of a dialectically constructed universe in metaphysics, and in theology the mind and power of God, now reduced to a dialectical entity.

Aristotle, in turn, laid some stress on actual particulars, but not for long. He was not content to dissect these, but must abstract them. Then he went on to define his abstractions, and not physical nature as it is, nor ethical and political motives as they are, nor metaphysical operations of specified scientific significance, nor God as Creator, for the so-called First Cause of what Aristotle calls nature is but the crowning abstraction in a system of abstractions. Aristotle's philosophical system was supposedly held together by a teleological principle, which pervaded all things from the "first bodies" to the highest and first cause. But as a comprehending, unifying principle, governing all areas of being and operation, Aristotle's teleology was of a questionable sort: for it contained a contradiction, because by definition the Stagirite had already rendered completely segregate the several regions over which it was to prevail, his metaphysics or theology, physics, ethics and politics, and the poietical sciences or arts.

Later writers under Stoic influence made an attempt to overcome Aristotle's discontinuities by bringing the operations of physical nature, human conduct, political rule, even the mind of God, within the orbit of an all-comprehending Law of Reason. However, as the extension of this principle increased, and the attempt was made to tie physical nature and God together as subjects under one law and rule, the terms and clauses became the more incomprehensible and illusory. The distinctions and exclusions required in such a case as this must of necessity dissipate any unity and authority within a law.

Bacon is a pluralist. Of philosophical opinions which make for pluralism Bacon recognizes three sorts. One of these, of which Aristotle is a supporter, affirms that nature is composed of individual substances, or entities. In this opinion Bacon agrees, but only up to the point where he argues that the objects of philosophical investigation are not particular substances, but common forms, or natures. In the *New Organon* he writes, "Though in nature nothing really exists beside individual bodies, performing pure individual acts according to a fixed law, yet in philosophy this very law, and the investigation, discovery, and explanation of it, is the foundation as well of knowledge as of operation. And it is this law, with its clauses, that I mean when I speak of *Forms*; a name which I rather adopt because it has grown into use and become familiar." It is Bacon's contention that philosophy is not concerned with particulars or individuals as such, but moves in the realm of universals. The universals which the investigator of nature seeks are forms or laws or causes, constitutive of and operative within material bodies.

A second kind of philosophical pluralism, which is also to be found in Aristotle, rests on a plurality of segregate sciences, each with distinctive principles and concepts, notions, terms, whose only bond of union is a rationale called analytic, or logic. With this, Bacon disagrees. It is his opinion that the natural sciences can be brought together through informing general axioms which are inherent within the subject matter of each and all of them. These principles are to be established inductively by a method not hitherto employed, a method which is not "logical" in character, and which operates only after the rejection of what hitherto have been received as the "first" and commanding principles of reason and the founding and segregating axioms of independent sciences.

A third sort of pluralism issues from a regard for the distinctive sources and appropriately distinctive knowledges of truly different subject matters. This is Bacon's kind of pluralism. His theology treats of the nature and will of God, the knowledge of which is given to man by Divine Revelation—a knowledge unto which man by use of his own faculties cannot attain. Bacon's political doctrine is premised on the principle of divinely bestowed sovereignty and initiative which comprehends rule by justice and law. This principle he finds in the repeated affirmations of Holy Writ, which are not to be weakened or reduced by any philosophical reconstruction of their placets. Bacon's philosophy of nature is discovered through natural inquiry. In this there is no legitimate place for a doctrine of a First Cause, which Aristotle accommodates through the services of a teleological metaphysics. The principles of nature as a body, or system, are not to be confused with what in tradition are taken to be the subjects of metaphysics, such as the four causes and matter and form. They belong only to the physics of materiate things. They are the very axioms of nature itself, and do not apply to God, nor to political sovereignty and subjection of political subjects under sovereign rule.

In the next place, Bacon rejects mind as a metaphysical principle, or entity. Mind has been made inherent within the intelligible world by Plato. In one of his latest dialogues, the *Philebus*, Plato assigns four "concauses" to the objects of inquiry: the indeterminate, the determinate, the "mixture" of these two, and *nous*, or reason—the determining principle within whatever is knowable. Plato also, in his last dialogue, the *Laws*, finds *nous*, or reason, within the elements, laws, and the cosmos generally. Aristotle, in turn, makes *nous* a kind of divine reason which actualizes in intelligence logical forms; he also makes logic a rational thing, the normal function of reason in demonstration; and he finds a *logos*, or rational principle, as something pervasive within each area of science. The Stoics identify the *nous* with their *logos*, and make this *logos* a reason within nature, man, and God. This reason they employ as an explanatory principle in three conjunctions, as the judgment of the knower, as the formal statement of judgment in the scientific proposition, and as the objective counterpart of judgment in the rational structure of the universe. With the theological Platonists, the *logoi*—the *logos* pluralized—become both ideas in the mind of God and seminal principles in nature. Causes are now reasons, and the world, as intelligible order, contains the rational principles of the Creator's mind. These several meanings of the *nous* and the *logos* and varied offices of reason are put into employment by a succession of Platonists, Peripatetics, and eclectic philosophers.

In the *Advancement of Learning* (1605), a work written when the author is embarking on his "voyage of discovery"—to use his own metaphor—and mentioning doctrines which he will later amend, he includes the statement that metaphysics handles "that which supposeth . . . in nature a reason, understanding, and platform." Then, almost immediately, Bacon goes on to say that "the natural philosophy of Democritus and some others, who did not suppose a mind or reason in the frame of things . . . seemeth to me . . . in particularities of physical causes more real and better enquired into than that of Aristotle and Plato." This qualifying of the earlier statement is what we should expect, if we bear in mind that metaphysics is being regarded by the author as universalized physics. In the Latin translation of the *Advancement of Learning*, the *De augmentis*, of 1623, Bacon lays stress on the greater "penetration" into nature by Democritus, the philosopher who "removed God and Mind from the structure of things, and attributed the form thereof to infinite essays and proofs of nature . . . and assigned the causes of particular things to the necessity of matter." In the same reference the author maintains that God in his wisdom has not "communicated to all natural figures and motions the characters and impressions of His providence [or knowledge]." In the early *Valerius Terminus* (1603-5) the author states that "God hath framed the mind of man as a glass capable of the image of the universal world, joying to receive the signature thereof"—"signature" and not mind of nature or of God. In the *New Organon* (1620), which contains his mature philosophy, Bacon states explicitly that what are sometimes taken to be the ideas of God in nature are properly to be regarded as the Creator's "seals" or "signets" on His creation. These are not, in manner or degree, divine ideas. The seals of nature are not reasons. The laws, processes, and structures of nature are not "logical" in the traditional meaning of the term. What is logical for Bacon belongs to a method which, he says, is a "machine" to control reason as a human faculty, and not to show a rationale inherent within nature. Bacon holds that the forms, or causes, or natures of philosophy are materiate, subject to the materiate laws of matter in motion. The structures and processes which scientific axioms embody are not of a rational or a mental, let alone a divine, order. The Creator has not put into nature His own mind, or any other sort of mind.

Bacon is so impressed by the greatness and majesty of God that he cannot entertain the opinion that the forms of matter are in any manner or degree participant in or even "imitative" of the ideas of the Creator. In the *Valerius Terminus* he writes: "If any man shall think by view and inquiry into . . . sensible and material things, to attain to any light for the revealing of the nature or will of God, he shall dangerously abuse himself. . . . God is only self-like, having nothing in common with any creature, otherwise than as in shadow and trope. Therefore attend His will as Himself openeth it, and give unto faith that which unto faith belongeth." Man at his creation "being a spirit newly inclosed in a body of earth, he was fitted to be allured with appetite of light and liberty of knowledge," yet, through his "intruding" by natural faculties "into God's secrets and mysteries," through his "presuming to come within the oracle of [Divine] knowledge, man transgressed and fell."

For Bacon there can be no "similitude" between man and God in the matter of knowledge, but only in goodness or charity, which "is nothing else but goodness put into action or applied." The rule of charity, which "comprehends and fastens all virtues together," is given in Revelation for the governing of that part of man which is made in the Divine Image. In the *De augmentis* Bacon explains: "We are bound to obey the divine law though we find a reluctation in our will, so are we to believe His word though we find a reluctation in our reason. . . .

"And this holds not only in those great mysteries which concern the Deity, the Creation, and the Redemption; but it pertains likewise to a more perfect interpretation of the moral law, 'Love your enemies'; 'do good to them that hate you,' and so on. . . . To which words this applause may well be applied, 'that they do not sound human'; since it is a voice beyond the light of nature."

"The use of human reason in matters of religion is of two sorts; the former in the explanation of the mystery, the latter in the inferences derived from it. With regard to the explanation of the mysteries, we see that God vouchsafes to descend to the weakness of our apprehension, by so expressing his mysteries that they may be most sensible to us. . . .

"But with regard to inferences . . . after the articles and principles of religion have been set in their true place, so as to be completely exempted from the examination of reason, it is then permitted us to derive and deduce inferences from them. . . . the first propositions are not only self-existent and self-supporting; but likewise unamenable to that reason which deduces consequent propositions. Nor yet does this hold in religion alone. . . . we see in games, as chess or the like, that the first rules and laws are merely positive, and at will; and that they must be received as they are, and not disputed; but how to play a skilful and winning game is scientific and rational. . . .

"But as the use of the human reason in things divine is of two kinds, so likewise in the use there are two kinds of excess; the one when it inquires too curiously into the manner of the mystery; the other when the same authority is attached to inferences as to principles."

When we bear in mind that Bacon has put reason, even as rationale, out of nature as system and has placed questions respecting the supreme rule of ethical conduct, the basis of political sovereignty, and the being, knowledge, and providence of God within revealed theology, we can the more readily comprehend some of the naturalistic implications of his classification of the parts of human knowledge obtainable by the exercise of human powers. This classification, which we have already stated in outline, is undoubtedly modelled on that of Aristotle. But Bacon's originality becomes immediately evident when we consider his radical modifications of the traditionally accepted Peripatetic system. According to Aristotle, there are three main sorts of science, the theoretical, the practical, and the "poietical" —the third having to do with the making of things. Each science, of whatever sort, has its own distinctive determining axioms, by which it is rendered separate from and independent of all the others. The sciences of the theoretical group include metaphysics, mathematics, and physics; these manifest several degrees of abstraction. Metaphysics is the most abstract and most universal of all the sciences, having to do with being *qua* being, which may be regarded, in several contexts of explanation in turn, as Pure Form, the First Cause, the First Mover, and God—the object of whose thought is Himself. This supreme science is founded on the metaphysical—as distinct from the logical—principle of identity: What is, is. From this principle is derived both being and unity, the latter convertible with being, as is also goodness which is being in act. The second of the theoretical sciences, mathematics, treats of quantity in abstraction from motion and matter, while the subject matter of the third, physics, consists of materiate things in motion. The motions of physics may be classified in a general way as generation and decay, augmentation, change in character, and local motion. Of the practical sciences, Aristotle names two, ethics and politics—in which ethics attains its end. While in the theoretical sciences the objects concerned cannot be other than they are, in those called practical the subject matter includes adventitious factors, such as choice and deliberate willing on the part of human agents. The third general sort of science includes the arts: medicine, cooking, architecture, husbandry, navigation, poetry, rhetoric, and so on. When describing these "poietical" sciences—those which have to do with making—Aristotle draws a distinction between nature and art. In the case of the latter, a secondary form is imposed on a primary, natural form—the form of a table, for example, or of a house, or the form of a tree. Some of the Peripatetics divide the arts into those of a higher, an "intellectual," sort, such as poetry and music, and those which are "manual," and lower, such as cooking, shoe-making, and husbandry. Aristotle recognized a science or art, namely analytic, later called logic, with its induction and deduction, which he did not place in any one of the divisions of his sciences because, in his view, it was assumed by all.

Aristotle's universe consists of fifty-five concentric spheres, with the earth at the centre. The outermost sphere is the *Primum Mobile*—the First Moved by the Prime Mover. This transmits motion to the remaining spheres in turn. The earth and terrestrial bodies are composed of four elements: fire, earth, air, and water. Terrestrial motion is rectilinear in character. Through this, the elements or "first bodies" tend to take up their respective appropriate places. Actually, the "first bodies" are never found in isolation, and the motions of earthly bodies are always combinations of several rectilinear motions. The element assigned by Aristotle to celestial bodies is a fifth essence, or quintessence, the "ether." Celestial motion is circular, without end or variation, as befits spheres near the First Mover. Their motions may appropriately be regarded as "imitations" of the motion of the *Primum Mobile*, the First Moved by God.

Materiate things are composed of matter and form. Matter in and by itself is formless, indeterminate, meaningless, deprived, potential. It is made significant when activated through the agency of form. In the motion of materiate bodies, four causes are to be distinguished: the material, that out of which something becomes; the formal, which brings what becomes out of privation into existence and significance; the efficient, which brings into act what without its operation remains potential; and the final, which is the actuality achieved when something becomes what it had had in it to become. Because the form is the activating agent upon matter, and also marks the end achieved through passage from potency to act, Aristotle sometimes reduces his four causes to two: the formal and the material.

Such is the system in part which Bacon learned at Cambridge. He was not taken with it. Soon he began to regard its logic, in ways already noted, as fruitless, and became unhappy over its divisions, its abstractions, and its interpretations of natural processes and causation. In a rebellion against the teaching of the Peripatetics, Bacon turned to Plato and the Pre-Socratics. He also began to acquaint himself with some more immediate predecessors and contemporaries. In Plato he found to his liking a system of truth wherein things ascended from multiplicity to unity, and also a principle of determination by which infinite particulars were brought within intelligible bounds. But to his disliking he also found in Plato a doctrine by which forms were set in opposition to an indeterminate matter. Going back beyond Plato, Bacon discovered that "almost all the ancients, as Empedocles, Anaxagoras, Anaximenes, Heraclitus, and Democritus, though in other respects they differed about the first matter, agreed in this, that they set down matter as active, as having some form, as dispensing that form, and as having the principle of motion in itself." Of these early thinkers, Democritus impressed him most of all. "The philosophy of Democritus," he said, "seems worthy to be rescued," both because of its freedom from final causes and its assertion of a formed and determinate matter, causal in its motion.

By the time Bacon prepares his first philosophical publication, the *Advancement of Learning*, he has rejected from his thinking the main parts and principles of the Peripatetic philosophy and has chosen alternatives of his own conceiving. These he cultivates during the next fifteen years. He will have nothing to do with any metaphysics or other natural science which professes to deal with the nature and the mind of God, with abstract being as such, with a First Cause or with a Prime Mover. Metaphysics is for him generalized physics, the science of formed matter in motion.

Bacon will not agree in the separation of fields of inquiry by means of axioms. He regards the principle of abstraction, on which the Peripatetics rely in aligning the sciences, as the source of "infinite error" and as one of the impediments in the way of scientific advancement. Aristotle's several motions are reduced by Bacon, as a philosophical materialist, to one, local motion. He will not countenance a separation of matter from form. Rejecting Aristotle's formal and final causes, he recognizes one efficient materiate cause active within formed matter. Bacon dismisses as useless things the four terrestrial elements and also the fifth element, the celestial quintessence. He regards the separation of the respective elements and motions of celestial and terrestrial bodies as a calamity in the history of astronomy. He notes that this separation is still being retained by some of those who profess a "new," heliocentric, theory.

In Bacon's classification of the sciences, mathematics is reduced in status from an independent science to an instrument of metaphysics and physics. The "poietical" sciences are merged with physics. Art and nature become one, both the products of the operation of common material causes. The practical sciences are put within "the Prerogative" of revealed theology. Political initiative and sovereignty are divine bestowals on rulers; the source of the governing principle and rule of ethics is Divine Revelation; all so-called principles of ethics are but "inferences" from this rule.

Bacon is extremely critical of Aristotle's teaching on the subject of ethics. It does not, in his opinion, touch the springs of human action. "We may," Bacon says, "discourse as much as we please," after the manner of Aristotle, "that the moral virtues are in the mind of man by habit, and not by nature, and we may make a formal distinction that generous spirits are won by doctrines and persuasions, and the vulgar sort by reward and punishment; or we may give it in precept that the mind like a crooked stick must be straightened by bending it the contrary way, and the like scattered glances and touches; but they would be very far from supplying the place of that which we require."

For an understanding of human motives, we could find more wisdom, says Bacon, if we turned from the philosophy of Aristotle to poetry and history. Machiavelli also has written informatively in this regard. In the works of poets and historians "we find painted forth with great life and dissected, how affections are kindled and excited, and how pacified and restrained, and how again contained from act and further degree; how they disclose themselves, though repressed and concealed; how they work; how they vary; how they are enwrapped one within another; how they fight and encounter one with another; and many other particularities of this kind amongst which this last is of special use in moral and civil matters."

Bacon has been attacking the Universities continuously for their employment in instruction of the Peripatetic logic and the doctrines and writings of Aristotle. His pleas for alternatives to these were often addressed directly to James and sometimes to Prince Charles. These entreaties produced no discernible effect in the reign of either of these sovereigns. However, during the days of the Commonwealth, Bacon's scheme for learning became the subject of common and vigorous debate. University curricula and exercises were made the objects of attack by pamphleteers and others who repeated what Bacon had written, often in the very words of the *Advancement of Learning*, the

New Organon, and the *New Atlantis*. No less a person than a renowned Oxford professor, Seth Ward—a member of the experimental "philosophical college" which became the Royal Society—found it necessary to publish a vindication of university practices in answer to the writings of William Dell and John Webster, who had stated in vehement language what others again had presented, in keeping with Bacon's criticism of learning, as "humble advices" to the Universities and Petitions to Parliament. Before long, plans for a new sort of institution of learning, which would give effect to Bacon's principles, were drawn up by such men as William Petty, Abraham Cowley, John Evelyn, and Robert Hooke. These innovators were one in thinking what Evelyn said, that "Solomon's House . . . however lofty, and to appearance Romantic, hath yet in it nothing impossible to be effected." John Amos Comenius was invited to England mainly for the purpose of reforming the schools of the kingdom according to Bacon's design. Oliver Cromwell warned the Universities that unless they adopted Baconian methods they would be closed. Plans were made to sequester cathedral funds for a "new" public education. Cromwell tried to place the Baconian Samuel Hartlib in the headship of an Oxford College. None of these plans came to fruition. Cromwell's attention was diverted by troubles in Ireland and at Westminster. The Universities refused to provide Hartlib with a post or to bring their curricula into conformity with what was now generally known as the "new learning."

Seth Ward, in his defence of the attitude of the Universities, had the following to say in his *Vindicae Academiarum*, a reply to Webster's *Academiarum Examen, or the Examination of Academies, Wherein is discussed and examined the Matter, Method, and Customs of Academick and Scolastick Learning, and the insufficiency thereof discovered and laid open* (1654): "There is one thing which this sort of pamphleteers insist on, which as it is pursued by my L. Verulam, so it carries weight with it, but it is very impertinently applied, either as an exception against us, or as a general rule to be imposed upon us in our academical institution. It is, that instead of verbal exercises, we should set upon experiments and observations, that we should lay aside our disputations, declamations, and public lectures, and betake ourselves to agriculture, mechanics, chemistry, and the like.

"It cannot be denied that this is the way, and the only way to perfect natural philosophy and medicine: so that whosoever intend to profess the one or the other, are to take that course, and I have not neglected occasionally to tell the world, that this way is pursued amongst us. But our academies are of a more general and comprehensive institution, and as there is a provision here made, that whosoever will be excellent in any kind, in any art, science, or language, may here receive assistance, and be led by the hand, till he come to be excellent; so is there a provision likewise, that men be not forced into particular ways, but may receive an institution, variously answerable to their genius and design.

"Of those very great numbers of youth, which come to our universities, how few are there, whose design is to be absolute in natural philosophy? Which of the nobility or gentry, desire when they send their sons hither, that they should be set to chemistry, or agriculture, or mechanics? Their removal is from hence commonly in two or three years, to the Inns of Court, and the desire of their friends is not, that they be engaged in those experimental things, but that their reason, and fancy, and carriage, be improved by lighter institutions and exercises, that they may become . . . graceful speakers, and be of an acceptable behaviour in their countries.

"I am persuaded, that all of these, who come hither for institution there is not one of many hundreds, who if they may have their option, will give themselves to be accomplished natural philosophers (such as will, ought certainly to follow this course). The pain is great, the reward but slender, unless we reckon in the pleasure of contemplation; that indeed is great and high, but therefore to draw all men that way, by reason of the pleasure, were to present a feast for all of custard or tart, and not to consult the variety of tastes, and tempers of our guests."

Although a member of the experimental "philosophical college," which for a period held extramural meetings at Oxford, Ward in the middle of the seventeenth century defended the use of Aristotle's works in ethics and politics and of manuals of traditional logic for pedagogical purposes within the University. In the pamphlet now quoted in part Ward states definitely that the logical works of Aristotle which comprise his "organon" were no longer being read at Oxford. He also expresses the doubt whether any appreciable number of fellows and tutors subscribe to the principles of Peripatetic physics and metaphysics. By the end of the century the opinion was general that, largely through the influence of Bacon and his disciples, the physical and metaphysical doctrines of Aristotle were no longer entertained by learned men in England. Nevertheless, Peripatetic teaching continued in the Universities, not as dogma, but as training in definition, organization of thought, and apt and clear speech; and as means, to acquaint students with the content of historic learning. The authorities of Oxford were not disposed to have their Greek and Latin communications polluted by the recipes and the vernacular, vulgar conversation of "burners of charcoal"—called chemists, apothecaries, farmers, and mechanics, however earnest and diligent these mixers of concoctions, tillers, and assemblers of machines might show themselves to be.

The scientific search which Bacon had begun was to be carried forward outside the Universities from the middle of the century. Members of the Royal Society undertook a "work," as their first historian said, "becoming the largeness of Bacon's wit to devise." These inquirers, at the bidding of the author whom their President, Robert Boyle, called "that profound naturalist . . . Verulam," took for their ambitious aim the investigation of every area of nature available to human observation and experiment. John Locke, whose scientific environment as a member of the Royal Society and whose study of the works of his philosophical progenitor made him one of the most thoroughly Baconian writers of the seventeenth century—specifically in doctrine, illustration, problem, and method—undertook the "historical" recording of the operations and structures of the human mind. Locke became, in turn, the progenitor of an ambitious family of epistemologists of a "psychologically" historical sort.

Not a few historians of philosophy would undoubtedly take issue with our placing of Locke in the Baconian tradition. Because of Locke's concern with "ideas" and "intuition" and his attempt to cope with the body-mind problem, he is often regarded as a disciple of Descartes (1596-1650), and his philosophy as a part of "Cartesianism." This is one of the causes of the contention that Descartes is the source of everything that is distinctively modern in the questions and the methods of modern philosophy. Let us pause, then, to look at some of the differences and similarities in outlook, doctrine, and issue between the two original philosophers of the Late Renaissance, René Descartes and Francis Bacon.

Both these thinkers are products of learning and remain critically aware of the fact. Both have been exposed in university discipline and instruction to practices and problems which had entered the schools of philosophy through successive revivals in learning: of verbal dialectic in the ninth century, of Platonic Augustinianism in the eleventh, of Arabian Aristotelianism in the twelfth, of Christian Aristotelianism in the thirteenth, and of Stoic eclecticism in a succession of ages from the time of Cicero. Neither thinks philosophically fertile the contendings among Scotists, Thomists, Occamists, and the followers of Bonaventure. Both turn from the study of books to consider what is involved in knowledge—in this case, of "nature"—Descartes to determine the character of the things which compose the mind's content and Bacon to control the mind's activities after its purge from "malignancies." Either rejects the main conceptions of the Peripatetics, Descartes after examining his own doubts and Bacon after condemning dialectical modes of thinking. Either is denied an explanation of the epistemological conjunction of subject and object, Descartes because of his absolute separation by definition of mind and body, and Bacon because of his placing the part of man made in the image of God within the domain of Revelation. Both find the Peripatetic logic an unsatisfactory method of inquiry, Descartes advancing an alternative logic of mathematical implication and Bacon providing an inductive directive. Both reject the Aristotelian alignment of the sciences through a doctrine of multiple axioms. Either, like Aristotle, professes a metaphysics. While the Peripatetics in the schools give the ontology of being *qua* being ascendancy over mathematics and physics, Descartes identifies the metaphysics of nature which he professes with mathematical continuities, and Bacon his with the physics of materiate forms. Both reduce Aristotle's varied sorts of motion—including generation, movement from place to place, change in character—to one sort, local, spatial motion. Neither considers contemporary astronomical hypotheses either sufficient for or essential to the formulating of a general philosophy. Neither thinker is, of course, wholly original in what he has to say; no philosopher since Thales, perhaps not even Thales, had ever been that. Descartes revives certain Augustinian conceptions, acquired at La Flèche. Bacon avowedly attempts a return to Pre-Socratic methods and conceptions, and draws, too— perhaps more than he would care to acknowledge—from Plato and the Platonists. Descartes and Bacon are both to prove themselves generative thinkers, yet not so much by the making of specific scientific discoveries, as through something more continuously seminal.

The progeny of Descartes is a succession from generation to

generation of a priori rationalists. Descartes, after entertaining doubt about the offices of sense and reason, takes refuge in mathematically clear and determined ideas. Having applied quantity to geometric forms, he rests his case on an ontology dialectically established. His philosophy emerges as a sort of Stoical, Augustinian Platonism. Its structures are not the products of the activities of a knowing *anima*, or soul, but the noetic content of a nonorganic *mens*, or mind. This content, so far as it serves science, is composed of innate ideas, mathematically coördinated. This content Descartes divides according to two categories, *res cogitans* and *res extensa*, thinking "substance" and extended "substance," by a defining which forbids intercourse between the two things defined. And while he states the former of his two "substances" in the form of the active participle, this "thinking" thing actually performs no operation; its "acts" are specified in terms of its structure—as in the later case of Kant's transcendental mind. By his establishment of a noetic content, Descartes solves to his own satisfaction the problem—a concern of Augustine and Francisco Suarez before him—of making available to human comprehension the *logoi* inherent within the principle of divine omiscience. Descartes' treatment of this question, we may add, is motivated not by an epistemological requirement, but rather by a theological preoccupation.

Thought's content, having been elevated by Descartes into the structure of the "universe," is bequeathed in this form to his philosophical heirs, the Continental rationalists. By them it is specified in such terms as divine attributes, transcendental ideas, transcendental categories, schemata of thought, all of which they find innate, as it were, certainly inherent, within a transcendental mind. Descartes, therefore, may properly be regarded as a "modern" who introduces into inquiry that epistemological puzzle whose solution is said to lie, by the Spinozists, the Kantians, and the logical idealists respectively, in the intellectual knowledge of God, the identification of human thought-structures with a transcendental understanding, the possession within human logic, in "degree" at least, of the Eternal Mind.

Bacon, following a thoroughly different line of thought, denies that man has capacity by natural inquiry to know in range or degree what God thinks or is. The assumption that man could do so is for Bacon the presumption and sin whereby Adam fell and forfeited his rule over the kingdom of nature. Bacon banishes from philosophy the *logos* and *logoi* of the Stoics and the Augustinians. He sees in philosophical objects only the structures and motions of formed matter. He reduces the transcendental status assigned by Plato and some sorts of Platonist to mathematics, making it an instrument in physical discovery. He relegates ontology to the verbal limbo of dialectic, and expels metaphysical theology from science achieved through human faculties. He puts distinctively human powers to work on the investigation of the created world for the recapturing of man's dominion over Nature.

After rejecting the dialectic procedures of the rationalists Bacon calls for "a true and lawful marriage between the empirical and the rational faculty," whose ill-starred divorce and separation have brought "confusion" into the philosophical life of mankind. He asks for a new sort of philosophy, whose "end, scope, office" will lie not in plausible, resolved, and admired discourse and argument, but in the understanding of particulars and the production of operative works for "the better endowment and help of man's life." The new philosopher will recognize that the subtlety of nature is greater than the subtlety of subtle words and arguments. His discoveries will not "float in air," but will "rest on the solid foundation of experience of every kind, and the same well examined and weighed." He will be satisfied with the recapture of that "parcel of the world... fitted to the comprehension of man's mind." His aim will be "the restitution and reinvesting (in great part) of man to the sovereignty and power [over Nature] which he had in his first state of creation."

The descendants of Descartes, because of the recognition by academics of the continuity of their thinking with *philosophia perennis*, were readily assimilated by learned institutions. Bacon's progeny, when looked at by academics in the "old way," were regarded as little more than mechanics. They were long to be denied admittance to the Universities. Their laboring faithfully, fearlessly, and fruitfully beyond the walls of learning, their industrious example, and the report of undeniable discoveries, eventually caused learned academics to relent. Finally the Baconians were reluctantly invited to enter the portals of the Universities. They arrived with vigor and authority. Step by step they brought about a great modification of university studies. The scientific curricula of modern universities—and modern research foundations; the varieties of and the relations among scientific subject matters; the sciences which employ induction and not simply speculation, experimentally and not verbally defined terms; the philosophies which hang upon the methods and discoveries of the inductive science; the adjusting of new means to new ends for the betterment of the lot of man as an inhabitant of the kingdom of nature with the status of ruler, but not yet in full control—these were to be some of the offspring of the greatest thinker of the English Renaissance. No Telesio, no Campanella, Descartes, Spinoza, Hume, Kant, Schopenhauer, or Hegel has ever produced, or ever could have produced, a like progeny. The more these philosophers, and their kinds, have meditated and have contemplated their concepts and definitions, the less, according to the disciples of Bacon, have they furthered the understanding and the conquest of nature. The more some of them have attempted to elevate to the realm of the a priori and transcendental what, the Baconians say, does not there belong, the more have they hindered man's exercise of his original birthright and his religious duty, the rule over the kingdom of nature.

Bacon's indebtedness to the ancients, notably to Democritus, Plato, and Aristotle is obviously great. His debt to the "philosophers of nature" among his more immediate predecessors and contemporaries is considerable—greater, perhaps, than is commonly supposed. While we know that Bacon was acquainted with their doctrines, in whole or in part, the questions of their influence upon him and his borrowing from them must remain in degree problematical. Certain facts, however, are evident: Bacon philosophizes in the manner of these "moderns," even if he rejects most of their elaborate terminologies. From them he has learned ways of approaching philosophy, problems to be considered by a "modern" philosopher, and some solutions of these problems. Generally speaking, Bacon ignores the Platonico-Aristotelian eclectics, John Pico, Pietro Pompanazzi, Juan Luis Vives, and the rest. He discerns in the "reports" of the observations and experiments of Roger Bacon of the thirteenth century a "good beginning" of inductive inquiry. He is aware of that author's doctrine of Idols, which is different from his own, and his stress on the offices of mathematics and language. Bacon acknowledges, too, that some recent chemists and alchemists have hit upon useful discoveries. As experimenters, he finds them comparable to the sons of a farmer who were told by their father to search in a field for hidden gold. After much digging the laborers failed to discover the object of their search, but by their tillage they did unwittingly cause an increase in the grain crop. Bacon praises William Gilbert (1571-1630) for his diligent, laborious, and fruitful observations of the loadstone, but he thinks that no scientist or philosopher as such would undertake to build a complete universe on the principle of magnetism. Like Descartes after him, Bacon entertains an enlightened scepticism of the "new" astronomy and its philosophical import. Even as Descartes would never have undertaken to propound a theory of the whole of nature on the results of his study of nerve structures, so neither he nor Bacon could suppose that a complete natural philosophy might be founded on some observations of the motions of the heavens. The "new" helio-centric theory, propounded by Nicolaus Copernicus (1473-1543), Galileo Galilei (1564-1642), and their disciples, is, Bacon observes, in fact not new. It was proposed by Pythagoras and has since been advocated by others. It is now being advanced again, but only as an hypothesis which can explain in simpler manner what the Ptolemaic hypothesis can also explain. There still re-main in the minds of some of its late advocates the queries whether the planets contain celestial intelligences, as Aristotle seemed to think they did, and whether they are composed of the same elements as the earth. Bacon notes with approval Galilei's rejection of the traditional opinion that the planets move in perfect circles, and he remarks in jest that in the Ptolemaic com-piling of cycles and epicycles, wheels many miles in circuit are required to carry a ball the size of a palm! Bacon disapproves of Galilei's account of the cause of tides: the incapacity of water to keep up with the velocities of the earth. Bacon's own views on this subject are transmitted by others to Gallilei, who in turn sends reasons for his explanation. Bacon hails Galilei's improve-ment and use of the telescope. This invention marks, in Bacon's opinion, one of the greatest advances in the history of astronomy. The telescope has provided evidence of the fact that the Milky Way is a collection of stars; has enabled an observer to descry the dances of the smaller stars about the greater planets; and has provided the grounds for new hypotheses about centres of mo-tions in the heavens.

Bacon is sympathetic to the appeal by contemporary astron-omers to the axiom of simplicity as a cause for choosing be-tween two opposing theories which both "save" phenomena. Now going beyond what these astronomers in general say, Bacon expresses the opinion that the "passions and desires" of matter are the same in both terrestrial and heavenly bodies, because there is evidence of an expansion of matter, its collection into masses, its contraction, cession, and attraction both on the surface and in the inner parts of the heavens and at their summit as well. His advice to astronomers—advice which is to be acted on by one member of the Royal Society, Isaac Newton (1642-1727)—is to the effect that they should pursue the hypothesis which suggests that there is a common matter with "common passions and desires" in both the earth and the heavens. The investigation of this problem, which is now made feasible by a "new commerce with the phenomena of the heavens," will entail, in Bacon's opinion, two things: the collecting of a massive natural history of phenomena and a doctrine of matter. Let there be arranged, then, pleads Bacon, a valid alliance between the new astronomy and a new philosophy of matter in such a manner that the former will not prejudice the facts, and the latter will affirm only what is explicable and demonstrable through the observation of phenomena in both heaven and earth.

Theophrastus Paracelsus (1493-1541), a physician, has attacked the philosophy of Aristotle and the medical systems of Galen and Avicenna, and condemned the methods of the three authors. Paracelsus professes a reliance on experiments and the histories of diseases. For the humors of the traditionalists among physicians and the four elements of the Peripatetics he substitutes three chemical elements: salt, sulphur, and mercury. Paracelsus also separates, initially but not ultimately, the operations of nature from divine acts in the Kingdom of Grace. Philosophy and science, he says, come from the light of nature, theology and wisdom from the revelation of faith. Philosophy and science by origin are ancient and pagan; they become Christian only by the end to which they are employed. The aim of a Christian philosophy is to bring to completion unfinished nature, which is under the dominion of man. This it can do by use of the applied science of medicine, the most comprehensive of all disciplines.

The creation, according to Paracelsus, contains an invisible astral body, or *spiritus,* and also a *limus terrae,* out of which the elements and all natural things, including man, issue. From created nature issue, too, the nutrition of organisms, sense, desire, and natural reason. Each work in nature displays an *archeus,* which is both an organizing and a transforming agent, the source of the virtues or functions in things; this is shown, for example, in the making of bread and wine and in the assimilation of food. Beyond the realm of nature lies soul, or the non-natural reason, which is the Breath of God, breathed into man by his Maker. This reason is the source and agent of man's moral virtue.

Man is a microcosm in whom are represented all the works of nature; and he is also a participant in what is divine. In the former conjunction, man is nourished through assimilation of metals, herbs, and animals; in the latter he becomes by faith the agent of divine goodness. The task of the physician is to make the ill man whole through the two great healers, nature and God, by drawing upon minerals, herbs, and animal substances on the one hand, and on divine goodness on the other.

Bacon, of course, is very critical of Paracelsus' statement of "medical" therapy, because if its mixing of the human and the divine. He finds the doctrine of the *limus terrae* very obscure. He rejects the new elements, salt, sulphur, and mercury. Like the four Peripatetic "first bodies" which they would supplant, these appear initially as things immediately available to sense but, on further inquiry, they prove to be mere terms of definition, things which never can by either direct or indirect observation, or by experimentation, be made available to sense. Bacon, however, has been struck by the attack of Paracelsus on Aristotle and the Peripatetic methods of demonstration, and by his separation of natural philosophy from the wisdom and the rule of virtue received in revelation by faith. He has been impressed with Paracelsus' regarding the rational part of man as the Breath of God, and his opinion that man can exercise dominion over nature by the employment of applied science. Bacon is sympathetic to Paracelsus' view that natural philosophy as such is neither pagan nor Christian. He has become interested in the Paracelsan kinship between man and the whole of nature. He proposes a doctrine of universal "perception," whereby man and nature "take hold" of each other in nutrition, in sensation, in knowledge, and in the act of producing operative works. Bacon, too, makes use of the *archeus*, calling it *spiritus*, and regarding it as a governing and integrative agent in the composing of material bodies.

Jerome Cardan (1501-1576), another recent thinker, is a systematic physician, very different from Paracelsus in outlook. He is an exponent of traditional medical systems, notably that of Galen. Cardan separates philosophy from theology, taking the aim of the former to be the understanding of nature, and the purpose of the latter the salvation of human souls. He considers both philosophy and theology extremely difficult undertakings, entailing abstruse inquiries; consequently, he thinks that their problems are not suited to the comprehension of the vulgar. As esoteric disciplines, these two studies should not be set forth in vernacular languages to the raising of uninformed disputes about ill-comprehended questions. Of sciences, Cardan regards mathematics as the chief, nothing less than the instrument of the Creator's wisdom in nature. Its prominence in the scheme of things is made evident by the amenability of the motions of the planets to quantitative calculation. Nature is regarded by Cardan as a system of parts related by sympathy and antipathy. Nature is possessed of a common, pervasive soul which manifests itself in heat at the level of sense. Set in opposition to heat, which may also be regarded as light, is cold, which belongs to passive, inert matter. Through the conjunction of these two opposites arise those mixtures which are natural things, possessing in varying degrees warmth, activity, and soul. The highest entity among natural things is man, who contains within him all that is found in minerals, plants, and animals. Man as a part of nature has both body and soul. As a creature capable of faith, likeness to God, and immortality, man is also in possession of *mens*, or mind.

Bacon disapproves of Cardan's dependence on traditional medical systems and his doctrine of sympathy and antipathy. He rejects outright his theories of passive matter and a world-soul. Yet Bacon probably learns several things from this predecessor. Certainly he is taken with the latter's manner of separating theology from natural philosophy and with his rejection of Aristotle's elements. He is in agreement with Cardan's separation of *mens* from those parts of man which belong to a science whose subjects include minerals, plants, and animals. He is impressed by the view in which *mens* is the recipient of what faith bestows. He thinks well of the assigning of a central place to mathematics in an explanation of nature. To the influence of Cardan's emphasis on the abstruse and esoteric character of scientific and theological questions may, perhaps, be attributed Bacon's disdain of the vernacular languages as vehicles of learning, his addressing some of his pieces *ad filios*, and his indicating in his early *Proem* to an interpretation of nature that his new induction should, in discretion, be revealed to but a capable few.

Of all the "novelists," the most impressive in Bacon's view is Bernardino Telesio (1508-1588). Telesio separates philosophy from theology, and contends that the office of the former is to understand the nature of the creation and not to expose the nature of the Creator. Philosophy, Telesio claims, must rely on the observation of particulars and not on "first principles." Even mathematical definitions must have objects of sense for their basis. The scientist should seek through experimentation the simplest explanations which will serve; his hypothesis should never go beyond what may be tried by observation and experiment. Such notions as a general sympathy and antipathy in nature and the four causes of Aristotle must always be held in suspicion. The doctrine of formal and final causes assumes in the beginning what cannot be demonstrated in the end. In place of Aristotle's four elements, or "first bodies," and their severally assigned motions, Telesio offers the principles of Heat and Cold as elements which act upon a motionless, characterless matter. Heat, for Telesio, is neither a first body nor the consequence of motion through activation of matter by form; it is motion itself, with a visible aspect of light. Cold is the principle of inertness, and, in contrast to heat, which has light, it may be regarded under the aspect of darkness. Matter is indifferently susceptible to either agent. Both agents are manifest in the condition of bodies; density is the effect of cold, rarity the effect of heat. Heat through rarity excites motion, and cold through density subdues it. Heat, rarity, light, and mobility are found in greater degree in celestial bodies, most of all in the sun; coldness, density, darkness, and immobility exist in degrees proportionate to distances from what is most hot. In the middle regions cold and heat compete, the latter trying to subdue the former. The things of nature produced in this conflict are each united through the agency of *spiritus,* which governs physical organization.

According to Bacon's interpretation of Telesio and his pupil Donius, these thinkers have "in part ... maintained" that the "sensible soul" of man is—to quote Bacon's statement—a "corporeal substance, attenuated and made invisible by heat; a breath ... compounded of the natures of flame and air, having the softness of air to receive impressions, and the vigour of fire to propagate its action; nourished partly by oily and partly by watery substances; clothed with the body, and in perfect animals residing chiefly in the head, running along the nerves, and refreshed and repaired by the spirituous blood of the arteries."

Bacon accepts Telesio's account of the soul as valid for that part of it which is produced in natural generation. He praises Telesio as an inquirer who initially undertakes the founding of an inductive philosophy on observation and experiment. Telesio's stress on density and rarity is, likely, the reason for

Bacon's emphasis on condensation and rarefaction among subjects for inductive inquiry. Bacon, however, deplores Telesio's failure to think through the nature of induction, and his tendency, in consequence, to rely, as his investigation proceeds, on principles theoretically derived. Telesio, explains Bacon, seizes upon the factors Heat and Cold because he recognizes them as major instruments of operation in nature and in art. Heat is essential to the growth, maturing, and propagation of organisms; it is indispensable in the arts and in the making of experiments in the laboratory. Bacon himself chooses the form of heat as the object of investigation when he provides his most detailed exemplification of inductive process. He incurs his fatal illness through experimenting on the use of cold in preserving flesh. Telesio, in Bacon's opinion, goes too far when he assumes, in keeping with his unproved principles, axioms not established by observation and experiment: that all celestial bodies are hot and all earthly bodies cold. Telesio is too intent on regarding heat, brightness, rarity, and mobility as inseparable "messmates"; because while air has rarity and mobility, it is not necessarily hot. The moon, while bright, is not heated; boiling water, while hot, is opaque. An opaque, cold, dense needle on a pivot in a compass can display quick motion. Telesio also fails to see that there are many operations in nature and art which show indifference to heat and cold. But the gravest of all mistakes on his part is the assumption of an inert matter. Telesio has failed to observe that even the most minute portion of actual, and not theoretical, matter possesses an inherent active virtue whereby it resists separation from its kind and refuses to be annihilated. We must turn away, then, says Bacon, from Telesio's imaginary inert and formless matter "to the atom; which is a true being," with formed matter, "dimension, place, resistance, appetite, motion, and emanations."

Another philosopher who, like Telesio, undertakes in the beginning to base a natural philosophy on what he calls "sense" and "history" is Thomas Campanella (1568-1639). He separates philosophy from theology, maintaining that theological truths cannot be established on the principles of physics, nor those of a philosophy of nature through appeals to Scripture. As a thinker, Campanella is faced with two "codices," the codex, or manuscript, of Holy Writ and the codex of writing on nature. These two codices, according to Campanella, require separate interpretations. Campanella professedly undertakes to complete that interpretation of the book of nature which Telesio has begun. To this end he, unlike Telesio, interposes between experimental philosophy and revealed theology a metaphysics which possesses its own principle of certainty and also contains certain "proprincipia," or primary principles, which Campanella finds basic to the physical sciences. Metaphysical certitude Campanella founds on the certainty of the existence of the thinking self. *Ens* (being) having been thus attested, *non-ens* (not-being), or *nihil*, follows from the limitation of this *ens*, a limitation attested by the finite character of the self's capacity in thinking and willing. *Ens* (being) contains the proprincipia potentiality, wisdom, and love. The proprincipia of *non-ens* (not-being) are impotency, ignorance, and hate, which mark the limits of the negation inherent within it. *Ens* contains eminently all that comes to be. Nature is the *ens* of the Creator operating under self-imposed negation. *Ens* includes within its essence an archetypal world which contains all possible creations, the world-soul, immortal human souls, or *mentes* (minds), and physical things. Each of these has within it the three proprincipia of both being and of not-being; they consequently possess capacity, knowledge, and desire, but only in limited degree. No object, not even the passive matter of Telesio, is completely inert. The planets, as physical bodies, are, according to Campanella, to be brought along with other bodies in nature under common proprincipia and not left segregate as the so-called heavenly intelligences of the Peripatetics are. While the other planets move around the

sun, as their *centrum amoris* (centre of love, or desire), the sun
as the most fiery, and therefore the most active, of all moves
around the earth as its *centrum odii* (centre of hate, or repugnance). Thus does Campanella attempt to merge the old and
new astronomical theories.

Bacon is greatly taken with Campanella's doctrine of the two
"codices." He thinks of nature as a "second scripture," requiring
a reverent approach by the interpreter. He is impressed also by
Campanella's stress on sense and natural history, which is its
product; but he regards the extension of the doctrines of Telesio
by Campanella as a continuation of the disposition to assert principles which are not inductively established by such a history,
nor rendered through induced operations available to sense as a
faculty which proves particular works. Bacon does not agree, of
course, in Campanella's establishing *ens*—as Descartes does afterwards—through reflection on the self as a thinking being. Bacon
is struck, however, by Campanella's attempt to find in physical
things evidence of a universal science and by his bringing celestial and earthly bodies within one system of matter and motion.
So great a regard has he for Campanella's use of proprincipia
that he incorporates within his own "first philosophy" being and
not-being and the possible and the not-possible. At times, Bacon
seems to agree with Campanella in regarding bodies as desiring
things, for he speaks of their "appetites," but, unlike Campanella,
he denies bodies knowledge, in any degree, and potentiality—as
distinct from possibility—as well. When Bacon adopts, and
adapts, Campanella's proprincipia he prefers the term "the possible" to "the potential" because of the association of the latter
term with Peripatetic doctrine. Bacon is firm in asserting that
everything which happens in nature is actual and never potential.
There are, of course, possibilities which are not yet actual in
nature; but the statement that these somehow exist as potentiali-
ties amounts, for Bacon, to a contradiction in terms. They may
be made actualities only through the operation of what is actual,
and not of what is potential and deprived.

Bacon is in agreement with Campanella when he regards mathematics as an "instrumental science." He takes note that Campanella's *Compendium of Physiology* (or *Natural Philosophy*) is published under the title *Prodromus totius philosophiae Campanellae* (*Forerunner of the Complete Philosophy of Campanella*). Bacon, in turn, calls the introductory fragment which he writes in representation of the Fifth Part of his Great Instauration *Prodromi sive anticipationes philosophiae secundae* (*Forerunners or Anticipations of the New Philosophy*).

Another novel philosopher is Giordano Bruno (1548-1600). He has associations with England. He gave lectures at Oxford on the principles of the Copernican astronomy, interpreting them through the teachings of Nicholas of Cusa (1401-1464). If these lectures were proscribed, Sir Philip Sidney was his patron, and he was favorably regarded by Queen Elizabeth. Bruno has attacked all philosophers, ancient, medieval, and recent; and while he considers the so-called reform of the Aristotelian logic by Peter Ramus (1517-1572) as pretentious and fruitless rhetoric, he finds the formal logic of Raymond Lully (1235-1315) helpful to memory and a useful means for organizing established principles. Bruno has discovered ethical teachings in the ancient poets and from their fables has acquired incentive for condemning the deduction of philosophical principles from the dogmas of revealed theology.

For Bruno, the subject matter of philosophy is nature. Nature is a unity, and this unity is the God of philosophy. Nature is divine through the presence of the One. God is in all things. The whole of nature is both materiate and besouled. The soul of nature is an all-pervasive inner cause. Matter in possession of soul and cause fills infinite space. Nature, or the universe, is a congruence of "atoms," which are the minima of matter. Each atom of matter possesses a unity analogous to the mathematical point. Such a point is not to be regarded as abstract, but as a minimal *prima pars* which contains within it the possible dimensions which become actualized in line and figure. Material entities are actualizations of possibilities within minimal monads. God, as *monas monadum,* the monad of monads, is the supreme philosophical unity, cause, principle, and the final explanation of all things in their attainment of possibilities.

Bacon looks upon the "natural theology" of Bruno as verbal artistry, but he nonetheless learns several things from the artist. Like Bruno, Bacon seeks and finds philosophical teaching in the ancient poets, including grounds for the separation of natural philosophy from revealed theology. He agrees with Bruno in a respect for Lully and a disdain of Ramus. It is probable that through Bruno's influence Bacon is led to treat Lully's logical scheme as a worthy instrument for aligning truths already discovered. Bacon does not, of course, think that Lully's representation of truths by chosen letters of the alphabet and pigments, and the manipulation of these in an elaborately constructed logical mechanism, can lead to any new discovery. Bacon is in agreement with Bruno's contention that nature when spatially regarded is seen to be a system of causes in motion. Bruno provides grounds for the elevation by Bacon of the Democritean theory of atoms into a doctrine of the form as entity with inherent law, cause, and activity.

From these several foregoing thinkers Bacon undoubtedly learns more than we have indicated; yet, taken either singly or together, their philosophical doctrines are never quite equivalent to Bacon's own. Bacon is neither an eclectic philosopher nor a detached historian of thought. Whatever he accepts is transformed by his own thinking in accord with his own distinctive principles. Bacon's main criticism of systematic philosophers generally, from Plato to Bruno, is advanced on the ground of their departure from induction. Bacon considers himself the author of a philosophy unique in its kind. This is a naturalism established from beginning to end through the employment of a specific inductive method, which never lapses into, nor takes refuge within, deduction. Whatever it asserts must be verified experimentally by sense in conjunction with reason. Sense tries the experiment which proves the axiom provided by reason. The axiom is not, then, a sense datum, nor is it composed of sense data; it is a universal definition demonstrable in most instances by particular processes in nature available to sense. If the definition as a direction can show an identical operation in fact, then that definition is a true axiom of science. If the definition is said to pertain to effecting causes which cannot be so demonstrated, as in the case of the principles of Telesio, say, the truth of the axiom is not demonstrated. In this regard, the more comprehensive and general axioms of science, which can suggest yet more comprehensive axioms, require special watching, for the aim of an inductive natural philosophy is the certification in the above manner, until the very end, of those most general principles which are presumed to command the widest causal operation in nature. It is Bacon's opinion that such general principles can be inductively proved and a full philosophy of nature thereby established.

Bacon, of course, never succeeds in providing a full inductive philosophy of nature; but he does, at every stage of his endeavor, resist the temptation to invent a speculative alternative which might pass for such a philosophy. Bacon does not succeed in preparing works in representation of the Fourth Part of the Great Instauration, which is to consist of exemplary Tables of axioms inductively discovered, and consequently can provide nothing of the Sixth Part, which is to contain a systematic philosophy. What this philosophy is to be, and not to be, the author of the *New Organon* can do no more than indicate, because inquiry has only begun. Its subject matter will, he says, comprehend all the structures and processes of nature. Its aim is to discover the forms, causes, and laws of natural operation and, having established these, to control nature in the production of operative works. This philosophy will not become a reality until the immense history on which it must be founded has been fully gathered, and until the axioms—whether lowest, middle, or highest—which sustain it have been inductively secured. No matter how properly its general axioms may be established, these are not at any stage to be considered an all-comprehensive and complete statement of the operations of God's whole natural creation. Nature can never be fully known until inductive inquiry is finally complete. There is to be no premature constructing of a theoretical system.

"God forbid," says Bacon, "that we should give out a dream of our own imagination for a pattern of the world; rather may He graciously grant to us to write an apocalypse or true vision of the footsteps of the Creator imprinted on His creatures." Care must be taken to see that the universe of nature is not endowed by investigators with final causes or with mind. There is in nature no mind or reason, logical, universal, or divine. Such appellations can properly mean nothing more than the "seals" or "signets" which the Creator has stamped upon his material creation, where they appear as material, and not rational, forms. The material universe is not divine in nature, but only in origin. Only from the placets of Divine Revelation—and not through inductive philosophy—does man learn that God is nature's Creator and that nature as a kingdom lies under man's dominion. Inductive science provides no basic rule for human conduct. Human rules for the use of nature's operative works are but inferences from a divinely originated and divinely imposed rule of charity, which is the foundation and the supreme principle of all human virtue.

INDEX

INDEX

Historia sympathiae et antipathiae rerum, 308
Historia ventorum, 314
Historia vitae et mortis, 308, 314
Historians of philosophy, 15-16
History and First Investigation of Sound and Hearing, 270
History of Dense and Rare, 309, 314
History of Heavy and Light, 308
History of Life and Death, 308, 314
History of Sulphur, Mercury and Salt, 308
History of the Reign of King Henry the Seventh, 230, 308
History of the Sympathy and Antipathy of Things, 308
History of Winds, 314
Hippocrates, 244, 250, 277
Hobart, Sir Henry, 128, 135, 151, 183
Hobbes, Thomas, 8, 15, 231
Honor, 46, 70, 128, 237
Hooker, Richard, 20-21, 73, 75, 81, 83
Howard, Charles, Baron of Effingham, Earl of Nottingham, 60, 204
Howard, Henry, Earl of Northampton, 66, 125
Howard, Lady Frances, niece of the Earl of Northampton, 187
Howard, Thomas, Earl of Suffolk, 136, 186, 204, 217, 226, 229, 240
Howard family and dependents, 203-4
Hume, David, 11, 12
Humphrey, Lawrence, 78, 79
Hypotheses, 12, 18, 258, 301; *see* Axioms

Ideas, history of, 16-17
Identity, principle of, 34, 252, 326
Idols, 13, 29, 243, 244, 258, 260-61, 288, 291-92; of the Cave, 258, 292, 293-94; of the Marketplace, 246, 258, 292, 294; of the Theatre, 246, 258, 292, 294-96; of the Tribe, 258, 292-93

Impositions, 129, 132, 135, 139, 142-44, 146, 156, 157-59, 185
In felicem memoriam reginae elizabethae, 96-98
Induction, 251, 252, 254, 257, 258, 269, 275-76, 279, 291, 297-300, 301, 304-7, 313, 318, 319, 346, 350, 351; Aristotelian, 275-76, 299-300; Bacon's not pure, 251, 297; Platonic, 11, 243, 298; *see* Method, new
Instauration, the Great, 13, 30, 107 ff., 137-38, 179, 180, 230, 231, 245-46, 248, 275, 315; its parts and ends, 260-63, 275-76, 288, 289, 351-52; first part, 288, 289-90; second part, 260-63, 275, 288, 289, 290 (*see* Method, new); third part, 260, 276, 288, 289, 290-91, 307, 309, 314; fourth part, 260, 276, 289, 291, 351; fifth part, 260, 289, 291, 349; sixth part, 260, 289, 291, 351
Inventions and inventors, 138, 246, cf. 274
Ireland, pacification of, 51-52

James I, 21, 26-30, 66, 73, 74, 99, 102, 104, 108-18, 122, 123, 126, 128, 134, 135, 138-47, 148-50, 152-62, 170-79, 185-86, 196, 199-200, 206-7, 209, 211-12, 218, 220, 222, 223, 227-30, 236, 248, 270, 310, 311, 316, 330; *see* Learning and political topics
Jewel, John, Bishop of Salisbury, 24, 87
Jonson, Ben, 36, 213, 238
Judges and the Sovereign, 116, 131-32, 135-36, 167, 169, 170-77, 193-94, 223
Justice, 70, 150; *see* Virtues, cardinal
Justinian, 180

Kant, Immanuel, 9, 336, 338
Kepler, Johannes, 20
Kingdoms, doctrine of the three separate, divine, natural, politi-